BEST
IN
SHOW

ALSO BY JOHN KENNETH MUIR

FROM APPLAUSE:

The Unseen Force: The Films of Sam Raimi (2004)

An Askew View: The Films of Kevin Smith (2002)

FROM MCFARLAND:

The Encyclopedia of Superheroes on Film and Television (2004)

Eaten Alive at a Chainsaw Massacre: The Films of Tobe Hooper (2002)

Horror Films of the 1970s (2002)

Terror Television (2001)

An Analytical Guide to TV's One Step Beyond (2001)

The Films of John Carpenter (2000)

A Critical History of Dr. Who on TV (1999)

Wes Craven: The Art of Horror (1998)

Exploring Space: 1999 (1997)

FROM POWYS MEDIA:

Space: 1999 — The Forsaken (2003)

BEST

— IN —

SHOW

The Films of
Christopher Guest and Company

JOHN KENNETH MUIR

APPLAUSE
THEATRE & CINEMA BOOKS

Best in Show:
The Films of Christopher Guest and Company
by John Kenneth Muir

Library of Congress Cataloging-in-Publication Data:
Muir, John Kenneth, 1969–
  Best in show : the films of Christopher Guest and
company / John Kenneth Muir.
      p. cm.
  Includes bibliographical references and index.
  ISBN 1-55783-609-4
  1. Guest, Christopher—Criticism and interpretation.
I. Title.

PN1998.3.G853M85 2004
791.4302'33'092—dc22

                              2004018986

British Library Cataloging-in-Publication Data
A catalog record of this book is available from the
British Library

APPLAUSE THEATRE & CINEMA BOOKS
151 West 46th Street, 8th Floor
New York, NY 10036
Phone: (212) 575-9265
Fax: (646) 562-5852
Email: info@applausepub.com
Internet: www.applausepub.com
Applause books are available through
your local bookstore, or you may order
at http://www.applausepub.com or
call Music Dispatch at 800-637-2852

Sales & Distribution
NORTH AMERICA:
  Hal Leonard Corp.
  7777 West Bluemound Road
  P.O. Box 13819
  Milwaukee, WI 53213
  Phone: (414) 774-3630
  Fax: (414) 774-3259
  Email: halinfo@halleonard.com
  Internet: www.halleonard.com

EUROPE:
  Roundhouse Publishing Ltd.
  Millstone, Limers Lane
  Northam, North Devon
  EX 39 2RG
  Phone: 01237-474474
  Fax: 01237-474774
  roundhouse.group@ukgateway.net

This book is for my father and mother,
Ken and Loretta Muir, and for my wife, Kathryn.

CONTENTS

ACKNOWLEDGMENTS

No man is an island, and that's especially true of writers. Every book is a team effort, and therefore I extend my deepest gratitude to the friends and comrades who helped make this text become a reality. First on that list is my agent, June Clark, who understood the project, realized why it would be fun and worthwhile, and then pursued it.

I would be nowhere without my wife, Kathryn, who so graciously gave up her weekends and evenings to help proofread the text and similarly encourage me through the whole process. My father, Ken Muir, also dug deep into his folk music record collection and shared dozens of albums to facilitate my research. For someone who had never listened to the Serendipity Singers, the Tripjacks, or the New Christy Minstrels, this was truly an eye-opening experience.

And then there are the fine actors and production people in Hollywood who so selflessly shared their time, thoughts, and insights with me on this project. It's no exaggeration to state that these eleven folks really made the difference on this book (and brought it up to eleven, in more ways than one): Harry Shearer, Fred Willard, Bob Balaban, Michael Hitchcock, Jim Piddock, Deborah Theaker, Paul Dooley, June Chadwick, Rob Covelman, Jerry Turman, and production designer Joseph T. Garrity. Thanks everybody!

Finally, my admiration goes out to each and every member of the incredible Christopher Guest repertory company, as well as the inscrutable but remarkable director himself. Because without their talent, silliness, humanity, and total ingenuity this book could not exist.

ONE STEP FURTHER: AN INTRODUCTION TO THE FILMS OF CHRISTOPHER GUEST AND COMPANY

"OUR ASPIRATIONS ARE OUR POSSIBILITIES," Samuel Johnson observed once reminding us that dreams are the fuel powering the human spirit. But aspirations can also be troublesome, especially when they are unrealistic or become obsessions.

In contemporary America, for example, one might argue that the *desire du jour*, the reigning national obsession, involves the achievement of Andy Warhol's elusive fifteen minutes of fame. Since the start of the twenty-first century, TV audiences have witnessed citizens eating buffalo testicles, enduring dress-downs from Donald Trump, and humiliating themselves before the reptilian glare of Simon Cowell, all for a shot at the media spotlight.

As we gawk at these cathode-ray spectacles, we might rightly ask, why do people do such things? What facet of modern life fosters this desire for celebrity, even among the most modestly talented folk? More to the point, does this pursuit of unattainable fame make us bad, silly, or merely very interesting?

Ironically, a few pithy meditations (if not answers) on the psychology of aspirations and the quest for celebrity have emerged from the very source that regularly bombards our heartland with images of people so cravenly seeking it.

Hollywood.

Since the mid-nineties, comedian, musician, and film director Christopher Guest, an artist who has reportedly avoided watching American television for two decades, has raised a mirror to the fame-seeking in a trilogy of low-budget, remarkably funny, and expertly acted films.

In his documentary-style comedies, *Waiting for Guffman* (1997), *Best in Show* (2000), and *A Mighty Wind* (2003), and even his more traditional narratives, the satirical *The Big Picture* (1989) and *Almost Heroes* (1998), the wannabe's quest for fame has emerged as the director's recurring, if perhaps subconscious, theme.

"I am drawn to people who have dreams that are slightly out of reach,"[1] Guest explains, with his typical talent for understatement. Insightful critics have been quick to pinpoint that the director's chosen terrain lies "wherever modest talent meets delusions of grandeur and cant serves as cover for a wobbly sense of self. A pretty broad swath of American culture, in other words."[2]

"Out here, every day," adds Fred Willard, a ubiquitous face in the Guest canon, "people have plans of what they are going to do. You listen to them, and they are real plans, and they're going to get on *American Idol*, or they're going to produce their own films, or they're going to put on a stage play, but everybody has a goal of what they're going to do."

"Certainly there is an aspect [of that] in all three of the movies we've done so far," chimes in Bob Balaban, who has also appeared in all the documentary-style features directed by Guest. "There's a certain core of characters that are just desperate to achieve something, and they're not particularly equipped to do it. You've got characters who are striving for something.

"In *Waiting for Guffman*, they're trying to put on the best show they possibly can. In *Best in Show*, they're trying to have their dogs be as good as they possibly can be," Balaban says. "And in *A Mighty Wind*, there's something else going on — we're really talking about a thing that died already, and all these people are left over who still do it."

Guest's dry demeanor in life and his keen eye for detail in art have made him the ideal talent at the ideal time to chart this ongoing national obsession with fame, and his frequent writing collaborator, Eugene Levy, has noted that Guest himself boasts "the characteristics of two irreconcilable worlds. He nails every emerging nuance of American popular culture almost as it happens, yet he's some sort of British blueblood with a certain disdain for drawing attention to himself."[3]

By "nailing the nuances" of human behavior, so to speak, Guest's films achieve something unique and entirely individual. Unlike the current crop of reality TV programs that, according to Guest, "seem to be about suffering and embarrassment,"4 the starry-eyed characters populating his films are treated with humor and empathy, never contempt.

Indeed, one might prescribe a healthy dosage of Guest's films as the antidote to reality TV, since they remind audiences that people are alike all over, and there but for the grace of God go any of us. Yes, *Waiting for Guffman*'s Corky St. Clair and his small-town brethren may be serious about their Broadway pretensions to the point of comic absurdity, but they are also disquietingly human, and therefore touching.

Where reality TV might invite us to laugh at a blond gold digger who isn't in on the joke that Evan Marriott isn't really rich, or that her new obnoxious, fat fiancee is really an actor, Guest's documentary-style comedies continue discovering new ways to make hapless characters appear inspiring in their "own uncomfortable humanity," and even sweet "in their simplicity."5

Despite the fact that they happen to be very strange.

"At the bottom of everything," notes actress and comedian Deborah Theaker, a member of Guest's acting troupe, "Chris's movies are incredibly romantic and idealistic. Everybody wants to be in the show and believes that they can do anything."

But then there's the flip side of that coin in his films, too, an acknowledgment that there are hurdles on the path to fame, and often they are self-imposed. "There's a melancholy underpinning to everybody's aspirations," Theaker says. "Very few dreams ever get realized. That's just the reality of life."

As Guest might inform us at this juncture, good comedy by his definition features a basis in reality and then "goes one step further,"6 a thesis that explains succinctly why his films generate such laughs, and why his characters may literally boast two left feet, like *Best in Show*'s Jerry Fleck, or believe that mankind is composed of materialized color, like *A Mighty Wind*'s Terry Bohner. These characteristics are comic exaggerations, to be sure, but by no means impossibilities. As critic David Ansen wrote in *Newsweek*, Guest "seems to know just how far he can stretch reality without losing the crucial texture of verisimilitude."7

"In my experience, we don't come close to describing how weird people in this world are," adds Guest, "I mean, there are whole conventions for people who like thimbles."8

"If you go back all the way to *Guffman*, you see that's true," says actor and improv veteran Paul Dooley, citing a specific example. "It would be very easy for the gay community to think that Corky St. Clair was making fun of gay people, and [the movie] was homophobic. But there is something about Chris's acting — and the acting of the other people, where even though they make fun of people, you don't dislike them or get mad at them for it. It doesn't seem mean-spirited.

"That's the key to Chris Guest's movies," Dooley continues. "I think the characters in Chris' movies are [somewhat] earthbound. They're types that we know. And their choices are a little eccentric, like Catherine O'Hara's character in *Best in Show*, who meets everyone she ever slept with in the past. That's not impossible."

"I think some of the sweetness of these movies comes from the naivete of the characters in them," suggests Balaban. "Most of them are somewhat misguided. They are trying to do something that they don't really know how to do, or they're doing it in a way that won't quite get them what they want. But there's something very endearing about it."

Indeed, the humor in the films is gentle enough to foster identification with the *dramatis personae*, yet sharp and true enough to be unerringly hilarious. In balancing this delicate equation of humor and reality, there's little doubt that Guest, his co-writer Eugene Levy, and the rest of their "cronies have invented a new kind of affectionate satire which is all but indistinguishable from an embrace,"9 as critic David Denby noted in the *New Yorker*.

"I don't think he's ever cruel with people," Willard points out. Bob Balaban says the same. "I don't see anybody being skewered. Skewering kind of implies a group satirizing something. I see it [these films] as basically affectionate and very human. For something that's so silly, it's also very real."

"You don't make judgments when you're in these things," Balaban stresses. "Christopher never does. There's no judgment made as to if you're a good character, or a bad character, or even if you're a funny character. You're just allowed to be, knowing that your framework will always be tilted in the humorous direction, if it can be."

No doubt a consistent theme, focus and tone are commendable in any film director's body of work, but the cinema of Christopher Guest remains remarkable, and worthy of book-length analysis, because the director has perfected the very format that best expresses it. And, as film critic Roger Ebert frequently writes, it isn't *what* a movie is about that's important, but *how* it is about it. In that regard, Guest has granted his audiences the simplest and most elegant entrance into the slightly bizarre world of his characters, by marrying his persistent theme to the format known far and wide as the *mockumentary*.

Now, quite frankly, that's a term Guest doesn't cotton to at *all* because, he insists, nobody in his films is ever mocked. "I call it comedy that's done in a documentary style," he stresses often. "People have adopted that term [mockumentary] because it's easy to use and say."[10]

Fair enough, as Alan Barrows (Guest's character in *A Mighty Wind*) might say, but the word "mock" need not be disparaging, for it boasts the second definition of "simulated" or "sham." Seeing as how these comedies masquerade as real documentaries, down to the clever use of manufactured archival materials and one-on-one interviews with "talking heads," one can detect a context in which the descriptor "mock" fits rather appropriately, without connoting any hostile or ugly intent on the part of the filmmakers. The films are surely mockumentaries in the sense that they ape and simulate in visuals and performance the documentary format ethos, particularly the "direct cinema" style of the early 1960s and 1970s — films such as D.A. Pennebaker's film on Bob Dylan's 1965 tour, *Don't Look Back* (1967), or the Maysles' concert film on the Rolling Stones, *Gimme Shelter* (1970).

In film, the documentary format is roughly equivalent to the non-fiction format in literature. That is, it lays out a story intended to represent reality. Film theorist John Grierson wrote that documentaries are "creative treatments of actuality"[11] and that they take their subjects from "the raw" and make them "more real than the acted article."[12]

In other words, real people living in real, unfolding situations are more accessible — more true — than actors working with written dialogue from a preconceived, highly detailed script.

The documentary format is instructive, too, in a comedy, because it encourages Guest's predilection to focus on the small details — something that a more traditional narrative like a typical Jim Carrey vehicle eschews. Consider the peculiar and oh-so-careful arrangement of office supplies on the desk of Bob Balaban's obsessive compulsive character in *A Mighty Wind*.

In this "creative treatment of actuality," such focus transmits essential and funny character information and attention to detail, while in a more linear, obviously fictional narrative the same shot might perhaps appear forced, heavy-handed, a shout to "look here." But since documentaries are meant by nature and design to convey very specific agendas and messages (like Michael Moore's didactic *Bowling for Columbine* [2002]), such pointed compositions fit perfectly in the realm of Guest's observational films.

"Guest has a gift for lingering on the seemingly innocuous small details of decor, mannerism, wardrobe, until a simple quirk turns touching,"[13] Georgia Brown wrote in the *Village Voice*, recognizing Guest's keen eye and his steadfast attention to seemingly small details. Or, stated in another fashion, the artist boasts the sensibility of a real documentarian. He prefers to report on a world that already exists (like professional dog shows or the world of folk music), rather than creating a new one. Once he's done so, he may pinpoint certain objects or characters, but really the burden of interpretation — in this case the important judgment, "Is it funny?" — rests with the individual viewer.

"I can truthfully say what I do is watch people and their behavior,"[14] Guest elaborates. It's as simple as that.

If we consider that the documentary format is the cinematic equivalent of reality, and Guest defines comedy as reality plus "one step further," it is clear then that the director has adopted the format that best captures both the humanity and the humor of his off-the-wall characters. Consequently, Guest's films are packed wall-to-wall with the hallmarks of the documentary format.

These include handheld, relatively static one-on-one interviews with the subjects (i.e., talking heads), not totally unlike the so-called "confessional" featured on some reality TV series, "live" background noise on the soundtrack, such as the amusingly passionate lovers in Mitch's motel in *A Mighty Wind*, and even the inescapable sense that the camera is capturing life as it unfolds before us, not *re-creating* dramatic moments or conflict that happened once in a character's life.

"Our films are created in much the same way as a real documentary," says Guest, "in that we shoot eighty hours of film for a ninety-minute movie."[15]

But Guest's films feel so unique, personal, and so much like documentaries for another reason. To maintain and enhance this heightened sense of reality, this notion of taking people in the raw and expressing their actual travails as is, he has executed what many producers — not to mention accountants — would no doubt consider a radical approach. He has willfully discarded the tradition of the intricate screenplay and asked his stable of regular performers (including, in alphabetical order, Lewis Arquette, Bob Balaban, Ed Begley Jr., Jennifer Coolidge, Paul Dooley, John Michael Higgins, Michael Hitchcock, Linda Kash, Don Lake, Eugene Levy, Jane Lynch, Michael McKean, Larry Miller, Catherine O'Hara, Parker Posey, Jim Piddock, Harry Shearer, Deborah Theaker, Fred Willard, and Scott Williamson) to improvise all of their dialogue.

That's right, working from just an outline and a few character cues — sometimes as few as two — these resourceful actors craft their own dialogue from whole cloth, fostering a spontaneity and freedom that sometimes feels revolutionary in the buttoned-down, storyboarded Hollywood of the computer-generated image (CGI) era. Recently, Larry David's award-winning HBO series, *Curb Your Enthusiasm* (2000–) has mimicked Guest's approach, though to somewhat more outrageous, over-the-top designs.

If the improvised approach sounds dangerous, well it is, because editor and director Guest doesn't ever know for certain what he will end up with when the film is completed. He has a sense of it, he is cognizant of the outline and aware of his overall purpose, but the specifics are left to the graces of these improvisors. And so Guest has also committed himself to something else genuinely rare these days. He has placed total faith in his performers.

"The word that comes to mind is trust," says Harry Shearer. "Chris trusts us. Castle Rock trusts Chris, and then we all trust the audience to get it. We don't have to pound it into their heads. We trust them to know what's funny about this stuff."

Still, why take the chance? For Guest, the answer is self-evident. There is no other way to forge this brand of observational comedy. "I personally don't think you can do it outside of the documentary concept," Guest reported in one interview. "I think [the format] sets the perfect structure to hang this on, and without that, you're lost."[16]

It helps, one supposes, that Guest has known most of his cohorts for many years, and that his films are relatively inexpensive to produce. "When you work as cheap as I do," the director admits, "the studio hands you the money and tells you to go off with your friends and have fun, which is basically what we do."[17]

"There are few very studios that would give somebody several million dollars without a script, and that's literally what Castle Rock is doing," adds Michael Hitchcock, another veteran of these documentary-style ventures. "Good for them."

To further offset the risk inherent in an improvised product, Guest again demonstrates an admirable quality inherent in any true artist's work: consistency. Specifically, the director has heretofore rigorously adhered to an overarching structure that shepherds his characters to precisely the places they need to go.

"All of Chris's films seem to do that," says production designer Joseph T. Garrity, who has worked on every one of Guest's movies. "The movies are all about some event that people have to prepare for in some way, and then about the hijinks of all these players coming together at the event itself."

Film scholar and critic Thomas Doherty described Guest's enduring structure in this way for an article published in *Cineaste*:

> However ragged and risky the improvisation method might seem, the bits and routines are buttressed by the sturdy pillars of a three-act structure — assembly, rehearsal, and show. As in a backstage musical, offstage melodrama and antics vie with proscenium performances through the Guest-Levy trilogy — a theatrical production (*Waiting for*

Guffman), a dog show (*Best in Show*), and a reunion concert (*A Mighty Wind*).[18]

The only note to add to this concise analysis of structure in Guest's documentary-style comedy is that each film ends with one other important moment, a coda accompanied by a tag line that (usually) reads "Six Months Later."

During these final moments, the story is wrapped up and interpreted by the subjects in much the same manner as a post-show analysis. If Guest were indeed mocking his characters, as many critics have accused, this coda would be totally superfluous because audiences wouldn't care in the slightest what happened to the protagonists.

Instead, the coda always serves as a kind of check-in with the characters after some time has passed, and is designed to let the audience know that pretty much all is well. Life goes on.

In *Guffman*, Corky St. Clair describes the "[have] your cake and eat it, too" part of his story, an upcoming audition for a Broadway revival of *My Fair Lady*; and in *Best in Show*, Jane Lynch's character, Christy Cummings, reflects on "the silver lining of this cloud" after losing the Mayflower Dog Show: the subsequent publication of *American Bitch*, her new magazine catering exclusively to the issues of lesbian pure-bred dog owners.

Their improvised remarks during these codas are not merely funny, but comforting, because nobody goes home hurting when the end credits roll. Even Catherine O'Hara's Mickey Crabbe, who ends up singing about penis clamps at a bladder-control trade show in *A Mighty Wind*, is delighted to feel like a musician again.

"People usually end up very happy in his movies, even though as outsiders looking in, we might say 'Oh my goodness, that's not so great where you got,' but they're happy with it," says Hitchcock. "So his characters aren't, in their own minds at least, tragic people at all. Even with Meg and Hamilton in *Best in Show*, though we lost the dog show, we switched wardrobes — we went to the Gap. We got a new dog and we were perfectly happy, and ready for the next year."

In fact, the comforting, almost predictable structure of the films in this trilogy has caused some critics to compare the Guest oeuvre to, of all things, the Andy Hardy film series produced for MGM in the 1930s and 1940s, starring Mickey Rooney, Judy Garland, and sometimes Lana Turner.

Set in the fictional Idaho town of Carvel (not Blaine, as in *Waiting for Guffman*), these films, directed by George B. Seitz, involved the adventures of the wholesome Hardy family, and more often than not involved putting on a show out in the barn, replete with catchy music like "It Never Rains But It Pours," and "Meet the Beat of My Heart."

Waiting for Guffman, especially with tunes like "A Penny for Your Thoughts" and "This Bulging River," has been called "reminiscent of such Depression-era 'backstage' musicals as *Love Finds Andy Hardy* (1938) and *Babes in Arms* (1939)."[19] Why? It exhibits the same passion for musical and theatrical performance as these classics, another consistent quality visible in Guest's films.

With determinedly comforting codas and subtle — and probably unintended — resemblance to such classic Americana, it is easy to understand why Guest believes his films do not seem cruel, nor mock human behavior. Affection still has a place at comedy's table, at least if Guest is the cook.

Sharp and yet somehow loving, the films of Christopher Guest are novel not merely because they visually express a consistent theme via the use of the documentary/mockumentary format, or because they are forged in an unusual manner, via the auspices of improvisation, but because they stand as a singular barrier against the mighty winds of twenty-first-century Hollywood trends.

More and more, film comedies are being perceived as packages. Which two stars can be shoehorned together for a profit? Jennifer Aniston and Ben Stiller? Ben Stiller and Drew Barrymore? Drew Barrymore and Adam Sandler? Comedy has become obsessed with out-of-control body functions, not human quirks or foibles. The Christopher Guest canon stands in stark contrast to this example, as Harry Shearer explains: "The humor [in Guest's films] happens as opposed to being extruded in an industrial process."[20]

Guest's human-centric movies also buck the trend to automate movies with ever-more-ingenious but somehow increasingly soulless special effects and staccato, overwrought editing.

"In the past ten years, film has become very unspontaneous," Christopher Guest told *Time* magazine in 2000, "whether it's using digital technology or being very storyboarded. This is the other end of the spectrum. Yes, it is just people talking, but that is just as exciting to me as a big wave [i.e., *The Perfect Storm*]."[21]

Because his humor is based on characters, not mechanics, because Guest observes his characters with both wit and compassion and "doesn't stop at their mannerisms or wardrobe," but works his way down to their "most primal insecurities,"[22] his films appeal to a more mature, thoughtful crowd than your average, mainstream comedies.

"Never, I think, have intellectuals been so alienated from American movies as now," social critic Philip Lopate writes of this contemporary epoch, "never has there been a period when they less expected to see in motion pictures a vestige of their own commitment to the life of the mind."[23]

Guest's movies are truly observational in nature and the essence of "character comedy," according to Jim Piddock, another radiant point of light in Guest's acting company, providing self-respecting grown-ups a reason to go to the movies again; a reason to go see a comedy.

"These movies bear repeated viewing because there's a lot of texture," says Shearer. "They're the opposite of most Hollywood comedies, which are focused on only one thing. If you're going for the big fart joke, you're not going to want somebody doing something in the corner of the frame to upstage it. To me, a lot of comedy is watching the people who are listening, as opposed to the people who are talking. I like the idea of watching an ensemble."

In a world dominated by adolescent humor, sitcoms, and reality television, this gift is precious, and critics have not been shy to proclaim that "one of the best things to happen to movie comedy in recent years is the Christopher Guest repertory company."[24]

Thus the director, along with collaborator Eugene Levy, has carved a unique niche in an industry renowned for conformity, and, in the words of one critic, become "the most successful comedian in Hollywood," since he's "making exactly the movies he wants to make, films that perfectly utilize his skills and the skills of those around him."[25] But Guest is more than just a successful filmmaker. To borrow the words of another critic, he is also "one of the best social satirists in the country."[26]

Considering the singular focus, format, and feel of Guest's documentary-style comedies, the purpose of this book is to attempt to document, as best as possible, the method behind Guest's comic madness. In making the effort, we'll also seek to understand the efficacy of the mockumentary format, and the difficult, step-by-step process of improvisation — two key elements that have made Guest's films not only accessible and smart, but so very funny.

Along the way, the book will also gaze at Guest's professional history, and the influences and experiences that led him to create films in such an individual manner. Several of Guest's comic conspirators also offer perspective, insight, and laughs about what it has been like working on these prestigious and popular films.

So let's take a deep breath, blow it out, wrestle that muse of theater and dance, and do a good show.

PART ONE

Base of Knowledge

1. A MAN OF CHARACTER(S)

THIS IS SPINAL TAP; THE BIG PICTURE; ATTACK OF THE 50 FT. WOMAN; ALMOST HEROES

AS DR. ALLAN PEARL OF BLAINE, MISSOURI, might explain it, Christopher Guest caught the entertainment bug early. It may be more accurate to state that the artist came by it honestly, as the grandchild of a novelist, and the son of Jean Hindes, a vice president and executive at CBS Records.[1] Guest's father was Peter Haden-Guest, of Saling in Essex, England, a one-time dancer and actor who inherited the title of baron from his celebrated father, Leslie Haden-Guest, a physician famous for his work in the field of children's health.[2]

Guest's parents courted and married while Peter was employed in New York City as an editor in the publications department for the United Nations, and Christopher Haden-Guest was born in the Big Apple on February 5, 1948.

From his earliest days, the young Guest, a frequent traveler between England and the United States, was a keen observer of people and human behavior. Gazing out windows, he would often "make up voices for the people as they walked by," paying close attention to their behavior, voices, and the way they walked.[3] In fact, the actor that Guest most admired was British comedian and chameleon Peter Sellers.

"He was a good actor, he was funny, and he did things that I want to do,"[4] Guest told *Back Stage West* in 2003, singling Sellers out as his boyhood idol. Among other praiseworthy attributes, Sellers was known for his total commitment to character, and for inhabiting these strange folks in films as diverse as *The Pink Panther* (1963) and *Dr. Strangelove* (1964).

But Guest's admiration of Sellers' work and predilection to observe and create funny personalities didn't necessarily mean that as a child he coveted the limelight. At age eleven, he appeared in a play at a camp in Vermont dressed in a bunny suit, and later reported experiencing some degree of stage fright.[5]

More in tune with his artistic temperament, Guest developed early an enduring love for music. He learned to play the clarinet first, and then moved on to the mandolin, like his hero Bill Monroe, the so-called father of bluegrass. Before long, Guest also mastered the guitar, and began an extensive collection of the instrument, not totally unlike his cinematic alter-ego of the 1980s, *Spinal Tap*'s Nigel Tufnel.

Talent wasn't just embedded in Guest's genes, it virtually surrounded him as he matured. His sometime babysitter was fifteen-year-old Mary Allin Travers, the female third of the folk trio legend, Peter, Paul and Mary.[6] And during the Greenwich Village folk explosion of the early sixties, a teenaged Guest strummed alongside his high school buddy, Arlo Guthrie, the eldest son of Woody and Marjorie Guthrie. This was just a few years before the incredible success of Arlo's album, *Alice's Restaurant* in 1967, and Guest promptly found himself ensconced in Greenwich Village venues such as the Gaslight and the Bitter End, jamming not just with Guthrie, but backing up other folk talents like Loudon Wainwright III.

After spending time in England, where he toiled on a BBC production of *Alice in Wonderland* (1966) directed by Jonathan Miller and featuring Peter Sellers, Peter Cook, Leo McKern, Michael Gough and John Gielgud, Guest returned to the states and enrolled at Bard College for one year.[7]

Guest transferred to the Tisch School of the Arts at New York University in his sophomore year, but soon found the establishment to be what he later dubbed "a mecca of pretension."[8] It was there in 1967, however, that Guest first encountered his future *Spinal Tap* bandmate, Michael McKean, a new transfer from Pittsburgh's Carnegie Tech and a talented musician with an extensive performing background.[9]

McKean had been asked to leave Carnegie Tech after skipping too many early-morning classes, reportedly due to chronic insomnia, so he became a drama major at NYU instead.[10] The two undergraduates roomed together, became good friends, and began composing songs while they were both still under twenty years old.[11]

Before long, Guest took his first steps into the world of professional theater. He began auditioning for plays and was cast in an off-Broadway production of *Little Murders*. This black comedy, set in a crime-ridden Manhattan, was the first effort by celebrated *Village Voice* satirist and cartoonist, Jules Feiffer. Directing the play was Second City icon Alan Arkin, and appearing in the show was a fresh-faced, young talent named Fred Willard.

A graduate of Chicago's Second City comedy troupe, Willard was quick on his feet and happy to be working in New York. He appeared in *Little Murders* shortly before co-founding the Ace Trucking Company improvisational group, which eventually made dozens of appearances on *The Ed Sullivan Show* (1948 – 1971) and *The Tonight Show* (1962 –). The group had begun its performing life by doing stints at the Bitter End, and Willard recalls one night when Neil Diamond played the small venue.

"It was 1969 or 1970 and I did *Little Murders* in New York," Willard remembers. "Christopher Guest was an understudy in the play, and I think I met him. I have a vague memory of him. I know his mother was a casting woman, and I don't think I was actually ever on stage with him. He reminded me of it, years later. He said, 'Do you remember we met doing *Little Murders*?' And I did remember him, and that's how I met Christopher, but we didn't become friends then."

But while Guest was enthusiastic to participate in the *Little Murders* company, the artist learned that some of his classmates — and teachers — at NYU didn't share the sentiment. They treated him with open disdain, informed him he required more training as an actor, and didn't even attend the show to support him.[12]

While Guest struggled to find fame and fortune on the New York stage, Michael McKean also fled the stifling environment of NYU. He dropped out and relocated to Los Angeles, where he and his friend actor David Lander, a Carnegie Tech student, met a fellow named Harry Shearer and formed an improv group known as the Credibility Gap.

But more on that later.

A NICE PLACE TO LAMPOON

At the start of the 1970s, Christopher Guest began accepting writing assignments for *National Lampoon Magazine*, for co-founder and editor Henry Beard and managing editor Tony Hendra. He continued to line up acting gigs both on Broadway (*Room Service* [1970], *Moonchildren* [1972]) and in bit parts in films like *The Hospital* (1971) and Peter Yates' heist movie, *The Hot Rock* (1972). It was in these early years of the decade that writer and comedian Paul Dooley first met Guest.

Dooley, who, in 1971, had just come off a very successful stint as the head writer of *The Electric Company*, the award-winning children's program on PBS, is famous to many generations of movie fans, not merely for his funny work in Guest films, but for such coming-of-age comedies as *Breaking Away* (1977) and John Hughes' *Sixteen Candles* (1984).

Other aficionados recognize Dooley for his accomplished work with director Robert Altman in the films *A Wedding* (1978), *A Perfect Couple* (1979), and *Popeye* (1980). But like Fred Willard, Dooley first knew of Guest through a particular family association. Guest's mother, Jean Hindes Guest, was once Dooley's agent. Dooley and Guest then worked together on a television production called *A Nice Place to Visit* (1972).

"I did a show on PBS back in New York, about thirty years ago, right after I did *Electric Company*, and a bunch of Second City people were in it," Dooley recalls. "We got together for a few days in a workshop to create a bunch of scenes, and then we did it for television on film."

Though this production isn't listed on the Internet Movie Database (www.IMDb.com), Dooley remembers that the project was filmed all around New York. "It was about a lot of different things, but the common threads were around New York, Central Park, the Bowery, and the Central Park Zoo," says Dooley. "Paul Benedict was in that one, too. [Guest] just showed up and did a couple of things with us while we were shooting. He was still pretty young then, and played his guitar in one scene."

The two talents also teamed briefly on the set of a famous Charles Bronson movie, *Death Wish* (1974). "He was a real young man," says Dooley. "I had a two-day part. I was a cop, and he was a young policeman, and probably had a one-day part. That was a long time ago. You really have to look for us."

But Guest was easier to pick out in another notable appearance. Under the auspices of Tony Hendra, the first managing editor of *National Lampoon Magazine* and, later, the not-quite-trustworthy band manager Ian Faith in *This Is Spinal Tap*, Guest appeared in an off-Broadway production entitled *Lemmings*.

A spoof of Woodstock, a concert that had some 300,000 attendees, this was an early production in the vein of *Spinal Tap*, satirizing popular musicians of the day like Joe Cocker, James Taylor, Crosby, Stills and Nash, and others. The title came from a descriptive line of dialogue heard in *Gimme Shelter*: "It's like the lemmings of the sea."

Along with Guest, *Lemmings* spotlighted such up-and-comers as John Belushi, Chevy Chase, Melissa Manchester, and Stockard Channing. Like the documentary-style comedies directed by Guest twenty-five years later, *Lemmings* also had no official script, and was totally improvised, other than the well-rehearsed music.

"The *Lampoon* show was never cute," said actress Alice Playten, who played a character named Golden Oldie in the revue. "It was extreme theater."[13]

Co-directed by Hendra and Sean Kelly, and with many songs composed by Guest himself, *Lemmings* commenced its theatrical run at the Village Gate on January 25, 1973, and ran for some 350 performances. Ostensibly set at The Woodchuck Festival, a free concert for millions of fans, *Lemmings* revolved around rock 'n' roll, and concepts like peace, love, and death, not entirely unlike the Rolling Stones Altamont concert film, *Gimme Shelter*, which gave *Lemmings* its title.

A high-energy, adrenalin-pumped John Belushi played the concert's whacked-out emcee and advised audiences that "the man next to you is your dinner." After the "Lemmings Lament," a bizarre anthem, Christopher Guest took the stage and delivered a dead-on, warbly imitation of folk icon Bob Dylan. He sang a cryptically worded tune called "Positively Wall Street," in which the unrepentant Dylan-figure told listeners not to look to him for any answers about life, let alone wisdom.

Following "Positively Wall Street" came Playten's dead-on parody of 1960s' biker songs like the Shangri-Las' "Leader of the Pack." Entitled "Pizza Man," the song was written by Guest, Sean Kelly, and Tony Hendra, and it highlighted the plight of a girl singing about her dead boyfriend, who, because of an accident on the road, ended up looking a lot like pizza.

After a few other songs, including Chevy Chase's performance of "Colorado," a John Denver-esque affair, Guest returned to prominence with yet another startlingly precise impression, this time of James Taylor. Entitled "Highway Toes," his song poked fun at Taylor's "Carolina in My Mind" with lyrics such as "Farewell to Carolina, where I left my frontal lobe."

Today, *Lemmings* is nothing less than a legendary venture because of all the talent it accumulated in one place ... virtually all of whom evolved into major movie stars. In *Wired*, Bob Woodward's controversial biography of John Belushi, the journalist recounted a tale about "a versatile musician and a talented mimic" named Chris Guest who, on some nights, saw his Taylor parody sabotaged by a scene-grabbing Belushi.[14]

Writing in *Harper's Magazine* in 2002, Tony Hendra described how shabbily these remarkable talents were treated back in the day by management. When Guest, Belushi and Chase asked for a raise from Matty Simmons of Twenty-First Century Communications (owner of *National Lampoon*), they were informed that they were "a dime a dozen."[15]

Hardly.

Still, Playten won an Obie for her work in *Lemmings*, and Guest himself was nominated for an Obie for best musical score. *Lemmings* is also generally credited with dramatically increasing *National Lampoon*'s circulation in mid-1973, and thus paving the way for several successful years in the pop-culture limelight.

While *Lemmings* granted Guest the opportunity to hone his musical abilities and his uncanny skill in mimicry, he also sharpened his writing instincts on *The National Lampoon Radio Hour*, a thirty-minute syndicated presentation sponsored by the magazine, and showcasing stars such as Richard Belzer, Bill Murray, Gilda Radner, John Belushi, Chevy Chase, and Guest himself.

The program included such parodies as "Front Row Center," an adaptation of Fyodor Dostoyevsky's *The Idiot*, with Bill Murray starring and Guest as the proper British narrator.[16] Like Peter Sellers before him, Guest was making a name for himself in radio before making the transition to film.

The Radio Hour ran for nearly sixty episodes before finally folding in 1974, and examples of Guest's work were excerpted on albums including *That's Not Funny, That's Sick*, *Radio Dinner*, and *Cold Turkey* (all of which garnered Grammy nominations).

As the 1970s continued, Guest became an increasingly in-demand comic writer, winning an Emmy for *The Lily Tomlin Show* in 1975 and writing for *The Chevy Chase Special*.

SYNCHRONICITY

While Christopher Guest followed his muse on the East Coast, connections that would some day impact his film career were being forged on the opposite side of the country.

By 1970, Michael McKean had left New York to seek his fame in California, and in February of that year he was introduced to Harry Shearer, a former child actor who had appeared in *Abbott and Costello Go to Mars* (1953) and *The Robe* (1953), and even played the role of Eddie Haskell in the pilot of *Leave It to Beaver* (1957 – 1963).

A political satirist with a quick mind and razor-sharp wit, Shearer was very much at the vanguard of American comedy as the Nixon administration became embroiled in the Watergate scandal. Like McKean and Guest, Shearer was not only a skilled musician, but an adroit improvisor and mimic, seemingly able to develop deep, layered, and realistic characterizations, often from the slightest premises.

Born in Los Angeles in 1943, Shearer was a political science major at UCLA before attending Harvard as a graduate student. He worked as a journalist for *Newsweek* in the mid-sixties, but very soon located more expressive outlets for his unique gifts. As in Guest's case, these outlets included radio, and Shearer was a founding member of the Credibility Gap, a troupe of satirists consisting of broadcaster Richard Beebe, Michael McKean, and David Lander.

This group hit the scene in 1968, was on the air daily on KRLA in Pasadena — often for three ten-minute shows, and always with new written material. The group debated such topics as killer bees and reckless driving with a deadpan sense of humor.

"He was a pretty impressive character," says McKean of Shearer, "Very funny and really eloquent with his anger."[17]

For Shearer, the topsy-turvy era of Watergate helped formulate some valuable philosophies about comedy, particularly his long-held belief that "comedy is good, reality is better."

"I was with a comedy group in the 1970s, and we did a lot of Nixon sketches," Shearer explains. "A lot of people were doing Nixon sketches in those days, and we kind of talked about it, and the group just didn't think that the people who were doing these 'Wow, wouldn't it be wild if Nixon got high? What if?' sketches were very funny or interesting. We were trying to do what was really going on.

"So I watched people that I worked with and admired, like Albert Brooks. He was very disciplined and every once in a while, maybe you could call him jokey, but his comedy came out of something very real."

Shearer was also impressed with Richard Pryor. "He got laughs from his heart attack. Over time, as a sort of hobby, I began collecting non-aired video of people just sort of being in strange situations, and observing real behavior. To me, that makes me laugh a lot more than 'The cop is a Martian and the deputy is an alien, and the kid is a dog!' and 'Wow, that's a fish out of water! Isn't that wild?!' All of these very hokey concepts."

Together, Shearer, McKean, and the others took the Credibility Gap's style of realism-based comedy to other venues in 1971, including popular record albums (1974's *A Great Gift Idea* and 1975's *The Bronze Age of Radio*) and comedy clubs such as the Troubadour and the Giant Pickle Barrel.[18]

It was around this time, circa 1974, that another important relationship was forged. Comedian Fred Willard was working in Los Angeles with his Ace Trucking Company. Despite some forty or fifty television appearances, a few of the group members were defecting to pursue solo careers, and consequently leaving a gaping hole in the act that only a (credibility) gap could fill.

"I'm a huge fan of Harry Shearer — anything he does," says Willard. "I think my connection with him started when I was in Ace Truck Company, and there was a comedy group out here in L.A. called the Credibility Gap. I saw them at what is now the Improvisation, but which was then called the Ash Grove, and I was so knocked out by what they were doing.

"By this time, we were just four guys," Willard continues. "We had lost a woman when we came back from London doing *The Tom Jones Show*, and two of the guys couldn't go on a trip to Chicago and Indiana, and were going to have to give up the dates."

Then Willard had an idea. "I said, 'Why don't we pool our resources with these guys from the Credibility Gap, and we'll do equal shares of our material?' And we did that. I became friendly with them, and we worked for about two weeks at Mr. Kelly's in Chicago, Milwaukee's Summerfest and a dinner theater in Versailles, Indiana.

"Over the years, I would run into them, or they would use me in some little project they were doing, and I think that was my [earliest] connection with *Spinal Tap*."

In 1975, Beebe left the Credibility Gap, and in 1976, it disbanded. McKean and Lander continued to work together, resurrecting two surly characters they had created together at Carnegie Tech College, Lenny and Ant'ny, for the ABC sitcom *Laverne and Shirley* (1976–1983). Renamed Lenny and Squiggy for the series, these two characters quickly became the sitcom's breakout stars.

In 1979, McKean and Lander worked on their own novelty musical album with Casablanca Records, *Lenny and the Squigtones*. The album asked the immortal question: "Is the world ready for Squigtomania?" and featured songs such as "Love is a Terrible Thing" and "So's Your Old Testament."

It was a nifty parody of fifties and early-sixties music, the age of *Laverne and Shirley*, but was also significant career-wise because it featured the earliest known credit for an enigmatic guitarist named Nigel Tufnel. That's right, Christopher Guest's British rocker actually made his debut on this Casablanca spin-off record, backing up his old college friend, Michael McKean.

Other important connections were made at the same time. McKean's *Laverne and Shirley* co-star was actress Penny Marshall, who back then was married to *All in the Family* (1971–1983) co-star, Rob Reiner. The son of comic legend Carl Reiner, Rob had been the brain trust behind an improvisational group called the Session at UCLA. Later a member of the Committee, another popular comedy group, Reiner was a successful comedy writer for *The Smothers Brothers Comedy Hour* (1967–1975) before making it big on Norman Lear's popular and controversial sitcom about Archie Bunker and family. He played Mike Stivic, known around the world as Meathead, a role for which he was honored with two Emmys.

Guest joined this circle of talent with appearances on *Laverne and Shirley* in 1976 and *All in the Family* in December of 1977. Then, in 1978, Rob Reiner teamed with Christopher Guest, Harry Shearer, Michael McKean, Billy Crystal, Martin Mull, Tom Leopold, and Johnny Brown for an ABC sketch comedy hour called *The T.V. Show*.

Fresh off *All in the Family*, Reiner appeared as a cast member and executive-produced the pilot with partner Phil Mishkin. Shearer also served as a producer, and Tom Trbovich directed all the segments, including a spoof of the popular ninety-minute, late-night rock series *The Midnight Special* (1973 – 1981). The special aired on June 24, 1979, and Reiner (as the Wolfman Jack–type announcer) introduced to the world a loud British rock band, a protean version of Spinal Tap.

The concept for this particular skit went back some years, to discussions Guest and McKean had shared at NYU about rock music and its stars. They pondered "how great and funny rock 'n' roll was when it had pomposity that didn't pay off," according to McKean. "You see it in all forms of music, but there was something about stadium rockers, when the stadium would go away and suddenly they're playing in little dives."[19]

From there, McKean and Guest developed a "hopeless English rockers sketch for cable TV,"[20] and, with Shearer's brilliant input, tweaked it into the trio as they appeared on *The T.V. Show.*

According to some resources, many of Nigel's prominent characteristics came out of the actor's stay in the Chateau Marmont in 1974, when Guest overheard a British rocker discussing his missing guitar.[21]

Playing the band members on *The T.V. Show* were Guest (as Nigel Tufnel), McKean (as David St. Hubbins), Shearer (as Derek Smalls) and Guest's friend, Loudon Wainwright III, on the keyboard. They performed a song entitled "Rock 'n' Roll Nightmare." Though the pilot never went to series status, it served an altogether more important purpose by uniting the creative forces of *This Is Spinal Tap.*

GUEST PERFORMANCES

The late 1970s and early 1980s found Christopher Guest jobbing about in small roles in a variety of feature films and TV mini-series. In 1978, he played a character in the Claudia Weill film *Girlfriends*, starring Melanie Mayron, and while on the set he met Bob Balaban, an actor who had made a splash in movies with a daring appearance in *Midnight Cowboy* (1969) and in Steven Spielberg's blockbuster *Close Encounters of the Third Kind* (1977).

"We were both actors in [*Girlfriends*]. There were two girls who were the stars of the movie, and we were the boyfriends," Balaban remembers. "I always had a good time with [Guest], and we got along really nicely." Nearly twenty years later, Guest would remember the experience and call Balaban to appear in *Waiting for Guffman*.

Guest also appeared as Jeb Stuart Magruder in the eight-hour TV mini-series based on former White House counsel John Dean's memoirs about

Watergate, *Blind Ambition* (1979), and in Walter Hill's epic western *The Long Riders* (1980).

In 1979, Guest gave voice to several animated characters in a French cartoon satire, originally rated X, entitled *Tarzoon, la Honte de la Jungle* (*Tarzoon, Shame of the Jungle*). Directed by Boris Szulzinger and animated by a Belgian artist named Picha, the film told the lewd story of ape-man Tarzoon, his monkey, Cheapo, and their effort to rescue the lady June from a tribe of penislike native tribesmen.

When the French film came to the United States for adaptation, several *Saturday Night Live* (1975 –) alumni toiled on the rewrite, including Anne Beatts and Michael O'Donoghue. Other performers on the project included Johny Weissmuller Jr., Bill Murray, and John Belushi. The American version, which Guest remembers as being heavily improvised in the recording sessions,[22] was quickly withdrawn from circulation after a limited theatrical release, in part because of copyright issues when the estate of the Tarzan creator Edgar Rice Burroughs allegedly complained.[23]

Perhaps Guest's strangest film from this era was *Heartbeeps* (1981), an eight-million dollar, science-fiction romance concerning two humanoid robots in love and on the run in the futuristic world of 1997. Directed by Allan Arkush, whose previous film was *Rock 'n' Roll High School* (1979), *Heartbeeps* starred the late Andy Kaufman as the robotic ValCom-17485 and Bernadette Peters as the mechanical woman, AquaCom-89045. Their R2D2-like child, named Phil, was given voice by the Grateful Dead's Jerry Garcia.

Billed fifth in this Universal production, Guest again co-starred with actress Melanie Mayron, this time portraying a fellow named Calvin who donned an orange jumpsuit and glasses, apparently resided in a junkyard, and cared for a pet raccoon named Rover. For Guest fans, the film's highlight was probably his ambush on the film's deep-voiced villain, a mobile robot and killing machine named Crimebuster.

Guest was soon back in more contemporary surroundings, working again with friend Rob Reiner on the TV movie *Million Dollar Infield* (1982). This effort starred Reiner and Guest as teammates on a Long Island softball team. Guest was a divorced guy named Bucky, and Bonnie Bedelia played co-producer Reiner's wife.

A sports-contest movie that foreshadowed some of the relationship angles of *The Big Chill* (1983), *Million Dollar Infield* also featured Shearer and Bruno Kirby, who would play limo driver Tommy Pischedda in *This Is Spinal Tap* soon thereafter.

Guest also appeared in another TV movie in 1982, *A Piano for Mrs. Cimino*, which starred the legendary Bette Davis.

IT'S A ROCK 'N' ROLL CREATION

This Is Spinal Tap, the rockumentary that shook the world, arrived in theaters in 1984, but it was a project that had been long in coming. Harry Shearer, Christopher Guest, Michael McKean, and Rob Reiner had worked on the concept for approximately four years before the first frame of film was ever shot. The group was particularly interested in crafting a rock 'n' roll movie that wasn't just funny, but *realistic* and — most important — accurate.

"The initial impulse for that was our mutual shared frustration when we saw all of these rock 'n' roll movies, and they kept getting it wrong," remembers Shearer. "People were supposedly playing guitars with their fingers in impossible positions, given what we were hearing. Forty million people in this country have taken guitar lessons, so why would you insult the audience quite that gratuitously if you don't have to?"

Unlike many actors, Guest, Shearer, and McKean didn't need to fake their performances, either instrumentally or vocally, and that meant they had a good shot at accurately observing and commenting on the crazy vicissitudes of the rock world.

"The idea was, 'Wouldn't it be fun to do a movie where people got this right for a change?'" says Shearer. "In the first instance, we didn't know if we wanted to focus on a band, or some backstage Rosencrantz and Guildenstern angle of a band, but then we realized the band was intrinsically more interesting, and funnier."

And there were certainly antecedents to lampoon. *Don't Look Back* (1967), by D.A. Pennebaker, was billed as a documentary, but few who watched it could legitimately deny that Bob Dylan put on quite a mannered performance for the camera, playing up his star "rebel" qualities to the utmost.

In 1978, director Martin Scorsese filmed a rock documentary about a group called the Band entitled *The Last Waltz.* He actually inserted himself into the proceedings, appearing as an on-screen guide, directing on-camera, calling retakes, and asking (mostly) inane questions of the group.

"The Scorsese model was there in *The Last Waltz,*" Shearer says. "It was something we were aware of, and we were certainly taking it into account."

As for the mockumentary form itself, it was a tricky and not-yet-fully evolved style back in the early eighties, when the *Tap* icons began exploring it. The Beatles' *A Hard Day's Night* (1964), directed by Richard Lester, looked at the backstage antics of the popular group with the band members playing themselves, but few audiences really took anything in it to be the cold, hard truth, in part because the film included carefully staged slapstick gags and featured comic buffoons like an old man, purportedly a relative of Paul McCartney, who was both a lech and a troublemaker.

In 1978, *The Rutles: All You Need Is Cash* explicitly mimicked the dress, hair, look, and style of the Beatles, but it was a very specific and obvious sort of put-on, not a wide-ranging look at the world of popular musicians.

Outside the music genre, the mockumentary — replete with location shooting and first-person interviews — had graced some low-budget horror films, including Charles Pierces' *The Legend of Boggy Creek* (1973). This was a particularly lame effort, since the film's creature was obviously a man in a suit and his attacks were mounted in lackluster fashion for the camera. For instance, a cat was so scared of the beast that it died of a heart attack — a fatal feline infarction. Not exactly stirring or believable material.

Even Woody Allen's *Zelig* (1983), an early and superior film of the *Forrest Gump* (1994) sub-genre that blended fake footage with historical, archival films, was only just being released as *Spinal Tap* was shooting, so it wasn't a role model for the struggling artists, either.

In many ways, *This Is Spinal Tap*, because of its realistic tone, and generalized references to a very particular world — hard rock — was forging new territory.

GIMME SOME MONEY

Seeking seed money to develop their initiative, the talents behind *Spinal Tap* were soon granted an audience with Sir Lew Grade, a British TV mogul who had seen great financial success in the 1960s and 1970s with dramas like Patrick McGoohan's *The Prisoner* (1967) and Gerry and Sylvia Anderson's epic *Space: 1999* (1975 – 1977).

At the commencement of the 1980s, Grade was the head of British TV production company ITC, but was also shifting heavily into the motion-picture world. His grandest and most expensive effort, and eventually his waterloo, was a thirty-five million dollar production of Clive Cussler's bestseller, *Raise the Titanic* (1980), a movie epic envisioned as "the most incredible undersea adventure of our time."

Marble Arch was the United States branch of Sir Grade's empire, and it put up some development money, approximately $60,000,[24] for the Spinal Tap brain trust to compose a script based on their concept. Yet when it came time to write the planned feature film, the group found themselves in something of a jam.

"We got a deal to write a script about this band, and sat in a hotel room for about three or four days — with me typing — trying to actually write a first-draft screenplay," Shearer remembers. "Then, at one point, we looked at each other and said, 'You know, this is supposed to be a sales tool in getting this movie made, and nobody is going to be able to read this and understand what we mean. This won't help us get the movie made.'"

And since Shearer, McKean, Guest, and Reiner were all doing okay financially at the time, the group decided instead to take Grade's script money and produce a demo reel instead.

"We knew we were making it in the documentary-style," explains Shearer. "We already made that choice. That was the going style for people looking at rock 'n' roll bands. So we were simultaneously making fun of a band and the adoring documentarian."

The group shot the demo over a four-day period, and Reiner began the task of editing it. All those involved felt a filmed presentation was a more compelling method of conveying their concept, but despite the effort and ingenuity they evidenced, there were no bites, and Grade's Marble Arch dropped out of the development process.

Studio after studio refused to produce the rockumentary. In many cases, executives wondered why anyone would make a movie about a band that nobody had ever even heard of. Even worse, some offered insipid advice that the moviemakers tweak their concept to be more like a traditional comedy, with broader, more easily understood jokes.

Of course, the latter notion was anathema to Shearer ("comedy is good, reality is better"), Guest (comedy is reality "plus one step further"), and the rest, all of whom were rapidly evolving their own unique comedy style and were itching to test it.

"Not to sound horribly pompous, but most movies lie, and they lie like sons of bitches," explains Shearer. "People now get so much of what they know about the world from movies, so it's nice every once in a while to tell them the truth about how things are."

That could have been *This Is Spinal Tap*'s mantra.

Fortunately, the filmmakers were finally given a helping hand by an old friend from Rob Reiner's *All in the Family* days. Emmy-winning producer Norman Lear had parlayed his television success in the 1970s and his profitable Tandem Enterprises into the high-stakes movie world beginning in 1982. His company purchased Avco-Embassy, a company responsible for several genre flicks, including John Carpenter's *The Fog* (1980) and *Escape from New York* (1981). Lear was the right man at the right time, and with Avco-Embassy's backing, *Spinal Tap* looked like it was indeed going to get made.

Budgeted at approximately two million dollars, *This Is Spinal Tap* geared up for production in the spring of 1982. Peter Smokler, a documentary cinematographer who had worked as a cameraman (with Robert Primes and *Star Wars*' George Lucas) on *Gimme Shelter*, joined the team as cinematographer, "wittily" re-creating the "grainy visual style of cinema verite"[25] in the process.

Still, that didn't mean the celebrated director of photography was comfortable with his work. Author Karl French reported in *This Is Spinal Tap: The Official Companion* that Smokler frequently sought re-assurance from director Reiner that he was doing the right thing by authentically re-creating the look of other rock documentaries.

"Trust me, this is funny," Reiner would tell him.[26]

DOIN' IT IN DOUBLY

It was at approximately this time that British actress June Chadwick, who later played the villainous Lydia on *V: The Series* (1984) and starred in films such as *Jumpin' Jack Flash* (1986), also became involved with *This Is Spinal Tap*.

"I think it was late in the stages of its development," she recalls. "They had apparently done this twenty-minute demo and were taking it around, showing it to people. And the consensus, they thought, was that there was no storyline to it, and they needed a storyline. So they came up with the storyline of my character [Jeanine Pettibone] coming in. They'd already formed the fictitious band before I came on the scene.

"I was booked to do — and I know this is really going to impress you — a movie called *Revenge of the Ninja*, and was in the process of practicing my limited martial arts, and the movie kept changing its locations and start date, so I slid side-wise, and hopefully upwards, to be in *This Is Spinal Tap*," she says.

"I went in and and met everybody, and I hadn't been over from England that long, and I had no idea who anyone was, which was fortunate, because I wasn't intimidated at this point. They asked me to come back and impro-vise with them, and I remember thinking, 'Oh yeah, right, let's see if these guys can do a cockney accent or a London accent. There's no way Americans can do that!' So I came back, and we sat around improvising and it was fun, and I had a good time."

With Chadwick involved as David St. Hubbins' meddling girlfriend, Jeanine, *This Is Spinal Tap* revved up. Chadwick remembers being comforted by the fact that there was at least something like a script to follow, although no specific dialogue.

"I was a bit clueless as to everything that was going on and how it was all going to be put together," she remembers. "There was a basic story, going from A to B, but no dialogue.

"I was given the fact that I was into horoscopes and yoga. I actually hadn't done yoga, so I went to have lessons and looked at some books and came up with the thing of sticking your tongue out, which is the lion pose, and is actually [a remedy] for a sore throat [St. Hubbins' condition in the film], which I thought was cool.

"As for the horoscopes, I read some books and basically learned things all wrong, if I could." she laughs. "You know, Saturn's in the house of the sixth moon, or something. I had no idea what I was talking about, and thought that was probably a good thing. So that was mainly the preparation I did. I thought it behooved me to not play stupid, but ignorant. It wasn't as if *I* thought I was ignorant, because obviously as the character I really thought that I knew exactly what I was doing. My preparation was also to come from the premise that I really cared about what happened to the band, because I cared what happened to my boyfriend. That's why I wanted to become the manager."

This Is Spinal Tap commenced a five-week shooting period in 1983. Chadwick remembers that the first days on the set were a bit intimidating. "In all honesty, it was frightening, because my first day on the set I had somebody saying I hadn't signed the contract and couldn't go to work until I signed, and my agent was unavailable.

"I was fairly green to all this, and so I was kind of panicky," Chadwick explains. "I remember really thinking that these boys were so clever, so clever and funny. At some point quite early on, I realized that and got to know their backgrounds. These guys were full-fledged comedy writers that had been doing this project for two years, and I was kind of wafting in and sitting in with them, somehow. So that factor was scary."

Despite all the gossip over the years about the inspiration for the role, Chadwick insists that, to her knowledge, Jeanine was not specifically modeled on Yoko Ono, the woman who reputedly broke up the Beatles.

Nor Anita Pallenberg.

"I didn't model this character on anybody," she says. "It sort of started to come together a little bit when I was doing homework on what she was into. So the astrology became really important. The yoga became really important. The fact that David had a sore throat and couldn't sing and needed yoga — because that's the only thing that would have got him better — was important to me.

"I didn't start to see anything until I had the tenth person say, 'Oh, it's a Yoko Ono character,' and I thought, 'Oh, maybe it is.' That was after the film," she recalls. "I remember going to the first screening and somebody said to me, 'Oh god, you're such a bitch,' and I was really hurt! 'I was? Really?' Now, over time, I say, 'Of course, I was.'"

Though *This Is Spinal Tap* was primarily improvised, Chadwick remembers a few occasions when rehearsals were involved. In particular, the scene in the diner in which Jeanine presents her strange sketches of Spinal Tap (as creatures based on the signs of the Zodiac) to the band. This is the so-called "doubly" scene, because of Jeanine's mispronunciation of the word "Dolby."

"The reason we had the rehearsal was because there were points that had to be put in," says Chadwick. "The problem with improvising is that when you get people that aren't necessarily able to do it very well, everybody wants to talk, and everybody talks on top of each other. I think it was smart of Rob to say, 'Let's rehearse this, so we know where the attention needs to be.' It was probably as much for the cameraman as it was for us, too."

Chadwick recalls the origin of that memorable turn of phrase: "That line was given to me by Chris Guest, and I thank him profusely for it each time I see him. No, I don't, but he very graciously said, 'It's the way you executed it that was funny.' Again, it was one of those things that once I was given it, there was no question that 'doubly' was the right phrase to use. So it was a combination of both of us, I suppose."

Chadwick remembers that one of the pleasures of working on *This Is Spinal Tap* was fully developing the character of Jeanine, down to her somewhat odd wardrobe, which became a subject for abuse in the film from the caustic mouth of Tony Hendra's Ian, who calls it "an Australian's nightmare."

"I considered myself quite trendy at the time," Chadwick says. "London was well ahead of L.A., and still is, and has always been a little avant-garde in its fashion, if you can put it that way. So a lot of the clothes were actually mine, but they were put together all wrong. What wouldn't go with what — and then [we'd] put it in there, and added something frightful to that, too. I was having so much fun with it. It was one of those things where I decided I looked really cool."

A FAN OF THE WHOLE GENRE

Another cast member appearing in *This Is Spinal Tap* was Fred Willard. "I had met Rob Reiner because I was doing a show called *Fernwood 2-Night* (1977 – 78) in the same studio where he was doing *All in the Family*, and we would pass each other all the time. I also worked with his then-wife, Penny Marshall, in *Laverne and Shirley*, where Michael McKean and David Lander were, and I had great respect for them, so I had a feeling when a part came up in *Spinal Tap* that it was Harry Shearer and Michael McKean that said, 'You've got to get Fred Willard for this.'"

Willard, however, wasn't interested in assuming the role of air force officer, Lt. Bob Hookstratten — at least at first. "I initially didn't want to do the part. My agent called and said, 'Rob Reiner is doing this movie about a heavy metal group, and you'd be an air force lieutenant that meets them.' I said, 'Oh, I'm tired of playing jackasses,' and my agent said, 'Rob would love for you to come out for a meeting,' and I really resisted it."

But Willard relented. "What could I lose meeting with Rob Reiner?" he asks. "So I got there, and his secretary said, 'Rob and Harry and everybody went for a coffee break, but they want you to see this little ten-minute film they've made.'"

Willard watched the documentary and was won over. "Watching it, I thought, 'I can't believe I'm watching improv! I can't believe this isn't a real documentary!' They came back from the break and I said, 'I have to be a part of this movie.' Rob said, 'Shall we talk about money and billing?' I said 'I don't care, I've just got to be in this movie.' So that's how I got the part. That kind of documentary style has always fascinated me."

WALKING THAT FINE LINE

When *This Is Spinal Tap* completed production, it featured appearances from Billy Crystal, Dana Carvey, Patrick Macnee, Fran Drescher, and others. Perhaps more to the point, there were more than one hundred hours of footage to sift through. There are many legends surrounding the making of *This Is Spinal Tap*, but the holy grail of *Tap* lore is probably the much-sought-after, four-and-a-half-hour "director's cut" first shown to the cast by Reiner after a series of previews that were much shorter.

McKean described this cut as "amazing," and noted that the cast saw "a lot of stuff we wanted to boot out, storylines that had to go. Some of that stuff resulted in a better movie. The removal of things gave us jokes we didn't know we had."[27]

When it was released in 1984, after nine long months of editing, *Spinal Tap* floored the critics. The film follows the members of Spinal Tap (and entourage) through every iteration of its disastrous North American tour. Matters go from bad to worse for the British rockers as gigs are canceled left and right, the band loses its way backstage, and later receives second billing on a marquee behind a puppet show. Petty rivalries are exposed in the group as lead singer David St. Hubbins' girlfriend, Jeanine, wheedles her way into the band's management, an act which causes David's best friend, Nigel, to leave in a huff. It is a band's death spiral caught on film for the ages.

"In a style reminiscent of Martin Scorsese's *The Last Waltz*, Reiner does take-offs on practically every rock cliche there is, with often hilarious results," wrote Ira Hellman for *People* magazine.[28] The movie has a "Swiftian sense of the ridiculous," according to critic John Nange, and is "especially trenchant in mimicking the vulgarity ... pretension ... and performing buffoonery that infects today's heavy rock underground."[29]

Newsweek's David Ansen realized the film was a "satire of the documentary form itself, complete with perfectly faded clips from old TV shows of the band in its mod and flower-child incarnations."[30]

More to the point, *This Is Spinal Tap* really stunned critics and industry outsiders because of one particular factor. It looked and felt terribly, painfully, awkwardly *real*.

"People were saying, 'Who is this band, and how come we haven't heard of them?'" Chadwick remembers.

In the words of narrator Marty DiBergi, the film evoked the sights, sounds, and smells of a rock band on the road, and that was always the intention, to express the actuality of that particular experience.

"That's one of the places where the bunch of us meet up in our sensibilities," Shearer acknowledges. "We do love that, the musicians who have said, 'Man, I can't watch *Spinal Tap*, it's too much like my life.' That's the highest compliment of all. It beats all the Oscar nominations we never got."

"I've had a lot of musicians say to me, 'Oh god, I couldn't watch that, it was too real,'" Chadwick repeats. "I give a lot of credit to Rob and Chris Guest and Harry Shearer and Michael. I think that they are comedy geniuses."

"We made up so little on *Spinal Tap*," Shearer acknowledges. "A vast majority of that movie was stuff that had happened to us on the road. The 'Kick My Ass' [scene] was a literal transcription of something that happened to Michael and me on the road. The air force base [scenes were based on] something that happened to our first keyboard player in his next band. I can go down the list for all the things that were real. Obviously, the scenario of a band that was almost destroyed by a woman — take your pick of how many times that has happened in rock 'n' roll!"

Over the years, a sort of cottage industry of speculation has sprung up around *This Is Spinal Tap*, with curious journalists and musicians attempting to determine who, precisely, Shearer, Guest, McKean, and Reiner were *really* alluding to in their rockumentary.

Like *Don't Look Back*, *This Is Spinal Tap* ponders the connections between business and artistry. In Pennebaker's film, the camera tracked Bob Dylan from a press conference to an informal meeting with his management and record company folks (like Spinal Tap's meeting with Sir Eton-Hogg of Polymer Records). Albert Grossman, Dylan's manager, is captured on film trying to arrange a performance for the BBC and is upset at the company's offer. It's a scene not so different from Ian's conversations with Bobbi Flekman (played by Fran Drescher). Later, Pennebaker's camera follows Dylan through a backstage maze as the icon gets lost trying to escape the building, again not unlike Spinal Tap's unfortunate experience.

Spinal Tap also adopts the stylistic flourishes of *The Last Waltz*. In both films, the band members are introduced while on stage performing, their names superimposed beneath them during a concert.

With Scorsese as the on-screen narrator in *The Last Waltz*, the members of the Band recount its byzantine history, replete with multiple name changes. Originally, the Band was known as the Crackers, but then became the Honkies — until they realized the latter moniker was "too street." In the early moments of Reiner's film, the members of Tap discuss their storied genesis as the Creatures, the Lovely Lads, the Originals, then the New Originals, then the Thamesmen, and so forth.

The Last Waltz also pauses to not-so-subtly assert that the members of the Band are actually "classically trained," because some members play the violin or speak Gaelic, affectations also reflected to an extent by Spinal Tap's quasi-historical number, "Stonehenge" and Nigel's (painful) soloing on the violin.

Another moment in *This Is Spinal Tap*, Derek's untimely confinement in a pod on stage, has been described as being reminiscent of Screamin' Jay Hawkin's performance of "I Put a Spell on You" in the Apollo Theater in 1956, when the artist became trapped in a coffin and famously lost control of his bowels.[31]

Groups as diverse as Foghat, Journey, and the Rolling Stones have all been named by scholars in relation to the events portrayed in *This Is Spinal Tap*, but Shearer, McKean, and Guest have persistently maintained that the film gazes not at these particular groups, but merely the conventions of the genre.

"It has always been a pastiche," Shearer asserts. "There are a lot of people walking around saying 'That's about us.' That's nice, but it's not true."[32]

The time setting for *Spinal Tap*, according to Shearer, "was the end of the roller-coaster ride that started in the late sixties, when rock 'n' roll was supposed to be this big social force, and by the time we made *Tap*, that had been clearly played out, but people were still walking around posing as if it were true. To me, that was part of the thematic thrust of the movie. The music has left the building."

A great running joke in *This Is Spinal Tap* involves the pervasive pretension of rock 'n' rollers in their choice of words and descriptions during interviews. This plays out in the film's speech, as uttered by Guest, Shearer, and McKean. They perfectly echo the circular logic and philosophical confusion exemplified by nearly every well-meaning but inarticulate rocker down through the ages.

"There's no ideas in *Time* magazine, there's just facts," Bob Dylan states cryptically in *Don't Look Back*. "Every word has its little letter and its big letter." *The Last Waltz*, according to Rick Danko of the Band, is "a "celebration of the beginning of the end of the beginning."

These elliptical and muddled remarks exemplify the sense that, in the music world at least, profundity is truly in the eye of the beholder, a notion circled delicately throughout *Spinal Tap*, from Nigel's declaration that there is "a fine line between stupid and clever" to Derek's description of himself as "lukewarm water," balancing the hot and cold geniuses of monsieurs Tufnel and St. Hubbins.

When describing the film, *School of Rock* (2003) star and comedian Jack Black noted that rock only really works well in film when movie creators make fun of it at the same time as they embrace it. "That's what *Spinal Tap* did, and that's why it's so fuckin' great."[33]

Mirroring that notion, Smokler's camera work, with its rough zooms, herky-jerky tracking shots, and "inflammatory" close-ups of the perpetually confused band members, captures the immediacy of the post-1950s documentary ethos laid down by Pennebaker, the Maysles, and other practitioners of the form. Smokler's camera work grants viewers a snapshot of life as it is unfolding, warts — and herpes — intact.

In the process, these lengthy takes, the awkward silences, and yes, the stammering and improvised dialogue, reduce the film's relative aesthetic distance from the viewer; the ability to distinguish what is real and what is staged.

"You're not going to make us into Spinal Tap, are you?"[34] the members of Depeche Mode once asked filmmaker Pennebaker when he set out to film a documentary on them. That's a sentiment that has no doubt been repeated, ad infinitum, among wary rock bands, and a testament to just how accurate the film really is.

"Getting it right gets it funny," Shearer says, and this was a lesson that he, Guest, and the others carried away from the film, even though it was not a financial success at the time. This style of work, based on the rigorous pillars of research and observation, and executed in naturalistic, spontaneous, improvisational style, resulted in a cinematic experience not only more immediate and true than traditional narratives, but much funnier as well. It is this style that would come to dominate Guest's film career in the late 1990s and early twenty-first century with his trilogy of documentary-style comedies.

On top of its significant influence within its creative circle, *This Is Spinal Tap* has emerged as one of the greatest cult films of all-time, contributing numerous catchphrases (like "there's a fine line between stupid and clever," and "this goes up to eleven") to the pop-culture lexicon.

It's a vindication of sorts.

"We're really proud of *Spinal Tap* because we basically had to will that film into being and into release, every step of the way," says Shearer. "There was absolutely no encouragement and no understanding, with the exception of Norman Lear, who said okay, fled the scene, and left the company [Avco-Embassy]. So we were just pushing that rug uphill all the time, and I think we're entitled to feel a little vindicated that we were right and all those assholes were wrong."

LIVE FROM NEW YORK

While *This Is Spinal Tap* played in theaters and garnered recognition on many critical top-ten lists for the year, Christopher Guest joined co-star Harry Shearer for a second venture. Along with Martin Short, they became regular "not ready for primetime players" on *Saturday Night Live* (*SNL*), but for just a single season.

This brief tenure occurred during one of the series' most tumultuous eras, when producer Lorne Michaels was no longer involved, and executive Dick Ebersol was his replacement. Ebersol brought aboard the established comedic stars because the series was faltering badly and needed an infusion of not just fresh blood, but *experienced* blood. Shearer had worked as a writer on the show once before, back in the mid-1970s, so he was familiar with the grind, but the environment was a new one for Guest.

A stint on *SNL* offered Guest the opportunity to write sketches, but also gain directing experience. Much of the material on the series in the 1984–85 season wasn't quite as live as the title indicated, and several short films were shot ahead of time. These were written and produced by the likes of Guest, Shearer, Billy Crystal, and Martin Short.

During his time there, Guest played a number of recurring characters, including the Weekend Update news anchor and Rajiv Vindaloo (in the "100,000 Jackpot Wad" sketch). Michael McKean also joined Shearer and Guest to reprise his *Spinal Tap* role, and the Folksmen, the folk music trio featured in *A Mighty Wind*, first surfaced during this one-season stint to sing "Old Joe's Place."

Guest also appeared in "Broadway Gumby Rose" with Billy Crystal and Martin Short, but perhaps his most memorable accomplishment was an effort with Shearer and Short on a format and theme they all enjoyed: a mock-documentary about aspiring, starry-eyed individuals.

"We did a quasi-documentary short film on *Saturday Night Live*, Chris and I and Marty Short, which was about male synchronized swimmers," Shearer recalls. "It was that same kind of theme. It's just one of the things that makes us laugh."

In the now classic sketch, Shearer plays Gerald, Short plays his swim partner, Lawrence, and Guest is their trainer. Gerald has quit his accounting firm to devote himself exclusively to the "sport" of male synchronized swimming, while a hapless Lawrence doesn't even know how to swim. Guest's coach character is a director of regional theater, "including Shakespeare in the park."[35]

The sketch aired on October 16, 1984, and became the subject *du jour* at watercoolers around the nation on the following Monday. Despite its lampooning nature, the skit also won admirers among the field it knowingly tweaked.

"It was probably the best publicity the sport ever got," reported one synchronized swimmer, though he noted that the sport was "nowhere near as flowery."36

"I was obsessed with the year he was on *Saturday Night Live*," actress Deborah Theaker admits. "I thought that the character work they did ... was superlative. I just had never seen anything like it."

Shearer, Guest, Short, and Crystal all won accolades for shoring up *Saturday Night Live*, but that didn't mean that Guest, with his ultra-serious temperament, necessarily made new friends.

"Chris Guest is impossible to talk to ... the man is an emotional desert," Elliot Wald, one of *SNL*'s writers at the time, told Tom Shales and James Andrew Miller for their book about the series, *Live from New York*. "He will not break his deadpan for any force on earth, so it is very hard to interact with him in a friendly way."37

Though Guest made use of the *SNL* experience to write and direct his film shorts, he departed the series — as promised, after one season — and later reflected on it without much affection. "We've done our time in the [*SNL*] pit, and basically nothing is spontaneous," he told *Seattle Weekly*'s Tim Appelo. "It's all read off cue cards, and nobody bothers to learn lines, because it's changed at the last minute."38

HIS FINGERS GO UP TO ELEVEN

After his stint on *Saturday Night Live*, Guest appeared in a number of films, including the remake of Roger Corman's *Little Shop of Horrors* (1986), directed by Frank Oz, and Robert Altman's *Beyond Therapy* (1987). But his most popular film from this period was no doubt Rob Reiner's adaptation of the William Goldman 1973 fantasy novel *The Princess Bride: S. Morgenstern's Classic Tale of True Love and High Adventures.*

A fifteen-million-dollar effort shot in the summer of 1986 at Shepperton Studios in England, the film stars Cary Elwes, Mandy Patinkin, Robin Wright, Peter Falk, Fred Savage, Andre the Giant, Wallace Shawn, Mel Smith, Carol Kane, and Guest's friend Billy Crystal, as Miracle Max.

Guest portrays the villainous Count Tyrone Rugen, an aristocrat with six fingers on one hand (making the total sum of the digits on his hands *eleven*). *Major domo* to Florin's Prince Humperdinck (Chris Sarandon), Count Rugen specializes in torture and swordplay, and has murdered the father of Inigo Montoya, Patinkin's character, spawning Montoya's lifelong quest for vengeance. Like *Spinal Tap*, *The Princess Bride* was only a moderate success when released in theaters in September 1987, but it soon became a cult classic, especially popular with college audiences.

Also like *Spinal Tap*, Reiner's new film became renowned for several lines of quotable dialogue, including Patinkin's immortal line, "My name is Inigo Montoya; you killed my father; prepare to die," and young Westley's constant refrain to Buttercup, "As you wish."

Fans of *This Is Spinal Tap* might also note that Marty DiBergi's Coral Sea naval cap appears briefly in the film's opening sequence. If you watch closely, you can see it for a split second, immediately to the right of Fred Savage's character as he sits up in bed and his mother kisses him on the forehead.

CALL MY SECRETARY, I'LL CALL YOU BACK

In 1988, Guest accepted a new challenge and prepared to direct his first feature film. The property he co-wrote and developed was called *The Big Picture*, the story of a young film student named Nick Chapman who, after winning the tenth annual Student Film Award, is seduced by Hollywood and forced to make compromises in his plans, vision, and even his personal life.

With a screenplay by Guest, Michael McKean, and Michael Varhol, *The Big Picture*'s knowing screenplay diagramed in often stark terms how a movie-loving, somewhat callow guy might lose everything important to him by attempting to become successful in the cutthroat, insincere world of Hollywood.

In particular, Nick sees his proposed Ingmar Bergman–like film, a bleak black-and-white affair about adult infidelity, cheapened and then transformed into a jiggling comedy called *Beach Nuts*, a sex farce featuring ghost stewardesses.

After losing his longtime girlfriend, his best buddy, and finally his project, Nick has to go back to basics, start over, and succeed on his own terms by doing good work and exhibiting a degree of patience.

The ubiquitous Kevin Bacon was cast in the film as Nick; Jennifer Jason Leigh is his avant-garde film student friend, Lydia; and Michael McKean plays Nick's cinematographer, a more mature fellow named Emmet Sumner, who is planning to shoot a movie called *Coffins from Hell*. Representing temptation is sultry Terri Hatcher as an ambitious ingenue named Gretchen Gorman, and the late J.T. Walsh was hired to play the controlling, mind-fucking studio head, Allen Habel.

It is Martin Short, however, who steals the show in an uncredited cameo as agent Neil Sussman, who memorably informs Nick, "I don't know you or your work ... but I think you have talent."

Fran Drescher, Polymer Record's Bobbi Flekman herself, also appeared briefly in one party sequence set at the 4.6-million-dollar estate of a movie mogul. Cameos from Elliott Gould, June Lockhart, Roddy McDowall, John Cleese, and Stephen Collins rounded out the picture.

The Big Picture was production designer Joseph T. Garrity's first assignment with Christopher Guest. After graduating from the American Film Institute (AFI) in Los Angeles, he served as a production designer for Cannon films. When he was interviewed for this book, Garrity was hard at work on a new Hilary Duff film, *Heart of Summer*. He recalled his first meeting with Guest, which occurred just a few years after his own student film days.

"What was fun about [*The Big Picture*] for me," says Garrity, "was that I had come from the American Film Institute about five years before the film was made in 1988, so I really connected with this film guy from a small town with no connections coming to the big city. Through his eyes, we see quite an array of characters. The people that make these movies — the assistants that work for these people — it's just amazing."

According to Garrity, Guest also identified closely with the material. "Chris and his writing partners were always pitching things, or in people's offices. They got to [see] a whole array of agents and the schmoozing that goes on. I have a real sense that Chris, although he's in the business, would rather be fly-fishing. He has a lovely house up in Idaho. Whenever he can get there, he goes there, and you see that in the Kevin Bacon character, where he goes out to the desert to get away from it all.

"What's really important is family and relationships," Garrity stresses, "and the business, though it's fascinating, can really turn you into jokes and caricatures. I think Kevin Bacon's character gets suckered into this, falls into this world, and loses very important people. I related to him, and I probably talked about that in the interview with Chris.

"We all dream about working on movies in our little towns in America, but very few of us get to do it. I remember at AFI I didn't even have a car — I bicycled to school — and I remember coming down from Graystone Mansion in Beverly Hills, where the school was, and just stopping and looking out over the city lights and saying, 'I can't believe I'm here. I can't believe this is really happening.' And I still think that."

And what were Garrity's initial impressions of Christopher Guest, an artist he has collaborated with successfully for more than fifteen years? "He's a curious fellow and a great guy," Garrity describes. "He's very quiet. The interview [for *The Big Picture*] was very peculiar. He came in the room and said, 'Well, here we are,' and I went, 'Uhhhh...' I felt like I had to make this go on, and, like him, I'm a very quiet person. I think that this is something that he likes about me, maybe — that I'm not always calling him; I'm not always trying to schmooze with him.

"He doesn't talk a lot," Garrity continues. "He'll kind of stare you down and look at you, and you'll wonder, 'What's he thinking?' Especially for new people. I feel very comfortable with him, and a lot of people say, 'Come with me, I need to talk to him about something,' or 'Help me get his attention.' He would prefer to work with fewer people; he would prefer that a movie was made with ten people."

Like *Spinal Tap*, many of the inside jokes in *The Big Picture* came specifically from Guest's experiences in the business, according to Garrity. One of the funniest and most oft-noted in reviews involved J.T. Walsh's unique office on the studio lot. Unlike its commonplace surroundings in the studio building, his office is decorated extravagantly in an over-the-top, southwestern motif.

"That was a big deal back then," Garrity remembers. "That look was happening, and I remember Chris telling me about all these offices that he went into. You'd go into a regular hallway, to a regular secretary's station, and then, from the point of the doorway, you'd enter an office where an interior designer came in and created this whole world of the Southwest, or whatever it was. Everyone was into this look, and it started at the threshold of the office and everything else was very ordinary.

"That's what we tried to do. Nick is called in, the door opens, and suddenly there's smoke in the room, there's atmosphere, there's the hot sun of the Southwest, and you're thinking, 'Where did this room come from?'"

The Big Picture also lampoons the stylistic excesses of many student films. "I think his comment there was that a lot of these kids were getting into prestigious film schools because of their parents," notes Garrity, because one of the students is a big-time agent's son. "He doesn't even know how to make movies, his father just gets him a lot of stars, and he thinks that will win him the prize, even though he is a terrible filmmaker.

"And then the other, heavier-set guy who is the Napoleon-like character is bombastic. His film is wide screen and over dramatic," concludes Garrity. "[Those are] just a bunch of details that come from student films that Chris has seen."

For instance, Lydia's student film is an avant-garde potpourri, crammed with strange symbols and nonsensical images. "We had fun with that. We just went nuts," Garrity recalls. "We put a door frame in the middle of the street, and she comes out of it for no reason with a leaf blower, and she was blowing her furniture on this limbo set that we did."

Nick Chapman's student film, a black-and-white magnum opus called *First Date*, intentionally resembles a German expressionist effort. "I called Kevin Bacon our little Orson Welles. We thought of him as very black and white," explains Garrity. "His house is black and white, his car is black and white, and we used grays, blacks, and whites for all his interiors.

"At the end [of the film], on the soundstage, we had snow machines going," Garrity remembers. "That was originally going to happen up in Big Bear state, on location, to take the house up into the mountains and do it there. But I said, 'Maybe he wouldn't do that.' I thought of Orson Welles and *Citizen Kane* (1946), and [how] all those sets were built. I thought he would want to have more control over the environment."

Guest liked the idea of filming the movie's conclusion on a soundstage, and ultimately that's how it happened.

"Chris is a great listener," says Garrity. "Sometimes he is very particular about what he wants, and sometimes he isn't at all. Sometimes he gives you no reaction whether he likes something or doesn't, and a lot of people who are newcomers with Chris wonder if he likes what they're doing."

Shot by cinematographer Jeffrey Jur and scored by Guest's friend David Nichtern, *The Big Picture* filmed around the exteriors of Warner Brothers Studio, and also at Raleigh Studios, near Paramount.

"It was a couple of different places turning into one studio," Garrity recalls. "We never named a studio. We were a little concerned about that, and who we were lampooning. But it was a general lampooning … and I don't think any of it was taking things too far beyond what it really is."

Maybe just reality, plus one step further.

When *The Big Picture* premiered in the fall of 1989, reviewers in general welcomed it as a clever and sly, but never cruel, view of the subject matter. "The picture shows none of the nastiness of such Hollywood satires as *Day of the Locust* (1975). It does hint at inside knowledge,"[39] wrote Ralph Novak in *People*.

"Guest's direction takes lots of interesting turns," noted the authors of *Comedy Central: The Essential Guide to Comedy*. "It's the ultimate movie parody."[40]

"Guest's heart is in the right place,"[41] Michael Wilmington added in the *Los Angeles Times*. "You'll get all the jokes even if you've never set foot in Los Angeles," concluded the *Nation*'s Stuart Klawans, "The problem, I think, is that everybody in the movie tries so hard. The filmmakers really want to be whimsical; they want to be original; they want you to know how hard it was to make a movie about themselves."[42]

Despite mostly positive notices, *The Big Picture*, a five-million-dollar venture, didn't draw large audiences, and failed to recoup its cost. Looking at it today, one can see how well it fits into Guest's oeuvre, a tenderhearted but sharply observant film about a starry-eyed someone hoping to make it and become famous.

Where the film differs from some of the director's other work (like *Waiting for Guffman*, for example) is that the character of Chapman is actually talented, and indeed has the right stuff to succeed in the industry, if only he remains true to himself. His primary conflicts are his desire for instant gratification and his propensity to sell out versus actually earning his laurels.

Also, it is an interesting distinction to note that, in general, Guest's documentary-style comedies are not really parodies or satires, but merely "fly on the wall" observations of one particular venue or another.

"Satire, as we all know, is a little bit on the bloodless side because the performers stand back from the characters and look at them and comment on them, comment on the scene, and the whole story," considers actor Paul Dooley. "That's the way it's done. It's much less emotional or heartfelt, because satire has a coldness in it. It's trying to make a point. It's more hostile than some comedy."

Guest may be tender with his leads in *The Big Picture*, but some aspects of the film, notably the portions concerning agents, studio executives, and studio "yes men," do lapse into satire. These moments seem more legitimately skewering than any moments in the documentary-style comedies, and deservedly so.

The student films presented at the opening awards ceremony also appear to satirize the conventions (or cliches) of the amateur-moviemaking world in much the same way that *This Is Spinal Tap* evokes the world of British rockers on a downward slide. Guest's camera captures this world, warts and all, replete with exaggerated, over-the-top angles, slightly off-balance editing, and basic, declarative line readings by non-professional actors. For anyone who has ever made an amateur film, these movies are a dead-on, perfect grace note in the film's bigger picture.

A FEW GOOD APPEARANCES

In the summer of 1991, CBS briefly aired a half-hour sitcom that was unlike anything the world had seen. The series, called *Morton and Hayes*, was devoted to the rebroadcasting of ostensibly classic films of the 1930s and early 1940s featuring a daffy, Abbott and Costello–like comedy duo, Chick Morton (Kevin Pollak) and Eddie Hayes (Bob Amaral).

One week, the hapless duo would appear in a ridiculous film noir, another week, a 1940s Universal-style horror film, and the next a jungle adventure. Fresh off the success of his Stephen King adaptation of *Misery* (1990), Rob Reiner created the series with his *T.V. Show* partner, Phil Mishkin, and also appeared as the admiring host of each series segment.

Christopher Guest and Michael McKean were heavily involved in the series, composing the show's original music and directing various installments. An executive producer, Guest also directed five of the six episodes. Among the series writers were Dick Blasucci, Joe Flaherty, Carl Gottlieb, McKean, and Guest.

Though the series disappeared from the airwaves by the end of August 1991, *Morton and Hayes* offered Guest an opportunity to direct several short features of various styles. He also worked with a number of friends who would later appear in his films, including Catherine O'Hara in "Daffy Dicks" (airdate: July 24, 1991), Lewis Arquette in "Society Saps" (airdate: August 7, 1991), and Paul Benedict in "The Vase Shop" (airdate: August 21, 1991).

Guest also appeared in the series in notable and diverse performances, including his most memorable character, El Supremo in "Oafs Overboard" (airdate: August 14, 1991). McKean starred in the horror pastiche, "The Bride of Mummula" (airdate: July 31, 1991), playing mad scientist Dr. Mummenschwantz.

Entertainment Weekly called *Morton and Hayes* "peculiar," and noted that the show "wasn't very funny," though Pollack was singled out as "terrific — brassy, amusingly insincere, endearingly shifty-eyed."[43] Though *Morton and Hayes* did generate a small and devoted fan following, it never became the success that CBS hoped for.

Still, the very premise reveals once more how Reiner, Guest, and cohorts always play with form, in this case creating a mock comedy team, replete with their archival films (the actual episodes) and career biographies. It was a shame that more people didn't get the joke.

That wasn't the problem, however, with 1992's *Return of Spinal Tap* (also known as the Twenty-fifth Anniversary London Sell-Out Tour.) By this time, fiction had become fact, and the presentation (which originally aired on TV) wasn't a documentary of a fake tour, but footage of a real concert at London's Royal Albert Hall, held in July of 1992. Hosted by Bob Geldof, this booking was the culmination of a world tour that had swept the group from Australia to Canada and beyond to publicize the release of their new record, *Break Like the Wind*, which actually made it to sixty-one on the *Billboard* album charts.[44]

It was a very good year for Spinal Tap. Not only was their album a hit, but their video for "Bitch School" made a stir on MTV.

"I was working at Canada's Much Music Premiere [the Canadian rock music equivalent of MTV] and the premiere of 'Bitch School' by Spinal Tap was on," Deb Theaker remembers. "My VCR didn't work, so I faked illness and raced up the street so I could see it."

Break Like the Wind, the new album, also featured a collaboration with Cher on the song "Just Begin Again" and guest appearances by Jeff Beck and Guns n' Roses' Slash. The television special included concert footage as well as new skits that followed up the events of the 1984 film. Nigel and David revisit their childhood home, an apartment in Squatney, and reminisce about how poor they were (Nigel's mum fixed them deep-fried cotton balls for supper). Derek fills audiences in on his father's Sani-Phone business, and reveals his involvement in some very unfortunate real estate deals.

Rob Reiner, Fred Willard, Paul Schaffer, and June Chadwick all resumed their movie roles, joined this time by Martin Short, Kenny Rogers, and Mel Torme, who sings a few bars of "Big Bottom." Critics called the TV special "pretty funny"[45] and "part of what has surely become the most elaborate joke in music history."[46]

Entertainment Weekly also honored *Tap*'s creators in 1992. In their October 16 issue, the magazine charted the "100 funniest movies on video" and ranked *This Is Spinal Tap* at number three, behind *Airplane* (1980) and *Some Like It Hot* (1959), and one slot ahead of Woody Allen's *Annie Hall* (1977). The article noted that the film "gets everything right — even tiny details like the contents of a backstage deli tray," and that it grasped the "essential ingredient for classic satire: a deep affection for the subject of ridicule."[47]

On December 11, 1992, movie audiences could see Christopher Guest in a role very different from that of Nigel Tufnel. He played the granite-faced and appropriately named Doctor Stone in Rob Reiner's forty-million-dollar Tom Cruise vehicle, *A Few Good Men*.[48] Based on a play by *West Wing* (1999 –) creator Aaron Sorkin, the film tells the story of a cocksure lawyer, Cruise, hired to defend two marines who, acting under secret orders, conduct a disciplinary code red on a fellow cadet at Guantanamo Bay, accidentally killing him.

Guest joined a cast that included Jack Nicholson, Demi Moore, Keifer Sutherland, and Kevin Bacon. His role consisted of one scene in the courtroom, wherein Commander Stone, an internist, appears on the witness stand to give testimony about poisons and coronaries. Wearing glasses and boasting an icy stare, few Spinal Tap fans would have recognized their favorite guitarist.

THE WORLD IS HER DOLLHOUSE

In 1958, director Nathan Juran and writer Mark Hanna brought drive-in audiences a sci-fi classic, or rather, anti-classic, entitled *Attack of the 50 Ft. Woman*. Like its brethren of the epoch, *Them* (1954), *The Amazing Colossal Man* (1957), and *Attack of the Giant Leeches* (1959), the film featured gigantism as a prominent theme, and made an explicit threat out of a giant, evil force, in this case a jilted woman bent on revenge. Actress Allison

Hayes played the lead, who, after being transformed into a giant by a bald alien fellow aboard a UFO, goes in search of her husband, Harry. The film is beloved by a generation of bad-movie fanatics around the world.

In 1993, Guest accepted the challenge of remaking the camp classic for HBO. With a script by Joseph Dougherty based on Mark Hanna's original work, the film came to represent a more comedic, feminist version of the campy original. *Blade Runner*'s (1982) Daryl Hannah headlined as the put-upon Nancy Archer, a timid but beautiful woman who comes to understand that the men in her life, including her cutthroat, businessman father (William Windom) and her perpetually philandering husband (Daniel Baldwin) make her feel "smaller and smaller."

Therapy with her shrink, Dr. Theodora Cushing (Frances Fisher) isn't working, and Nancy's husband is having a continuing and very public dalliance with the local floozy, Honey (Christi Conaway). All this changes, however, when Nancy grows to enormous proportions and becomes empowered to stand up to the male oppressors in her life. In the end, it is the giantess who gets the last laugh, abducting her husband on a UFO and enrolling him in interminable sensitivity training courses.

Joseph Garrity served as production designer on the Debra Hill–produced project, and remembers his first thoughts upon seeing the 1958 source material. "I didn't particularly care for it," he remembers. "Chris didn't write this, but he felt there was something he could bring to it, like *Almost Heroes*."

One of those things Guest brought to the project was his fine sense of accuracy. His film work always begins with a concentration on homework, research, and preparation. Consequently, the attention to detail and film history in his version of *Attack of the 50 Ft. Woman* (1993) is remarkable, especially if one happens to be a fan of the genre. For instance, early in the film, a minor character, a prospector named Hard Luck Eddie, makes a pertinent comment about the desert winds making "the power lines sing," and this is a direct allusion to the cinema of director Jack Arnold and his classic film, *It Came from Outer Space* (1953).

In another scene, a character makes reference to an "amazing, colossal" object, an homage to *The Amazing Colossal Man*, about a man who grows to amazing proportions, just like poor Nancy.

Character names in the film also reference classic fifties horror films. Dr. Cushing is named after the legendary Peter Cushing, who starred in more horror movies than any man in history, and Nancy's choice of caterers, Arkoff and Corman, are named for two great exploitation producers of the fifties, sixties, and seventies. Roger Corman was behind such gems as *It Conquered the World* (1956), *Day the World Ended* (1956), and *Attack of the Crab Monsters* (1957), while the late Samuel Z. Arkoff shepherded to the silver screen initiatives such as *The She Creature* (1965), *Teenage Caveman*

(1958), *Earth vs. the Spider* (1958), and *Attack of the Puppet People* (1958). Not coincidentally, all of these films were contemporaries of Juran's original *Attack of the* 50 *Ft. Woman.*

Like the original film, Guest's version also commenced with a deadly serious narrator, in this case Paul Benedict, playing Dr. Loeb. Though there were some notable alterations in the remake, including the fact that two characters (a doctor and a police deputy) originally played by men were portrayed by women, it was respectful, if not slavish, to its bizarre source material.

Perhaps more significantly, all the sets and special effects were created to almost subconsciously evoke the atmosphere of a 1950s-era production. "We wanted to have that feeling that we were making a 1950s movie, and then confuse it with the fact that there's a cell phone. Nancy has a cell phone in the car, but she's driving a 1950s Cadillac," explains Garrity.

"A lot of those sets were obviously sets with painted backdrops, and there was a real desire to use effects and lenses that were used when they made these movies back then," continued Garrity. "We built the desert set where the saucer landed, and it was obviously a set built inside, with a backdrop where it was always twilight. We just moved rocks around for different parts of the desert and we had this forced perspective of the road going into the distance over the horizon."

Gene Warren was the man who designed many of the film's special effects. He built a highly detailed miniature of Nancy's hometown, based on the real towns where the film was shot. The "giant" effects involving Daryl Hannah were all accomplished with the camera, according to Garrity. "There's a special lens that keeps the foreground in focus and the background person in focus, so that it can look like a giant hand coming down into the picture. It's just a matter of eye lines," he explains.

In one complicated sequence, Daryl Hannah's Nancy luxuriates in a backyard pool. In actuality, the actress was sitting in a bathtub, and her portion of the shot aligned perfectly with Daniel Baldwin, who was standing by a real pool side. Hannah was some 200 feet away from Baldwin in reality, but they share the same shot and the correct perspective is maintained in the film.

"It was amazing in-camera stuff. Nothing was done after the fact," Garrity recalls. "It's the way they did it back in the fifties, and it was part of getting that feel, so it was a lot of fun."

HBO was happy with the results too, and *Attack of the* 50 *Ft. Woman* proved to be one of their highest rated programs of the year when it aired from 8:00 to 9:30 p.m. on December 11, 1993. "We pulled it off," Garrity says. "It was very popular at the time."

That said, some critics didn't find the feminist twist on the subject matter particularly comedic, and weren't certain what to make of the timeless, but vaguely 1950s, aura.

"Part of the problem is that the gents who made this movie were clearly conflicted about how they should present their material," wrote critic Kathi Maio. "They wanted to put a modern, trendy spin on an old story, but they couldn't bear to leave the '50s behind."[49]

Time magazine's Ginia Bellafante noted the project's good intentions to "spoof '90s notions of male insecurity and female empowerment" but concluded only that the film "means to be funny."[50] Sci-fi and horror authority John Stanley was disappointed and mystified that the filmmakers "didn't improve on an old B movie."[51]

Attack of the 50 Ft. Woman is a fun production to watch in the context of Guest's professional history, not merely because it shows his ubiquitous attention to details, but because it hints at his future endeavors. The film commences at a visitor center, where tourists sit down to watch a documentary presentation about Nancy's strange experience. On screen, Dr. Loeb welcomes his prospective viewers, addressing himself to "the morbidly curious," and the style is very similar to the interview or confessional component of the documentary-style comedies. "Everything you are about to see is absolutely true," Loeb tells us, and then the story proper, filled with nice homages to the 1950s (including images of the original film on a drive-in theater screen), begins.

The film also has some very funny sight gags. Feeding and caring for a fifty-foot woman is not a task to be taken lightly, and at one point the camera tracks a caravan of tanker trucks as they deliver supplies to Nancy, including name-brand products like those of Revlon. Then, of course, in drives a truck with the label Summer's Eve plastered on its side.

ALMOST LEGENDS

Christopher Guest spent a good portion of the years following *Attack of the 50 Ft. Woman* as a director on his first documentary-style project, *Waiting for Guffman*. Shot in Lockhart, Texas, over almost thirty days in early 1995, the film took over a year to edit. Between *Waiting for Guffman* and the second chapter of the so-called mockumentary trilogy, *Best in Show*, Guest directed a mainstream comedy that is his last traditional narrative to date, a film called *Almost Heroes* (1998).

Originally known as *Edwards and Hunt*, *Almost Heroes* is a tale from American history (sort of), about two hapless wannabe pioneers who believe that, with a little good luck, they can beat Lewis and Clark to the Pacific. A prissy gentleman, Leslie Edwards, and his hard-drinking tracker, Bartholomew Hunt, set out in 1804 with a useless translator (Eugene Levy) and his wife, an Indian beauty, to conquer the pathway to the uncharted West. On the difficult journey, they face angry bears, a crazy Spaniard, dangerous waterfalls, deadly diseases, conquistadors, and other terrors.

With a script by Mark Nutter, Tom Wolfe, and Boyd Hale, *Almost Heroes* was actually a period comedy that seemed like an intentional throwback to the antics of Laurel and Hardy, or at least Abbott and Costello, with its fat guy/thin guy dynamic. Though Hugh Grant was originally sought for the role of the dandy Edwards, he turned down the part, as did Bill Murray, whom Christopher Guest met with concerning the role. Finally, Matthew Perry, star of the sitcom *Friends* (1994–2004), signed up for the role of the doofus Edwards, and the late Chris Farley starred as his ruffian partner, Hunt.

"Working with him was intimidating as hell at first," Perry said of Guest, a man he considers perhaps the funniest in the world. "If you make Christopher Guest laugh, which is something that rarely happens, you're in a good mood for about two weeks."[52]

Guest's Spinal Tap bandmates were also involved in *Almost Heroes* in background capacities. Shearer's voice can be heard as the film's voice-over narrator, and McKean is listed in the credits as a "project consultant."

"I responded to the intelligence and humor of the script, plus the fact that it was a period comedy," Guest reported in the film's production notes. "There just aren't that many movies made anymore with people in costumes filmed in different locations that also feature bears and conquistadors."[53]

For Garrity, working on a period film involved much research and — again — homework. "The humor of the movie was that these goofballs were in front of a very real historical context and environment," he explains. "We weren't being funny at all in the art department. We were researching; we were being very accurate. We talked with people, we called historians, we had pictures sent from Missouri, and it was serious business. We were doing a historical film.

"The hope was that if Lewis and Clark were in the movie, it would have worked just fine. It could have been a drama, but the fact was, these were stupid people. It was like Laurel and Hardy in this historical epic, that's where the humor was."

Shooting the thirty-million-dollar epic was a real test of stamina in many cases. There were four long weeks of shooting out in forests in the Big Bear region of Northern California, and the crew also shot in Redding, near Mount Shasta, where the production built a little town to represent St. Louis in 1804. Down river from that set, the team constructed an Indian village.

No doubt, the biggest concern on *Almost Heroes* was the sweltering summer heat. "It was a very hot summer, and people were in these thick costumes," Garrity remembers. "Heat isn't good for comedy; Chris worried about his actors. I think Chris Farley almost fainted a couple of times. It was very, very hot, and Chris [Guest] said, 'This isn't going to help us at all.' He knew it wasn't a good thing and felt bad about his people having to be funny in buckskins or furs in 105 degree weather."

There was some additional shooting near the coast, in Eureka, and sets were also constructed indoors, including an artificial forest for some of the nighttime campfire sequences. Another interior involved a fancy party in the backyard of a mansion (replete with topiary), where the audience would have been introduced to Perry's sweetheart, played by Parker Posey.

Unfortunately, the whole scene was eventually cut from the film, as was the film's original ending. In the final release, Parker appears only as a portrait in a locket that Edwards keeps close at hand.

Although actor Chris Farley was reputed to have serious problems with alcohol, all indications are that he was on good behavior for the shoot. "He was actually completely straight while making the movie,"[54] Perry asserted in *Entertainment Weekly*.

Eugene Levy found Farley to be a funny co-star, and noted that "Take one, he'd come in with his fly unbuttoned. Take two, his pants would be down around his knees. Take three, he'd basically moon his way through the scene."[55]

"He was hilarious and a lot of fun," Garrity adds.

Almost Heroes completed filming in the fall of 1996, but the picture sat on the shelf for over a year. It was produced by Turner Pictures, but the release date was significantly delayed, pending Turner's merger with Time Warner. Sadly, the long wait granted the comedy no favors, and on December 18, 1997, before *Almost Heroes* ever saw life in cinemas, Chris Farley, just thirty-three years old, was found dead in his apartment in Chicago, apparently of a multiple drug overdose.

"He was such a talented man, and he basically killed himself," says Garrity sadly. "Chris [Guest] had seen it with other people he knows, and he said, 'What a waste.' I know he was very upset by it; more than he would show, I think, to most people. It was just a loss of a great talent, and it was stupid."

By its May, 1998, release date, the movie's star Farley had been dead nearly six months, so the film was suddenly perceived very differently by critics and audiences alike. Essentially a lark and a silly buddy comedy, the film, advertised with the tag line "Almost History ... Almost Legends ... Mostly Ridiculous," was now known instead as a great comedian's final film appearance.

It didn't help, either, that Farley's character, Hunt, spent much of *Almost Heroes* in a drunken state, an unfortunate reminder of the conditions of the actor's tragic passing.

The comedy didn't do big business. It grossed only six million dollars by the end of July, a meager return on a thirty-million-dollar investment.

Worse, critics tore the film apart.

"*Almost Heroes* wants to be a funny road movie with Farley and Perry the latest Hope and Crosby, or, more likely, the newest Abbott and Costello. The skinny guy and the fat guy bouncing jokes off each other. But what Perry and Farley are given to do isn't funny. It's old,"[56] critic Beverley Buehrer concluded.

"*Almost Heroes* is Christopher Guest's directorial follow-up to last year's hilarious *Waiting for Guffman*, and it has nothing of the latter film's nuance or heart, but then, Guest also wrote *Guffman*,"[57] said *Boston Globe* critic Cate McQuaide. *Entertainment Weekly*'s Owen Gleiberman branded the film with a grade of F and said it was "as bad as any comedy" he'd seen in the "post–*Animal House* era."[58]

Today, any strong negative reaction to *Almost Heroes* seems a bit out of proportion. The film is precisely what it sets out to be: a silly and entertaining romp. Watching it is not an unpleasant or degrading experience (like most Adam Sandler movies), and some gags really build to genuine laughter, including Farley's repeated, frustrating attempts to steal the much-needed eggs of a protective eagle.

The script also boasts some outlandish one-liners ("You smell like something that's been passed through the system of an old woman") and showcases Farley's outrageous demeanor at least as effectively, and perhaps even more so, than some of his earlier features.

Even in terms of Christopher Guest's recurrent themes and obsessions, the film offers some merit. The snobby Edwards and the never-say-die Hunt may be blithering idiots, but by god, they're going to make it to the Pacific and show the world that they have value. They are dreamers and would-be achievers, just like the folks of *Guffman*'s Blaine, Missouri, or the stalwart Flecks in *Best in Show*. The story may not be told with the same subtlety and realism that fans have come to expect of Guest, but it's the same overall song, merely in a different key.

Just weeks after *Almost Heroes*' release, Guest, Shearer, and McKean could be heard, though not seen, in another big, mainstream summer release, Joe Dante's fantasy adventure, *Small Soldiers* (1998).

The Tap threesome played Slam-Fist (Guest), Insaniac (McKean), and Punch-It (Shearer), three Gorgonite action figures implanted with military computer chips that grant them sentience. A young kid has to save them from a dastardly commando elite force — also composed of action figures — bent on killing them.

TWENTY-FIRST-CENTURY GUEST

The year 2000 brought Guest's second documentary-style effort, *Best in Show*, and, like a phoenix rising from the ashes, *This Is Spinal Tap* shone in another sustained moment of glory. A special edition DVD was released, the out-of-print, Criterion laser-disc edition of the film sold for over one hundred dollars on e-Bay,[59] and on September 5, 2000, the film finally had the theatrical premiere it had missed back in 1984.

"I saw it at the premiere and hadn't seen it in a long time," June Chadwick says. "It was interesting, because I could watch it and completely step back from it. It still holds up today. I think rock 'n' rollers are the same. The wardrobe doesn't date it. In fact, nothing dates it — except when it goes back to the sixties."

The film also benefitted from a new MGM release with a remix of its soundtrack by Chace Productions in Burbank. Mark Rozett was in charge of the assignment and collaborated with Michael McKean and Harry Shearer on the project. They all felt they had to tread lightly to preserve the film's original qualities.

"There was the feeling that the documentary nature of the show should be left pretty much intact," Rozett explained. "Any enhancement of the dialogue sequences should, at most, be minimal. Where they were really looking to see an enhancement of the show was in the music."[60]

The outcome? "Sex Farm" and its ilk sounded clearer — and louder — than ever.

And the hits keep coming. In 2001, Spinal Tap re-formed one more time for a concert at prestigious Carnegie Hall, where the Folksmen opened for them. In 2002, the Library of Congress added *This Is Spinal Tap* to its prestigious National Film Registry, an honor reserved only for a select few films that continue to have "cultural, historical, or aesthetic significance."[61]

In 2003, the year of *A Mighty Wind*, Rob Reiner's directing debut continued to reach new heights of acclaim when *Rolling Stone* named it "the best rock movie ever."[62]

The first years of the twenty-first century have found the members of Tap busier than ever. Michael McKean appeared in Guest's *Best in Show* and *A Mighty Wind*, played a recurring part on *The X-Files* (1992–2002) and *The Lone Gunmen* (2001) as the villainous Morris Fletcher, and in May 2004, McKean won the coveted role of Edna Turnblad in *Hairspray* on Broadway, replacing Harvey Fierstein.[63]

The third member of the band, Harry Shearer, has been just as busy. He continues to voice several characters on *The Simpsons* (1990–), broadcast his own political radio show, *Le Show*, and in 2000 also embarked on a new challenge, directing his first feature film, *Teddy Bears' Picnic*.

"It's a fictionalized comedy version of a real group of people and a real situation," Shearer explains, "which is this very high-level retreat populated by the highest level of people in the American government and business structure that happens in Northern California every summer. The story is very simply how they react when the secrecy of the retreat is threatened by a local TV station in San Francisco.

"It's not in the improvisational-style, very deliberately for three reasons," he continues. "One: I didn't have the budget to shoot enough to make that plausible. Two: I felt that it's Chris's style now, and I didn't want to encroach. And three: most crucially, given what I've told you about the storyline, there's no way even an unmentioned camera could be watching these events. It would violate some sense of 'Why are they concerned, when this camera's watching?' It had to be a more traditional narrative, pretty much for that reason alone."

THE COLORS OF HIS HEART

This narrative history of Christopher Guest's professional career has encompassed his directorial assignments and participation in a number of films and television efforts of all stripes, but there is another side of Guest worth examining.

Virtually every person interviewed for this text mentioned not only Guest's skill as a director, but also as a character actor, and thus it seemed appropriate to conclude this section with a few thoughts on the artist as a performer, from the folks who have worked with him closely so often.

Deborah Theaker suggests that those seeking to understand Guest might do best to start with the actor's boyhood idol, Peter Sellers. "I actually think that much like Peter Sellers, he channels his characters," she explains. "It's quite spooky. It's almost supernatural when you're in the room with him, because you think, 'Where is that voice coming from?'"

Jim Piddock agrees. Peter Sellers, he believes, is a "good comparison," though he also notes that Guest is even "more deadpan." "His performances are fascinating," Piddock describes with admiration. "He just... goes."

"When I was looking through *Vanity Fair* a few months back, there was a picture of Catherine O'Hara, Eugene Levy, and Christopher Guest, and I could tell that it was Christopher Guest as Alan Barrows, and not Chris being himself, just by the way he held his mouth," Theaker adds. "Everything about him is so subtle, but very deeply felt. It's not a caricature — ever. It's not as thin as the characters people do on *Saturday Night Live*. It's fully fleshed out, every time he does something."

Guest has been known for delving whole-hog into his characters, whether that means dyeing his hair a crazy shade of red (a decision he later regretted[64]) for *Best in Show,* or shaving a considerable swath of his hair right down the middle, as he did for *A Mighty Wind.*

"He's a handsome guy and you certainly can't tell in the last three films," Theaker says. "It's a complete absence of vanity — just the bad wigs and weird outfits — so it has to be the same for everybody."

"Christopher has something that most people don't have, because they're not born with it, and I don't think you can learn it," says Bob Balaban. "He has a staggering ability to get [into] a character. When Christopher does a character, he doesn't just talk a certain way, and move and think. The inside of his heart turns colors, depending on who he's supposed to be.

"It's like being a mimic, I suppose," Balaban muses. "It's a gift. He's strikingly interested in differentiations between characters, and we can't all do it the way he can, but seeing him do it does encourage that in yourself."

Fred Willard recalls, "He once said in an interview, 'Fred Willard, I think, comes from another planet.' The interviewer told me that and I said, 'Chris Guest says I come from another planet? That other planet he must be talking about is Earth!' Because he is in another world."

Guest is not merely a tremendous character actor; the artist has also made a concerted effort to pass his knowledge, expertise, and success on to the next generation, whether it be by sharing knowledge with aspiring filmmakers and screenwriters at the 2003 Times BFI London film festival, or discovering young new talents and bringing them into the repertory company.[65]

"He's discovered so many people that he's seen at the Groundlings, or other places, and decided that they're so talented that he needs to nurture that," Deborah Theaker says. "There's this stereotype of the neurotic comedian, and he's the furthest thing from that. He's generous and he inspires all these people, and if he sees someone ... if he likes their work, he never forgets it and makes a point of working with them.

"I consider him the godfather of comedy," she declares. "He's incredibly loyal."

2. THE ARCANE ART OF IMPROVISATION

OR, A STEP-BY-STEP GUIDE TO MAKING AN IMPROVISED MOVIE

MOVIEMAKING IS A DICEY ENTERPRISE in even the most ideal circumstances, those rare occasions when all the myriad elements — including screenplay, cast, and art design — are carefully established and appear locked safely in place. That's because there always remains some of those uncertainties that Secretary of Defense Donald Rumsfeld might dub "unknown unknowns," or rather, "the things we don't know we don't know."

Alternatively, and in hopefully more illuminating terms, a film's production could be all sunshine and roses, and then, *bam!* Suddenly, the director must be replaced (Paul Shrader and *Exorcist IV: The Beginning* [2004]), or the lead actress unexpectedly bows out (Nicole Kidman and *Panic Room* [2002]), or heaven forbid, the whole script suddenly requires a total rewrite (Wes Craven's aptly named *Cursed* [2005]).

Just imagine the ulcers on any of those sets.

But now consider a totally different route, and one that boasts a completely different set of challenges. Consider the notion that you've committed to the total improvisation of a ninety-minute feature film. This doesn't mean you forge a motion picture in the manner that director Mike Leigh (*Secrets and Lies* [1996]) might, improvising from a tightly structured outline during a six-month period of rehearsals, all before principal photography begins.[1]

Instead, in the case of Guest's documentary-style comedies, you improvise *every* individual moment on the spot, on set. This means you can't rely on carefully written dialogue, or even the sense memory, as Corky St. Clair might say, of previous rehearsals.

How would you improvise intelligent, meaningful, and true dialogue on the spot? What's the process involved? Isn't the pressure to be funny so great that a creeping anxiety just crushes the naturalism of the performances?

These are just a few pertinent questions that a layperson might ask about the labyrinthian process of improvising a movie in this unique fashion, and thus the inclusion of this chapter, a closer examination of what actor Michael McKean once termed the "arcane art"[2] of improvisation, specifically as it applies to the cinema of Christopher Guest.

"It's really an interesting phenomenon," Bob Balaban notes about the process, and the impressive results it has yielded in these documentary-style comedies.

"You almost can't talk about it too articulately. So much of it is between the lines — it's how Christopher is — and the fact that he manages to put this assortment of people together with these stories, ideas, and things, and his uncanny ability not to say anything, and often allow some action to occur. And then he also knows when not to. It's amazing to watch."

"I still hear so many times, 'Was that improvised?'" relates actor Michael Hitchcock. "I think that's actually a compliment to the films. They should be enjoyed that way, because I don't think you get an A for effort. You can't flash on the screen before the films begin, 'These films are improvised, so give us a break!' They have to hold up on their own. I like it when I hear that, when people say, 'I had no idea it was improvised. I thought it was all scripted,' because that means that as actors, we did our jobs; that Chris and Eugene did their jobs at the beginning with the writing by creating these wonderful characters, and of course, in the editing process and everything else."

So, with the insights of many in the repertory company guiding us along the way, here is a rough step-by-step outline of how it all seems to work.

Kind of.

THE BEAT GOES ON

Like all great works of art, a Christopher Guest project begins with a concept — a story. That story may involve a small town's preparations for a sesquicentennial celebration (*Waiting for Guffman*), a group of pet owners rallying for an important dog show (*Best in Show*), or a reunion concert for some over-the-hill folk music acts (*A Mighty Wind*). Usually, the concept or story chosen involves something close to Christopher Guest's heart, something he already knows a great deal about (music), or even something that just intrigues him (dog owners, strange hobbies).

That's why we have every right to expect the auteur's next film to revolve around a competitive and slightly off-kilter band of fly-fishers in Idaho.

But seriously, it all gets rolling when Guest and his co-writer on these projects, Eugene Levy, hunker down, sometimes at Guest's idyllic log cabin in Idaho,[3] sometimes at a rented office in California. There, they dig in and start developing characters, ideas, and a structure that will make their latest story memorable, true, and funny. Unlike many comedies, the goal of these artists is not to magically divine what particular jokes make America's teenagers guffaw, but to create realistic views of characters and their universe, and, in the case of Levy and Guest, make each other laugh.

Collaborating on these scripts involves a tremendous amount of research. For instance, in prepping *A Mighty Wind*, Guest and Levy not only listened to dozens of folk music albums, but developed elaborate histories of the groups they intended to showcase, details like group members, changed band names, breakups, and so forth.

Again, Guest has proposed the theorem that comedy is reality plus "one step further," so it is vitally important in the formative days of these projects that the reality quotient of that equation be ironed out. This detailed, research-heavy approach was actually forged back in the 1980s on *This Is Spinal Tap*.

"The sense that people have is that improvising is somehow simpler or easier than so-called regular acting, but in fact, one of the first things we did was write the entire history of the band, and of all the members of the band, so that any time we were sitting around, either in interview situations or in scenes, we knew exactly what the characters would say, so that there wouldn't be any unexpected moments," Harry Shearer recalls. "So that was the very first step we took, making sure we had a shared base of knowledge."

Not coincidentally, research and intense scripting — Shearer's "base of knowledge" — is also essential in the straight documentary format these films mimic so well. As W. Hugh Baddely wrote in his text concerning the production of documentaries, "the treatment [screenplay] must be sufficiently detailed to indicate the method of presentation — the style of the film."[4] In other words, research is the bedrock that precedes all efforts.

The scripts formulated by Guest and Levy are tightly structured, featuring a concrete start, middle, and climax. Every scene is noted and charted on a marker-board outline as it develops, otherwise actors won't have the parameters they need in any given scene once it comes time to shoot.

"You have to know what happens," Guest stresses. "We know all the plot points, what you don't know is how it's going to be said, because the dialogue hasn't been found."[5]

The formative stages of the script or outline of the movie is a period of great creativity and hard work, a time when Guest, a notoriously serious personality, really comes to life.

"He's got a very dry demeanor in real life. You can't tell what he's thinking," Levy says, "but in a writing session, he works himself into a frothing at the mouth."[6]

"There is something inherently funnier about this way of working," Guest says of the process. "It stimulates something in me and the other people that a conventionally scripted comedy would not."[7]

After roughly six-to-eight weeks, the script is completed, the character arcs mapped, and the details ironed out. The final result is a lengthy script that "looks like a script," according to actor John Michael Higgins, except that it "doesn't have dialogue in it. There are descriptions of what happens, but no lines are given to the actors."[8]

This script or outline then becomes the blueprint of the film, and an essential resource for the performers.

"On Larry David's show [*Curb Your Enthusiasm*] and on Chris's films, there is an outline," Paul Dooley confirms. "Chris lets you look at the outline, but Larry doesn't. Larry keeps it to himself. He and the directors and producers look at it between scenes. 'Well, now we have to do this,' and they share it with the cameraman, but they don't give it to the cast because we don't need to know."

Finally, once the story is set, parallel tracks commence: the designing of the film, and casting. Let's tackle production design first.

A WRESTLING MATCH WITH THE MUSE OF THEATER

"The screenplay is what we're all working from," Joe Garrity explains. "It tells us the story in words. The actors tell the story by performance, and the cameraman does it by where he places the camera — the composition of the shot — and the lighting. And we [production designers] put in, with our backgrounds, the choices of color, and the locations that are picked.

"[In general, production design] is about knowing the characters and about discussing them with the director, and then coming up with the backgrounds of people and creating the story through our tools — which include furniture, wallpaper, paint, and shapes of rooms. It's a collaborative thing. We all have to work in the same playbox.

"The hardest thing is to get a director who understands it; who is playing the same game you are, and who thinks about things like the use of color, and the use of certain shapes — rounded, for instance, as opposed to sharp-edged — and that 'this color won't work here, but it will work later,' and to manage that, and keep everybody who needs to know about it aware of it ."

Unlike traditional film, however, the actors in these documentary-style comedies bring a great deal to the table early on, including their own unique ideas about wardrobe and props. For instance, Parker Posey and Michael Hitchcock in *Best in Show* wanted their home to be decorated with items from catalogs, since their characters had been dubbed "catalog people."

Also unlike conventional film, the Guest-Levy scripts are very brief in length in comparison with "regular" screenplays, anywhere from ten to twenty-five pages. Brevity may indeed be the soul of wit, but it doesn't preclude the inclusion of important details and instructions for the production designer or other crew.

"Every scene has a scene number, and you can schedule it," Garrity reports. The script follows the story from point A to point Z, and is often referred to as a blueprint by those involved. This unconventional script format has been known to create some problems with talents who have never worked with Guest before.

"When we shot *Best in Show*," Michael McKean told Craig Mathieson in an interview with *The Age*, "I arrived in Vancouver about a week in and Chris said to me, 'I can't make the assistant director understand the process. He keeps asking me how many pages we're going to shoot today.'"[9]

"Assistant directors will ask Chris, 'How long will this scene take?' because there's no page count," Garrity confirms. "You can't count the dialogue and figure out how long it will take, so he tells them 'Oh, this will probably take half a day.'"

On a normal set, three pages of script may be completed on a good day, but on one of these films, the equivalent of twenty to twenty-five pages might be shot. So it's a whole different scope, and that is important to comprehend.

"You understand that you might be in Corky's loft on days three and four, for instance, so we know what needs to be done, and when," Garrity stresses. "Chris always encourages us to talk with the actors, which we do, to find out what they're thinking and what they're planning to do. If there's something they need to have, we'll make sure it's there. Prop people are always very nervous about that."

A production designer's job is also to be flexible in choosing locations and settings.

"The funniest thing is always what's real," Garrity considers. "Pictures aren't perfectly hung on walls. People have no taste, and that's real. You walk into a house and say, 'What happened here?' Nobody designed it — it just happened. You try to get that quality, where things aren't perfectly symmetrical, and you leave things alone. You don't have to do anything, sometimes. You might walk into a location, and look at each other, and Chris just says, 'Leave it.'

"The strangest things strike him as being funny," adds Garrity. "Like a house with a palm tree sticking out of the back, or a telephone pole with wires filling the sky in the background. Something odd, but something real."

Garrity finds this mindset very appealing, and also very truthful. "I come from ordinary suburbia, middle America. I know what it is, but a lot of Hollywood films gloss it over and over-produce it with flowers and wall-paper, and it becomes a Hollywood version of reality — and they can't stop themselves. But here, you want to leave it. Mostly on Chris's films it's location driven, and the real job is the event at the end [the show]. That's where the very little money we have usually goes."

THE IMPORTANT THING IS, YOU FIND THEM.

Though it may disappoint aspiring thespians, the scripts masterminded by Christopher Guest and Eugene Levy are nearly always designed with specific players in mind, the talented group forming Guest's (informal) repertory company. If you're a fan of these films, you know these folks when you see 'em, and you're always glad they're there.

"We approach the script from the point of view of performance. The characters are very much tailored for the actors and actresses — some of whom I've worked with for thirty years — who we want for the parts,"[10] Guest reports. Describing these actors as a "rare breed," the director notes that "You can't train them. You can do this or you can't."[11]

"His casting is his forte — getting actors who can do the improv work that he likes to do," suggests Roberto Shaefer, Guest's director of photography on *Waiting for Guffman*, *Best in Show*, and a series of commercials. "Working with Chris is always fun. Everybody laughs a lot."[12]

Established Hollywood personalities like Robert Redford, Harrison Ford, Tom Cruise, or even TV's *Seventh Heaven* star Stephen Collins — who Guest actually turned down for a role[13] — need not apply.

This doesn't mean that Guest isn't open to new talent, as witnessed by the arrival of Jennifer Coolidge, Jane Lynch, John Michael Higgins, Rachael Harris, Chris Moynihan, and other additions to the troupe since the year 2000, only that those talents cast in his movies must meet the needs of the story first, and not bring along the baggage of being a traditional star or celebrity.

There's no discrimination here, either. This is merely a blanket policy, and it applies even to Guest's oldest, dearest friends. For instance, Fred Willard recalls a conversation he had with Guest during the casting stages of *Waiting for Guffman*.

"I think I was one of the first people he contacted to be in it," Willard remembers. "Chris said he ran it by his friends, and I would be the lead in the movie. My head was really getting pretty big then; [he said] that Marty Short loved the idea [for the movie]. [Short] said, 'I love it, when do I start?' and Chris said, 'No Martin, I want people who aren't that recognizable.'"

Why? A familiar face undercuts the reality of the film, and without reality, how can you have reality plus "one step further"?

While casting his movies, Guest gains a feel for the talents of prospective participants almost surreptitiously. He observes actors closely during a casual interview, but often there is nothing that would be considered a formal audition. Instead, Guest attempts to suss out sensibilities and determine if they have something in common in how they see comedy or a character.

"Basically, I just sit and talk to them," Guest has declared. "Within half an hour, I've got a very good idea of whether they'll be able to do this type of work."[14]

"I got a call through Eugene Levy, whom I've known for years," Jim Piddock remembers regarding his first association with *Best in Show* in 1999. He then met with Guest and they "just chatted."

"There was no audition," Piddock recalls. "We met a few times just to get on the same page with the character [Trevor Beckwith]. It became more a question of figuring things out, date-wise, because I was writing and directing a series for the BBC."

Deborah Theaker tells a similar story. "I was down here in L.A. in 1990 working with Robin Duke and Ryan Stiles in the Second City company, and Chris came to see the show. The next day, I had a message that I was supposed to meet him and Norman Lear. He hadn't even met me, but he thought I was good enough that he recommended me for the lead in a TV series [*Jodie Hartman: The News and the Storyteller.*]

"I was living in a hotel, and didn't drive at all," Theaker recalls, "and I got this message at the box office that I was supposed to go meet Norman Lear and Christopher Guest, so I took a few buses — which he thought was hilarious, that I had to bus it over. I'd never been to California and I didn't know you had to drive.

"As I was leaving the audition, in the hallway he said, 'I think you're really talented, and I'll definitely want to work with you.' And so over the years I'd be in Toronto, and it was in the middle of winter, and I'd get phone calls from people on his behalf to find out if I was available for things."

Some six years after that initial meeting, Christopher Guest remembered Theaker and called her to meet with him regarding *Waiting for Guffman*. "I don't know if it was an audition," Theaker admits. "To this day, I'm not really sure what happened. I just got a call to go see him and Eugene. They are just the nicest guys.

"So I got a call to go to Castle Rock one day, and I didn't really know what was going on. He [Guest] was just telling me [about] what the film was, and I gathered once I left that they already had me in mind to be in the movie, and were just telling me about it."

WHAT ARE YOUR FEELINGS, RIGHT NOW, WITH YOUR EYES CLOSED?

In addition to laying the foundations for production design, the Levy-Guest screenplays also involve those conceptual jokes, like "catalog people" or the amp that goes to eleven, and these details serve as guides for the actors now cast in the film, so that they may forge their characters.

"Chris basically called me up and said two things," Piddock says, recalling the genesis of his character, Leonard Crabbe, in *A Mighty Wind*: "'He's a model train enthusiast and a catheter salesman.'"

Theaker remembers Guest's description of Gwen Fabin-Blunt in *Waiting for Guffman*: "He said to me, 'She's the sort of woman who wears pantyhose with open-toed sandals,' and I said, 'Oh, I see, of course!'"

"I was guided by Christopher's note that described my mother as being very overly protective," adds Balaban, regarding his *Mighty Wind* character, Jonathan Steinbloom. "That was a real guide to me as to whom my character might turn into."

The result in that case was a characterization that expressed Steinbloom's obsessiveness and compulsion about everything from the arrangement of items on his desk to the health and safety issues regarding a decorative bouquet. "His mother probably created a lot of fear in him," Balaban explains sympathetically.

With the script prepared, the actors now cast are then, according to Shearer, "responsible for inventing more intimate details of [their] characters, and bringing them to the set.

"Chris and Eugene write the overall framework and crucial backstory elements, and then we bring in other things that help build the texture and detail of the characters. It's very collaborative. It's not people standing around ad-libbing, which is what people sometimes think."

"You don't know too much what's going on, you just enjoy the fact that you're going to work with wonderful people who are enormously fun to work with, and that it's going to be ... *dangerous*," Balaban says.

But in some senses, good casting in a comedy like Guest's involves not merely finding the right people, or matching the right people with the right conceptual jokes, but also finding the right dynamic *between* players. For lack of a better word, you might call this intangible quality *chemistry*.

For instance, one of many high points in *Best in Show* was the dog show finale, a set piece that involved Jim Piddock and Fred Willard as emcees of the Mayflower Dog Show. Their work together in that extended sequence represented a perfect blend of different — and complementary, comedic styles, and Piddock believes that detecting in advance that very type of dynamic is part of Guest's genius as both a director and a comedian.

"I think it really is chemistry. A good balance, a smart judgment," says Piddock. "One of the things Chris said to me is 'You are rather like me. You are a re-actor as well as an actor. You enjoy reacting.' I said, 'That's true.' My experience with comedy is that you get the laugh with the reaction as much as the action, and I don't mind that.

"In this case, I knew I had to be the straight man, because with Fred there's no point in doing otherwise," Piddock notes with affection. "It's sort of like a tennis match — having two people who are great playing close to the net, and nobody in the back of the court. There's no point in having someone who does what Fred does [acting] with him. It would just be competition. I think every funny guy needs a straight guy, and to me it's funnier to see that. Fred is so great at what he does, he really is. The hard part is just not laughing."

"You're thrilled when other actors do something and you can react," Balaban agrees. "You look forward to being in a scene with Fred Willard because he's such an explosion, and you have to hold on and pay attention and try not to get blown away by the force of the hurricane — which is really fun. It wouldn't be fun if Fred were piggy, but Fred is a very giving person. You wouldn't think so seeing his characters, because they're so obnoxious and pushy, but Fred isn't that way at all. He is a very generous actor, so when he does these things, you are just blown away. He just sucks you into his reality so quickly, and that's a pleasure. You don't have to work."

"Let me say this about both of them," Willard replies, "they are both wonderful people to work with, and wonderful straight men. In *Best of Show*, if Jim Piddock had tried to be silly, it would have fallen apart, and the same with Bob Balaban.

"They went on a tour for *A Mighty Wind* and did a stage show all over the country, and the only one I was able to do was the one here in L.A., and Bob Balaban was the host," Willard relates. "I came out and said, 'Bob, I'm just going to come up and start being the jackass that I am, and I might start putting you down, do you mind? He said, 'No, no, no, I love it!' I just walked out and started doing this long stream of jokes and asides, and he would just look at me and say, 'Uh huh, uh huh, well...' and he didn't try to top me or anything, and I just loved doing it."

As a result of such camaraderie, being cast in a Christopher Guest film is not only fun and exhilarating, but also something of a gift for the performers, at least according to *Legally Blonde*'s (2003) Jennifer Coolidge, the actress who played Sherri Ann Ward-Cabot in *Best in Show* and Amber in *A Mighty Wind*. "[Being allowed] to create your own dialogue and character, that is the ultimate compliment."[15]

Michael Hitchcock concurs. "It is the most rewarding aspect of my professional career, because as an actor you get to help create your character ... you even pick out your wardrobe and hair and how you look, and that just doesn't happen on anything else. Certainly not to that degree. It's an incredibly rewarding experience."

"The thing is, you don't ever want to do anything else," Theaker admits ruefully. "When you work in a regular sitcom, you're ruined. When you read dialogue on the page, it is never the same. I have a hard time, since working with Chris and Eugene, saying a lot of that dialogue. There's some stuff now I just can't do because it doesn't sound realistic. It sounds like jokes, setup, punchline, delivery. Formulaic and tired. It's not my rhythm."

THIS IS THE DAY OF THE SHOW, Y'ALL!

Once the film is cast and the right mixes are formulated, it's time to put your money where your mouth is — to get to the set and improvise a character who best fits the story and who stays faithful to the established backstory. As one might guess, that's a pretty daunting charge. "[Making this type of film] is really exhilarating," Parker Posey told the *Sydney Morning Herald*. "The first day is hard, then we all get into it."[16]

"It's nerve-wracking in the beginning," Theaker agrees, "because you are looking to see what props are available, and what's going on. [Chris] doesn't block you out — you can move freely. You have a general idea where you're supposed to be for the shot, so there's that element of it."

Others echo the same sentiment. "I knew that's how it worked," Piddock notes, "but once the reality set in, it was sheer terror. It is terrifying — and I'm not the only one who feels that way."

"I'm glad somebody else agrees that it was terrifying," adds June Chadwick, who portrayed Jeanine in *This Is Spinal Tap*. "Working in the theater, at least in England, I did some improv. I also took a class with Harvey Lembeck. He had a class at Paramount, and on the advice of a manager, I attended it. It was completely terrifying to me. Because a lot of people — including studio executives, came in and stood at the back of this very large auditorium. Harvey would call you up, say one word to you, and then you'd have to go on stage and improv on that one word with zero! So the fact that there was an entire script on *Spinal Tap* was actually a relief."

Making matters more harrowing, there is usually very little, if any, rehearsal on these films. "Christopher makes the assumption that you'll figure out some material," Balaban reports, "and if you don't, that's okay, he just won't have you in the picture that much. It's very Zen-like, this experience."[17]

"Around town, with professionals, you hear, 'Oh everybody has pre-planned everything, which is just not the case. At all," Hitchcock stresses. "I've heard that comment from Hollywood insiders who are just sure everyone has rehearsed it, but we don't. It's totally exhilarating, and at the same time, totally scary."

The result? "You're looking for anything to bounce off of," Balaban elaborates. "Obviously, you initiate certain things as well, and you learn during your month there, or week there, or whatever it turns out to be. You get an instinct as to what's going on. You try not to do it with your head, but with your heart — or whatever part of you isn't operating when your head is operating. You don't write these things in your head, you just try to say, 'I know where I'm coming from, I have an idea who I am, let's see what they're going to do to me right now.' That's what improvising is, I suppose."

Deliberate, extended rehearsal "would ruin the spontaneity of the riff," Theaker adds. "There is no rehearsal. Now on *Guffman* and *A Mighty Wind*, the actors did have to rehearse and create the music well in advance for the premise to work, but that was it."

"We would just have conversations about things," Theaker recalls of the period leading up to the shoot, a period on conventional films when a rehearsal might occur. "The odd phone call here and there before things began. 'What do you want to be named?' 'What do you want to do for a living?' That sort of thing."

Chadwick suggests that for her, getting to the set and physically appearing as the character, in costume, was a great boost to the improvisation process.

"It started to come together when I put the wardrobe together," she acknowledges. "Once you get the shoes on, it's a big deal. It wraps you up in your skin, and you start wearing the person."

Chadwick's other advice about improvisation is to stay loose. "You can't plan your reaction," she says. "You can't plan what you're going to say. You have to react in character. You can have an idea of things that — if you can fit them, you will fit them — but that doesn't always happen."

Indeed, it is probably impossible to anticipate what may come out of another improviser's lips once the word "action" is called, a fact Jim Piddock knows very well. He remembers meeting with Fred Willard for the first time on location for *Best in Show*, not much more than a day before they were to begin shooting.

"Fred is a very clever preparer, I think," Piddock notes. By that, he means that Willard didn't let the cat out of the bag and tell him anything about what he intended to do once the cameras rolled.

"It's scary, but it's much better that way," Piddock acknowledges. "Because then you don't have to play genuine reaction — you *are* genuinely reacting. It's much more fun."

That's another key element of improvisation. Although it appears spontaneous and off-the-cuff, it comes from a deep understanding of character and nuance, and often that does mean intense preparation. Which is entirely different from rehearsal, and much more like homework.

"Fred really did teach me that you can prepare, if your character would prepare," Balaban notes. "There are many things you need to know about your life if you're going to bring them in. It's so much more fun when you don't tell anyone about them, if they don't need to know. If you're singing a duet, you better practice it together, but if you're coming in and saying things that nobody else knows, you can just think of a million things that might amuse you that are part of your background. You don't write them down, because they have to come out depending on the scenes that happen between you.

"My character was giving a big speech at the opening of the concert in *A Mighty Wind*," Balaban elaborates. "My character *would* practice his speech and know it, and have notes. That's why I came in with my huge piece of paper there. My character wasn't used to doing this, so I thought it would be lying to say that he made up a big introduction to this event. He would never do that. It was televised, and he would prepare. The way that Fred came in with a battery of strange questions about dogs in *Best in Show*? You just want to do that, and Fred taught me it's not bad to prepare. It can be a wonderful thing to do."

"If your character would prepare, you should prepare," Willard explains. On *Waiting for Guffman*, Willard created a whole background about his character's track and field days, and where he and Catherine O'Hara's character had met.

In *Best in Show*, he also conducted research for Buck Laughlin's outrageous string of one-liners and faux-pas. "In the airport on the way up [to Vancouver], I bought a men's weight-lifting magazine because I wanted to do that joke about how many pounds I can bench press," Willard notes, "and I didn't know anything about it, and wanted it to be in the right ballpark."

And the hazards of no preparation?

"When we were doing *Waiting for Guffman*, I tried to contact Catherine O'Hara," Willard recalls, "and I called her several times and said, 'Catherine, we should talk about the background of our relationship, and plan out what we've done,' and she never got back to me. So on the first day, we were driving out to the set and she said, 'I'm sorry I never got back to you,' and after the first day, she was a little bowled over, because I just started in."

What happened?

"For most of the actors, it was their first scene in the movie. Ron, Sheila, and the other Blaine Players were in a library because — in the film — they'd been kicked out of their rehearsal space. This also explains why one scene of the characters practicing Corky's funky dance is set in what appears to be a car dealership, another impromptu rehearsal space.

"There were people in the library looking at books, and we were getting ready to be directed by Corky," Willard sets the scene. "The camera was up in the balcony, and the next thing we know is 'Action!'

"So I said something to the effect of, 'I've always wondered if you take a book out of the library and lose it, do you pay fines for the rest of your life?' Then that led to something else. So afterwards, Catherine said, 'Fred, I think you have a pretty good idea there; I better prepare a little stuff about our background.'"

But, of course, no matter how much homework one does, it is also quite easy to be thrown by someone as adept with this process, and in generating laughs, as is Mr. Willard.

"There were a few times where I tried not to smile a lot, though that was a very legitimate response in that situation," Piddock explains. "One would be amused ... and then sort of gradually less amused. That's funny because it gives you an arc."

"You'll notice I never appear in a film with him," Guest told reporter Andrew L. Urban, "because the one time I did ... if you watch closely, you can see my shoulders shaking with laughter."[18]

In a similar vein, June Chadwick remembers her first day on the set of *This Is Spinal Tap*, suddenly thrown into improvisation among seasoned pros like Guest, McKean, and Shearer. "At my first entrance, when I come in and talk into the microphone, and they're all on stage looking at the album, I said, 'Hello, darling,' and came down to the stage.

"Well, we all stood around looking at this album cover [*Smell the Glove*], and they each would get it and turn it over and then pass it from one to the other, and turn it over again — and they're all looking for artwork on it, but there was nothing.

"It was one of those things that starts out a little bit funny, and then just friggin' builds and builds until it was more than ridiculous," Chadwick recollects. "It was too stunning, this stark black cover. I remember at one point I really thought I was going to lose it, so I thought of my education — which was horrible — so I could literally take my mind absolutely out of the scene and not listen. Because if I had listened, I think I would have gone. And nothing can be repeated."

Indeed, according to Christopher Guest, one quarter of all the footage used in *Spinal Tap* is from the first take, fully 50 percent from the second take.[19] That doesn't leave much wiggle room for do-overs.

On the other hand, even takes that do go well, i.e., without laughter, are not necessarily guaranteed to be successful. Not every improv run is golden, and actually, that's okay too.

To wit, Theaker remembers an occasion on *A Mighty Wind* when, as Corky might say, the elements just weren't coming together. "Chris had one scene set up where Catherine and I are trading stories about man trouble, and she's saying, 'I don't know what to think about Mitch,' and I ask if she's married. She asks me, and I say, 'I was once, for six hours ... we were just different people.'

"We had this whole girl-talk thing that could have been hilarious, but we both felt it at the time, and as soon as they called 'cut,' we were both like, 'Oh, jeez, sorry.' You just felt we didn't have it, and we both knew it.

"Sometimes you're talked out," Theaker notes, "or you can't think of much to say, or it seems so ordinary and mundane that it doesn't have any artistic value. I was disappointed, because I adore Catherine, and she's always been so gracious and charming with me. I wanted so badly to have a great scene with her; we both did. It just didn't go anywhere. I'm sure it's not on the dvd and it'll never see the light of day."

CHANGE YOUR INSTINCTS, OR AT LEAST IGNORE THEM

Christopher Guest has likened the process of improvisation to a jazz solo.

"I really like to use the analogy of a jazz player who basically stands up on stage and plays, yet people don't question that there is no music that they are reading from," he explains. "This is really the same thing, but we're actors and we're really jamming, with people soloing occasionally."[20]

That's an apt comparison, but during many moments in the documentary-style comedies, the actors aren't soloing so much as finding themselves involved in a duet (or neuftet), and this means understanding the nature of the other actors you are playing with.

"There's a dynamic based on who's in it," Paul Dooley explains. "Some people are slow talkers. Some people are dominant. Many people are very physical. Then there are the people who are almost entirely verbal. I've worked with people who I think are better than I am, and that just makes you want to play on their level.

"In a jazz band," says Dooley adopting Guest's analogy, "there's more than two people playing, and they give each other solos and take moments, but they still play together, and against each other, and in counter-point. I think the worst scenes in improv are usually with more than two people and the best scenes are with two. Because there's a natural sense of 'When I finish saying something, you pick up the cue.' Whereas if there is one person talking and two people might pick up the cue, you might have a lot of overlap."

Willard agrees that scenes with two people can be the most rewarding. "They are the best. I think that the one-person confessional thing, in baseball terms, is like going out to the batting range and you can keep putting coins in and keep hitting, hitting, hitting. But when you get in the game, that's when you're playing with other performers — and you don't know how the game will go. And when it goes great, nothing could ever be more wonderful than one line leading to another. You have to shut off any sensory thing in your brain and just go with it, and your worst fear is that suddenly you're going to dry up."

Theaker offers another analogy for the give and take between improvisors on these projects. "It's like knowing when to pass the ball when you're on the court playing basketball. You can always tell people who have come from stand-up comedy who are trying to improvise because they'll go for jokes, or they'll steamroll or bulldoze, or not let you get a word in edgewise.

The great improvisers *listen* and respond. They don't know what their bits are going to be in advance, they just respond in the moment. So you have to have trust. When you're working with people like Mike Hitchcock and Larry Miller — whose comic timing is so great — everybody just embraces their reality and really listens. You can see everybody listening in each scene ... nobody is trying to get their licks in to be the show dog."

Of course, there are likely few places in the world where trust is in shorter supply than Hollywood. "It's amazing, given the nature of the business we're in," Theaker admits. "Quite the opposite is expected. Because it's the shiners in regular sitcoms who draw the applause and the attention. But in this type of work, it isn't. You're there to create the fabric. When you get your moment, you take it — or other people give you the moment. And if you don't get a genuine moment, Chris puts it together in editing."

"There's not pressure," Harry Shearer establishes. "The zeitgeist of the thing is not to try to get laughs. It's to try to tell these stories and make these scenes real. It's not pressure in that sense. You can go through a whole scene where you feel it is not right for you to say anything, and if you don't need to say anything to move the story along, that's perfectly fine.

"My favorite example of that is about two-thirds of Catherine O'Hara's improvising in *A Mighty Wind*," Shearer says. "It's all in the looks she's giving to Eugene's character. She's not saying anything, but yet it's all there — without her having to say a word. The thing that you feel in Chris' movies is this incredible atmosphere of trust. And that's what is missing in an awful lot of other situations. There's such a crippling absence of trust."

In fact, Guest fosters not merely trust, but a sense of empowerment on his sets. "Instead of the responsibility for storytelling being on the writer, and the actors are just there to say their lines and hopefully not bump into the furniture, everybody shares the responsibility for storytelling in these movies," Shearer elaborates.

"Your job is not to get laughs, but to help tell the story. And that may be talking, and it may be listening, and it may be by ostensibly doing nothing — if that's what your character would be doing at that moment. It's not like *Whose Line Is It Anyway?* (1998–) where you have to get a laugh every ten seconds."

"These movies are such a luxury," O'Hara told the *Saint Paul Pioneer Press*. "No one tells you how to behave from scene to scene, and that makes it feel so much more real."[21]

They're such a luxury, in fact, that the actors, who are usually only required for eight to ten days of a twenty-five-day shoot, often hang out after they complete their scenes just to watch one another in action.[22]

In all, it could be described as a sort of mutual admiration society, as well as a graduate-level class in improvisation and acting. Also, unlike most movies, the actors don't hide in their trailers between shots, either.

"At lunch, everybody sits down and trades stories," Theaker reveals. "It's like going to a barbeque at [Guest's] house. I would sit with Bob Balaban, who is such a fascinating person as well, and it's such a nice environment. I've been on so many sets that are fraught with tension, and this is the opposite."

In fact, stopping an improvised scene once in progress is sometimes more difficult than creating one out of whole cloth. "We could chat and chat and chat until the cows come home," Theaker says, "and they can try to shut us up so they can finish the day. That's the reason this style of comedy works, because you find the right players, or the right musicians, to strike that note."

"Everyone in those movies, I have such respect for," Willard agrees. "When I went into it, I had great respect for Christopher Guest and I loved Eugene Levy from SCTV [Second City TV, 1974 – 1981], and Catherine, but as I got to work with these people, I got to see the things they would do on the days I wasn't there, and I just couldn't believe what I was seeing on screen.

"One of the most brilliant acting things I've ever seen ... was in *Best in Show*, when Eugene and Catherine find out that the hotel room they have is a broom closet. They all stand in the room, and the manager is Ed Begley, and I'm still amazed by that scene. I know it was improvised, I know they had to prepare something, but I look at that scene and it is beyond brilliant. When Ed Begley explains they are going to be in the broom closet, and they ask where the ladies' room is, and he says, 'Well, you go downstairs across the lobby,' and Catherine looks up, and all of a sudden a little smile comes across her face, and she says, 'Oh, that'll be fine.' That just gave me little goose bumps. What a wonderful acting moment. I think she's one of the best actresses out there today — not just comic actresses, but actresses."

THIS YEAR CORKY WILL BE DIRECTING THE SHOW – WHICH IS ... DIFFERENT ...

The artists interviewed for this book share in common an admiration for Christopher Guest and his skill directing these atypical documentary-style features. If improvising can be likened to music, then the role of director in the process is something akin to that of conductor. He leads, he oversees, he keeps things rolling in tempo, but he also leaves space for individual contributions.

"Chris is a very laconic guy. Always has been," Shearer says. "The great thing about Chris as director — unlike Chris in real life — [is] you're never in any doubt about what he thinks. Because as a director you *have* to tell people what you think. He's extremely generous. He's very calm. He's also extremely funny and extremely smart, so you can't really ask for a better experience in terms of acting in a movie than that."

"He doesn't overdirect," Piddock adds. "He just sets you up. It's almost wordless. Chris will clarify and then let it go. He's very supportive."

"I think it boils down to personality. There are directors who are great at doing crane shots and other things, but ultimately it's about material, casting, and all those subtle things, and you don't even realize how the director necessarily influenced you," Balaban considers. "But in most cases you really are influenced by the personality of the director, if he's a good one. In Chris' case, there's a level of taste and intelligence, and absolute honesty that I think really encourages the same in the actors. He doesn't talk too much, but when he does, his words are informed by his unique personality, and it really does find its way into the movies all over the place.

"He doesn't like easy jokes, he likes behavior," Balaban stresses. "He's kind of like Mike Nichols in that sense, who's also a terrific improvisor. I think it's just his love of human behavior."

"He's very soft-spoken and infinitely kind," Theaker says of Guest. "There's a lot of tension on any shoot because of deadlines, but he'll give you a pat on the back or a hug. I call him Pappy, which is weird because that's what Martin Short calls him too — because he seems like such a dad. He's very nurturing … I've never seen him scream at anybody; I've never seen him lose his cool. He's old-school — a gentleman of the old school.

"If I was very nervous or getting stuck on something, he would take me aside and talk quietly and say, 'Well, what about this? Do you think she would be feeling this?' He never says 'That was wrong, it doesn't work,'" Theaker says. "There's never anything that isn't nurturing or isn't for-warding the story when he's talking to people or doing the work."

"Most directors I've worked with — Soderbergh, Altman, Chris Nolan — they don't tell you very much what they want," Dooley adds. "They mainly tell you if you've gotten it wrong. Chris rarely tells you what to do."

Theaker is able to provide some examples of Guest's directing style, which, on occasion, includes the role of interviewer, asking direct questions that may spur a valuable run, or bring forward illuminating aspects of a character. "[On *Guffman*,] Chris would occasionally stop and say things like, 'This is a matrilineal thing, it started with the mother.'

"He would also do things like ask, 'What if?' [For example] 'Maybe you've started the local chapter of the Daughters of Blaine?' He would throw ideas out, but never get real specific about it. It was like an excavation of whatever nugget of information that would feed the plot or inform the character."

Guest also carefully nurtures a relaxed setting for the actors, one where concentration isn't shattered, and performance takes precedence over camera acrobatics and setups.

"I couldn't even tell you where the camera was when he was shooting," Theaker notes with appreciation. "He gets within your eye-line so that you're talking to him directly in those interview segments. And I wasn't even aware sometimes that there was a second angle.

"You're not at all focused on what is going on with the camera, which also means that you have to check your vanity at the door," Theaker notes with a laugh, reflecting on her tearful, often sans makeup, *Mighty Wind* character, Naomi Steinbloom. "I want to be pretty. I want to be a pretty girl and look good, but here it's all about the characters. Chris doesn't care what anyone looks like, he just wants it to be real."

Guest does one other thing to assure a safe and productive environment, according to Michael Hitchcock. "Agents and managers and studio executives are not invited. They're not really allowed on the set, so you have a freedom to fail. Everything that comes out of everybody's mouth, all the time, isn't gold. You have to have that freedom to fail, because improvisation, by its very nature, is like baseball — you're not going to hit a thousand all the time. He makes it a very nurturing set. He's picked his people and stands back a little, and lets them do what they do."

Another director who utilizes the improvisation approach, albeit in somewhat different terms, is Robert Altman, with whom Balaban worked very closely on the celebrated, highly acclaimed drama *Gosford Park* (2002).

"Basically there is, in a funny way, a great similarity between the two of them," Balaban says. "Not that their movies end up being anything alike. Their interests are quite different, too, you must understand, so the similarity is that they both have a certain basic approach to actors, which is that they make an assumption that improves everybody's performance dramatically. And that is this: if he's chosen you in the first place, you probably know something about your part that nobody else knows, so even the director doesn't know. It's going to be buried inside of you, and it's got to be nurtured, and you have to feel like you can do anything in front of these people: Take risks, take chances, make a fool of yourself. It's an atmosphere that breeds some wonderful performances much of the time.

"Robert's approach to a written scene is, 'Let's just get it on its feet, and you will find it.' He'll spend a couple of hours with you just working through a scene, making some general suggestions, letting you come up with ideas and stuff. You actually approach the scenes with Robert Altman as if they weren't scripted — but of course, there is a script [with dialogue.]

"Ultimately, in *Gosford Park* the parts that were improvised were exactly like Christopher Guest's [projects]. When we were in a large party with twenty-seven people and the camera was wandering around us, you can't just wait for your line to begin speaking, because the camera will see you just waiting for your line. So we spent hours and hours milling around in the room, literally not even knowing if Robert was watching us or not, talking to Maggie Smith, having conversations with people.

"And that was exactly like Christopher, because you definitely have the feeling that anything you do would be okay. It's also true in the Christopher Guest movies that you're not always 100 percent sure when you're on camera, necessarily. It could be zooming in; it could be going wider. There are two cameras sometimes, so you have that extra element that you feel very private. No one yells 'cut' and 'action' too much, you're just doing your thing for five or ten minutes. It wears you down, so you can't be all that self conscious eventually, and you do get lost in what you're doing, in a very good sense.

"I think there are some real similarities, but Robert's movies are scripted, 90 percent sometimes, 40 percent sometimes, and Christopher's aren't scripted in terms of dialogue at all. So I think that's the main difference. In Christopher's case, the movie can take a left turn, and just end up on the left turn if he wanted it to.

"In Robert's case that might happen briefly, but it doesn't happen too much. In *Gosford Park*, probably the end result of the movie was certainly that 80 or 90 percent was exactly how it had been written, but then there were the improvised things in group scenes, mostly people talking at the same time."

As directors, Altman and Guest share another quirk, too. They tend not to limit what the audience sees in a frame, if they have a choice. "[Robert] has this wandering shooting style so that you feel like you're in the room with everybody," Balaban says. "Your eye is very seldom restricted to one thing that's happening. There's so much going on in the frame, and it's a moving frame, and the actors are moving around."

Shearer notes that both he and Guest share a parallel sensibility, one that's a deliberate throwback to more old-fashioned, less aggressively edited comedies. "We like giving the audience a chance to decide what to look at," he explains.

"There are a lot fewer reaction shots in both [Guest's] movies and my movie [*Teddy Bears' Picnic*] than you see in normal Hollywood comedies.

You can see the reaction in process rather than in a cut, which is a manufactured reaction," Shearer reflects. "So you can watch the movie three times, and it's a different movie each time, because your eyes can move to different things."

The benefit of this style is not only a heightened sense of realism, but in this age of by-the-numbers moviemaking, a feeling that the work is unique, quirky, and highly individual.

"Everybody doesn't have to be making movies in the same style," Shearer emphasizes. "If you're trying to entertain the MTV-generation kids, you do a lot of cuts and a lot of close-ups and a lot of exaggerated shots. But if you're doing movies for grown-ups, maybe you can trust them a little more. The word goes back to trust. We all trust the audience to get it."

And the actors trust the director, with good reason, as Monique Prud'Homme, costume designer on *Best in Show* reported to the *Vancouver Province*. "Christopher loves his actors, he supports them. A lot of directors love action, they love stunts, they love effects," she says. "Most of them don't even like actors, they don't know how to talk to them."[23]

Christopher Guest also has one terrific resource that not all directors are fortunate enough to have: backup. He has a stalwart, clever, and responsible partner in Eugene Levy.

"On the set, he is the one that is down to business," Willard reports. "He's always concerned. 'Did we get that scene?' 'Wait a minute, should we go back and cover this?' He's really the down-to-earth, nuts-and-bolts guy. Chris is kind of 'Let's go, let's move on' and Eugene is like, 'Wait, Christopher we didn't get an angle here.'

"But what Christopher does is very supportive. There's never a negative. It's never, 'Oh no, no, let's do that again,'" Willard considers. "I couldn't have more respect for him. He's a genius."

CHECKING IN (AND WAITING TO GET A MESSAGE FROM YOURSELF)

Even under the tutelage and guidance of a nurturing director, improvising is strenuous work, and sometimes during a shoot it helps to get feedback of a different type, to get a sense that your efforts are panning out and coming across on screen.

Both Guest and *This Is Spinal Tap* director Rob Reiner are known to be extremely generous when it comes to permitting actors to watch the dailies.

June Chadwick, for one, believes dailies are a very useful tool, given the right mind-set.

"Rob allowed us to see dailies on *Spinal Tap*," she reports. "I think a lot of times, people don't like to see dailies, but I found them tremendously helpful because I was watching myself and thinking. When you're on camera, sometimes you think you're doing amazing work, and it's actually too much. Or sometimes you think you're doing nothing, and it is fabulous. As you progress, hopefully you learn a little bit more about that. But I saw myself in dailies and there were certain things I was doing where I thought, 'Oh yeah, I'll keep doing that, I like it.' Or, 'I don't like that at all! I'll avoid that.' So dailies are helpful. They reassured me to stick with something I started with, I think. If anything, it was like, 'Oh, I don't need to do much more than that.' If I hadn't seen the dailies, I might have been much more paranoid."

"I can only say that I loved watching the dailies in *Waiting for Guffman*," Balaban says. "We all did it. We were all staying at a hotel together — it was fantastic! You do learn from them. I was helped by learning so much about the world my character lived in. I got to learn what everybody else was doing, and how they were doing it, and what their lives looked like. You get into the style and tone of the movie that way, because it gives you better insight into the range of possibilities in a way that I think is really helpful."

"I did it twice," Theaker remembers about watching dailies, "but I found it difficult to sit through. That's the thing in Chris' movies — it's all character-driven, so I'm not exactly playing a babe. So to cry that much and be so swollen and cry through most of the shoot of *A Mighty Wind* with no makeup on — I would only do that for him."

"As far as *Best in Show* goes, Parker and I chose not to watch ourselves when they were showing our scenes," Michael Hitchcock explains. "Just because I get a little self conscious. I still think that I have a chin ... and I'm much more handsome in my mind. I don't want it to throw me. I do love watching other people, and I love watching the process with Chris, and to get that opportunity is very rare."

"I don't like them," Willard comments on the dailies. "I watched them one night, and I got nervous, and didn't want to watch them again, because, for one thing, I can't even watch myself in a movie for a long time. You start to think about what was on your mind. Maybe you were hungry when you did a scene, or you were cold, or you got some disappointing news.

"There's two sides. I think the ideal thing would be if you could do a scene, and then watch it right away and do it again. But if it's the end of the day, and it's in the can, and it didn't come off right, you're just depressed. I only watched one night [in Texas] and I didn't watch anymore. I said, 'Let Chris be God and choose and just hope that it's coming out okay.'"

AND THEY TELL A FASCINATING STORY

Christopher Guest has also been known, on occasion, to invite actors to join him in the editing room and watch how his movies are compiled. Not surprisingly, the editing process is a long and arduous one. Sometimes, more than eighty hours of footage must be trimmed down to tell a coherent tale of eighty to ninety minutes. That's a tremendous amount of footage to sift through, and subsequently there are many difficult decisions to make about what stays and what goes. The editing process on these documentary-style films can take as long as a year, and Guest often works ten to twelve hour days alongside the editor.

"I don't see anything until I sit down with an editor," Guest reported in *Time* magazine. "I'll just look at everything and start talking and taking notes. But unlike a real documentary, where you don't know the story until you shoot, we know what the story is. We have to pick scenes that tell the story."[24]

On *A Mighty Wind* and *Best in Show*, Guest collaborated with Robert Leighton, Rob Reiner's film editor on films such as *When Harry Met Sally* (1989), *Misery*, *A Few Good Men*, and *Alex and Emma* (2003). On *Guffman*, Guest shared the job with Andy Blumenthal.

"Editing is always the final rewrite of a movie," Harry Shearer says. "I had to laugh when the Writer's Guild, in their last negotiation, wanted the right to be present on the set. If that doesn't tell you how little they know about the motion-picture-making process — being on the set is so insignificant. If I were trying to make that claim now — and I'm not — I'd ask to be present during editing. Because that's when the movie really gets reshaped and re-formed. In both improvisational and non-improvisational style, you learn a lot in the editing process.

"The crucial job of editing is to know how much of the storytelling you don't need," Shearer continues. "Almost always, unless you're making an incoherent big action movie, you've shot more storytelling than you need, because you're never sure that the audience can follow what you're doing. So you put in some of that, and then watch it with people. There's a thing you feel in the room when the audience has been told something one more time than they need to be told it. So their interest momentarily flags and is withdrawn. 'I know this already. Let's get on with it.' You feel that in the room with them, so the editing process in both cases is taking stuff out until you've really got the essential spine of the story and nothing more. And then, hopefully, some laughs along the way.

"The difference is that if you're doing a movie Chris' way — the improvisational way — your editing process is much, much, much, much longer," Shearer explains. "You're really building the movie from scratch. With a traditional script, you have an outline for an editor to string together a rough view of the movie. In an improvised situation, you're really building from brick one when you start editing, so it takes much more time. But in both cases your job is essentially the same: getting rid of anything that slows down the flow, anything beyond the minimum necessary to move the story along. You don't want to overload your movie, you want to keep up the pace — especially in a comedy. In drama, you can linger over loving shots of leaves and stuff forever, but in comedy you really have to keep it moving."

"He shoots seventy hours of footage and uses ninety minutes. It can't ever be more than ninety minutes," Garrity explains. "He feels that with a comedy, that's as long as he wants to stay with it. So everything has to compress down. It takes him a long time to do that, sometimes more than six months of paring down."

Dooley concurs that editing is a much more difficult process in the documentary-style comedies of Guest. "Editing is hard with improvisational people. That's why sometimes you'll do three takes. And when that happens, you begin to refine it and iron it out a little bit. You know when someone is going to come in with his line. You still overlap, but it's a little cleaner.

"Instead of editing one line out, like you do in another kind of a movie, for a close-up and reaction shot of one sentence, Chris can do an edit where he picks up three or four sentences, and then make an edit where there's a pause."

It's not an easy task by any metric, sifting through multiple takes and so many hours of footage. "We do a vast amount of material for every moment that ends up in the movie. We've done a day or something. The ratio is enormous," Balaban stresses. "In all movies, they usually do a number of takes and a number of angles, but in these movies, you'll do a twelve-minute take of something that might end up literally lasting a second or two, or being thrown out."

The group, however, is in safe hands with Guest. Dooley suggests that Guest's experience as a comedian actually helps to preserve the individual rhythms of the performers once the footage lands in the editing room for cropping.

"You don't find a whole lot of quick cuts, which you find now in almost every movie, where they cut it to death, actually. They're just so afraid of staying on one static shot for as much as thirty seconds. It's an editor's medium, finally," Dooley laments.

"Editors can save a scene, and editors can time a scene and pace a scene and make things funnier than they are, but they can also make them less funny than they are. You can have the best timing in the world — you can be Jack Benny — but if the timing is left up to the editor, it won't be Jack Benny's timing anymore. Sometimes editing is the enemy of timing."

The tools of the documentary format also permit Guest to be creative in the editing process, not just with pace and timing, but with the film's jokes and visual flourishes. If he desires to cloak an awkward zoom during a talking-head interview, he can cut away to what is known as the B-roll, archival footage of photographs, album covers, black-and-white TV performances, or virtually any "document" illustrating the points being made by the actors in the scene. The cutting in of the B-roll is especially relevant in these comedies because it often consists of a punch line, a succinct punctuation for a subtle joke.

In *A Mighty Wind*, Bob Balaban discusses how Steinbloom's protective mother required that he don protective gear at all times, even while playing seemingly innocuous games, such as chess. At this point, there is a cut away from Balaban, and the B-roll hammers home the joke, revealing an old black-and-white photo of a young boy sitting before a chessboard, a football helmet over his head.

Another example of the B-roll's efficacy occurs in *Best in Show*, when Jerry Fleck (Levy) refers to himself as a Casanova-type, and then the B-roll cuts in, revealing a very un-Casanova-like shot of the young Jerry, garbed in a sky-blue tuxedo and awkward glasses, his eyes crossed. In this case, the B-roll has been used as a humorous contrast rather than as supporting data, undercutting Jerry's (deluded) assertion about himself.

Essentially, a B-roll gives the director and cutter options at the editing bench, and sometimes a voice-over and archival footage can bridge the seams during an overlong or meandering interview sequence, trimming the fat as it were, and getting right to the good stuff.

In editing these documentaries, Guest also deploys an editing strategy that scholar Jason Middleton has termed "cutting on the absurd," a technique that Middleton feels "positions viewers to laugh at and laugh with the subjects, to occupy a position that can be at once derisory and sympathetic."[25]

Again, the pertinent example might be that B-roll insertion of the goofy-looking photo of Jerry in *Best in Show*. The film cuts to the youthful, un-surefooted Mr. Fleck, and audiences can recognize the absurdity of Jerry's claims to be a Casanova, yet at the same time, the photo doesn't make one despise the fellow. It merely cues viewers in that he doesn't have an objective view of himself or perhaps his dreams.

Sometimes, the art of cutting also involves holding on a scene for longer than is generally comfortable, allowing audiences to feel the awkwardness of the moment, and to dwell on what they have just witnessed unfolding.

In *Best in Show*, Christy Cummings and Sherri Ann sit down together for an interview, and Sherri describes Christy as the dog's disciplinarian,

Christy counters that Sherri provides unconditional love. Then Cummings adds that this is indeed how it was in her family of origin, with her unconditionally loving mom — at least until her mom committed suicide in 1981.

Instead of clipping off this scene directly after Christy's admission, the scene holds pat with these two for a few seconds, and the joke settles in. There is time to reflect on the remark, and the moment feels a little awkward, i.e., like life. Such a moment, and its impact, might have been missed with a tighter editing style.

Also, the pause after the joke or comment allows audiences to feel as though they have discovered the humor for themselves. By holding on the scene, the editing makes us all feel like we've found the moment.

The editing in the documentary-style comedies is vital, because it is the period of filmmaking in which the improvised runs are sharpened, where archival footage is inserted to both support and contrast the opinions of the participants, and moments can be lingered on or trimmed to add laughs, pathos, or reflection. Alongside Robert Leighton and Andy Blumenthal, this is where Guest really shapes his films.

The very format of the documentary permits a director to exercise a more imaginative degree of interpretation over his material than does the traditional narrative, and that's why one can feel secure making the assertion that Guest is an auteur in the traditional sense. His chosen format empowers him to wield a high degree of control over his art, a dominance that even his own conventional comedies like *The Big Picture* and *Almost Heroes* don't seem to evidence nearly as powerfully.

THAT LESS IS MORE STYLE OF ACTING

The words "final cut" have a scary ring, and that is especially true regarding improvisational comedy. Remember, roughly eighty hours of footage are shot on a film like *Best in Show*, and only eighty minutes survive. That means that the majority of material lensed — even if it is golden — will be cut. The criterion? If something doesn't serve the story, it is gone with the wind.

"It's very surprising what ends up in the final cut, and it usually has to do with good storytelling," John Michael Higgins notes in an interview. "There are so many great bits that aren't used in the film. I think there are nine characters cut out of the film [*A Mighty Wind*] entirely. Whole subplots, sets, locations, storylines."[26]

"Watching one of [Guest's] movies for the first time is like Elisabeth Kubler-Ross's five stages of loss," Theaker compares. "You work your way from anger and denial toward acceptance.

"Honestly, among each other, when we first see the screen — the finished product — there are tremendously hurt feelings that we suppress and hide. We buck up and carry on," Theaker says, "because in our mind it is so vivid when you're doing it that you're sure it's been committed to film, or that you're part of the story. It becomes so very real that when you see the edited product, you still carry all those scenes you did in your mind's eye."

"We all go through that," Balaban agrees. "We did learn after the first one that no matter what you thought, or what was great, or how it felt while you were there, you must put your life in the filmmaker's hands, and try not to judge it too much, because you're always going to be missing your favorite three moments."

"It's terribly hard," Willard says. "I think some of the others have accepted it a little better than I have. I've always hated to watch things where you've done brilliant moments, but they're not up there on the screen."

Theaker says it takes her "a good three or four viewings" to make the shift from denial to acceptance. "I always appreciate everybody else's work on the first viewing, but I'm always deeply disturbed by what's not there," she says. "But in the end, you realize that Chris is totally democratic. [The cuts] are only there to serve the story. There's never anything personal about what's been edited. It's actually smart and brilliant in the editing choices.

"It's a fine balance," Theaker continues, "and Chris works very hard to achieve that. He never hits a wrong note when he edits. I never question his judgment."

Fred Willard illustrates the point. "I mentioned to Michael McKean once, 'I know you're a Vincent Price fan. I was just watching *House of Wax* (1953) last night, and it was quite an interesting movie with 3-D.' He said, 'It's funny you mention that, because in *Best in Show* we did a twenty-minute thing where Michael Higgins and I were sitting around in character watching *House of Wax* and commenting on it.' And I said, 'But it didn't end up in the movie?' and he said, 'No.' I would have loved to see that scene.

"Everyone just puts in everything that they've got, and Chris uses what he needs. I think that's why his movies are so successful. Everybody says, 'I've seen that movie five or six times,' and it's not a two-and-a-half-hour movie, so you can watch it again and again, and he gives everyone their shot. When I hear what he's cut out from other actors, I say, 'I don't feel so bad now.'"

Besides, there's always the next movie.

"It's like playing with the jazz greats," Theaker explains. "Just to be on the team is enough. If you don't get your licks this time, you know that Chris is such a generous person by nature that he will feature you somewhere, somehow, later on, because he always does. He makes sure everybody gets their focus. Be it a year down the line, or several years down the line."

"To me, it's fascinating to see how these films are crafted, and what has remained, and what subplots have been dropped due to time, or maybe they didn't work as well as they hoped," says Michael Hitchcock. "I've never really had a sense of loss, but I can understand how some people can. Frances Fisher, who got completely cut out of *Waiting for Guffman,* I'm sure had a sense of loss, but that's also the reality of these movies, and the fun of them, too. You shoot so much material, and since it's a documentary, it is shot that way and has to be edited that way."

For those who mourn specific cut moments, Balaban suggests that they never really disappear at all. "Everything that doesn't end up in the movie that you love? It gets in anyway; it's part of the reality of the characters. It's *emerged*," he describes. "You just see this little tip of the iceberg of these characters that have lived a whole life. There are arguments and discussions and events that happened to you that you don't have to see literally in the movie to experience these characters. They all look like they came from somewhere; they all know how they feel about each other. Those aren't decisions that get made, those are because all the things that don't remain in the movie inform what does remain. It's really an interesting thing. It's a 'less is more' philosophy, and it works really well."

One example of this philosophy occurs in the scenes in *A Mighty Wind* involving the Steinbloom siblings (Balaban, Theaker, and Don Lake). The relationships seem rife with barely concealed conflicts and irritations, even though not that much of the family's scenes remain in the movie.

"You could have had an hour of Steinbloom family activity, but instead you have three minutes," Balaban explains, "but you felt all those vibrations anyway, and they're real. It's kind of like an orchestra. You sense resonances and different things and you don't always have to hear the whole piece to get a lot of it."

Fred Willard appreciates the fact that Guest must balance many elements in the editing room, and gladly leaves him to the task. "If I were to edit, it would be seventy minutes of me and fifteen minutes of plot. Every actor feels that way, it's not just me," he laughs. "But I still like to bug Christopher about it. I'll say, 'You know, Chris, I can come down and show you how to edit, if you want to save some of my stuff.' And he says, 'Yeah, okay Fred.'"

THE SILVER LINING IN THIS CLOUD

Despite the winnowing process that leaves many great character moments on the cutting room floor, the improvisation process on Guest's documentary-style films remains an enormously effective process by which to make the film's characters seem real. And when all is said and done, that is the most important thing — to accurately reflect the strange experience we all know as life.

"Sometimes when you improvise, it really does have the quality of real life," says Dooley, "because you don't really know what you're going to say next. So its sort of like you stammer. Dialogue is usually clear and crisp, and you deliver it the same way each time. That's how it is conceived and written. But in improv, you can show character and get a kind of naturalism by being as stammering as you would be in real life, if you're telling a story.

"Any story told in real life, or any sort of dialogue, if you listen in on the people on the bus, or the subway, or at dinner — it's never clean. You don't finish one sentence and start the next. Everything is overlapped in life. You have lots of half-sentences and interruptions, and that's what it's really like. Improv gets that feeling because we do interrupt each other and we do ramble on."

"I think [improvising] works really well in Christopher's case, because the documentary interviews take care of so much. You get everybody's background in them," says Balaban. "You can actually deal with plot in them, if you have to, so that the scenes between people don't usually have to carry much story weight. It's very hard to improvise story, because story is something everybody has to agree on and know where its going, and where it came from.

"I think the fact that it's labeled a documentary, and it has a rather strict format, really serves this idea that as an actor you're not writing the story, you're just experiencing it. You don't have to make large leaps. You don't have to decide in the middle of a scene, 'We're going to Colorado to get the wagon ready.' Mostly, the scenes are allowed to be as leisurely as they want to be, because there's no giant urge to make a story happen. A lot of that takes place with the interviews," Balaban explains.

"There's a great freedom in not having to go anywhere."

DON'T TRY THIS AT HOME (OR YOU MIGHT END UP WITH A STINKY PRODUCT)
Improvising may indeed be an arcane and intricate art, especially if you come from the world of traditional film acting, not to mention one that works best in the hands (and voices) of experts.

"So many people are trying to make what they call improvised movies now," Balaban says, "and some of them are perfectly good and some aren't, but everybody does it differently. To some people, it's an improvised movie if you write down everything that everybody's doing moment to moment and then just have somebody say, 'I'm going to use the words "I'm going there" instead of "I went there."'"

Despite such differences in definition, Paul Dooley believes that some improvisation technique can be learned. "I think most people can learn it. I've actually taught some classes," he says. "Senior citizens and children are the best at it, because they have no inhibitions. Improvisation is kind of like play. Kids are already good at play. They're highly imaginative and haven't been stunted by living. As an adult, you're used to being embarrassed. You think you're going to be judged by people."

"It's really about a kind of obliteration of self. Don't come in with pre-conceived notions," Balaban recommends. "The most fun thing I can say about the entire process is that you've got to have your antennae really tuned up. You have to be aware not just with your ears, but with your instincts. 'What's in the air right now? Let's hook into that.' You don't bring your own hook and apply it, you really look at what's happening and go with the flow. There's a group thing that starts to happen. When it does, it's like heroin. You just crave being around it, and you crave being around the people that helped generate it."

"These are talented actors who see something around them, it sparks their imagination, and they go with it," Garrity describes. "I don't really know how they do it. Chris tells me he completely forgets what he said afterward. It's an 'in the moment' thing, and if I asked him what he said this morning, he would have forgotten it. It just goes in and comes out."

"The best actors I know are scared to death of improvisation and don't improvise," Willard reveals, "and some of the best improvisors I know don't go on to become wonderful actors. It's a strange talent, like being able to juggle, or shoot an apple on somebody's head. If you can do it, get into your character and just go. *Get into your character* — that sounds like a cliche, but it's true. Be the character, and have your character's hopes and faults, and be as real as you can be."

Harry Shearer gets the last word on the improvisational approach, and the efficacy of it in these films. "To me, nothing is funnier than humans, and the way we actually behave. You don't need to dress it up or extend it with a lot of imaginative flights. You just need to be a good observer. That's the toughest thing, apparently, because people find it much easier to go into a room and talk about or sell things that are 'what ifs' rather than get comedy out of how people really are."

PART TWO

The Documentary-Style Comedies

3. THE ELEMENTS ARE COMING TOGETHER, SIR

WAITING FOR GUFFMAN (1997)

THERE'S A GOOD REASON
SOME TALENT REMAINS UNDISCOVERED.

CASTLE ROCK ENTERTAINMENT PRESENTS
A PALE MORNING DUN PRODUCTION, *WAITING FOR GUFFMAN*.

DIRECTED BY: Christopher Guest

WRITTEN BY: Christopher Guest, Eugene Levy

PRODUCED BY: Karen Murphy

DIRECTOR OF PHOTOGRAPHY: Roberto Schaefer

PRODUCTION DESIGNER: Joseph T. Garrity

FILM EDITOR: Andy Blumenthal

COSTUME DESIGNER: Julie Carnahan

MUSIC AND LYRICS BY: Michael McKean, Harry Shearer, and Christopher Guest

ASSOCIATE PRODUCER: Ginger Sledge

UNIT PRODUCTION MANAGER: Helen Pollak

FIRST ASSISTANT DIRECTOR: Liz Ryan

ART DIRECTOR: John Frick

MUSIC PRODUCED AND ARRANGED BY: Jeffery Vanston

STARRING (IN ORDER OF APPEARANCE)

LEWIS ARQUETTE: Clifford Wooley
BOB BALABAN: Lloyd Miller
CHRISTOPHER GUEST: Corky St. Clair
MATT KEESLAR: Johnny Savage
EUGENE LEVY: Dr. Allan Pearl
CATHERINE O'HARA: Sheila Albertson
PARKER POSEY: Libby Mae Brown
FRED WILLARD: Ron Albertson
DEBORAH THEAKER: Gwen Fabin-Blunt
LINDA KASH: Mrs. Pearl
MICHAEL HITCHCOCK: Steve Sark
LARRY MILLER: Glenn Welsch, Mayor
DON LAKE: Phil Burgess, Blaine Historian
DAVID CROSS: UFO Expert
TURK PIPKIN: Ping-Pong-Ball Juggler
JERRY TURMAN: Raging Bull Auditioner
PAUL DOOLEY: UFO Abductee
BRIAN DOYLE-MURRAY: Red Savage
PAUL BENEDICT: Not Guffman

FILMED IN LOCKHART AND AUSTIN, TEXAS AND LOS ANGELES, CALIFORNIA

IT'S THE STORY OF BLAINE ...

IN THE SMALL TOWN OF BLAINE, MISSOURI, the City Council prepares to celebrate the sesquicentennial anniversary of their little hamlet, a town settled in 1845, visited by extraterrestrials in 1946, and famous for its manufacture of footstools.

In honor of this momentous occasion, Off-Broadway exile, Blaine High School drama teacher, and founding member of the Blaine Community Players, Corky St. Clair, mounts a lavish theatrical tribute entitled *Red, White and Blaine*. Cast in this historical musical revue is Clifford Wooley, the local taxidermist; Dr. Allan Pearl, the town dentist; two very confident performers (and travel agents), Ron and Sheila Albertson; the Dairy Queen ingenue, Libby Mae Brown; and hunky mechanic Johnny Savage.

Corky's hopes for a triumphant return to Broadway are fueled when a prominent New York producer from the Oppenheimer Group, Mort Guffman, sends notice that he plans to attend the debut of *Red, White and Blaine*. However, Corky quits the show in a tussle with the City Council over budgetary issues, leaving the task to the uninspired musical director, Lloyd Miller.

After a last-minute plea from the mayor, Steve Stark, and Gwen Fabin-Blunt, a descendant of the town's founder and local hero, Blaine Fabin, Corky makes a triumphant return to the production.

But then, on the day of the show, a cast member drops out suddenly, leaving the flamboyant Corky no alternative but to appear in the show himself.

ASSEMBLING THE GANG

Shortly after production on HBO's successful *Attack of the 50 Ft. Woman*, a thoughtful Christopher Guest was contemplating his future in the film industry, and the shape it might take.

"It was harder and more complicated, that film," production designer Joseph Garrity recalls. "It was about effects and miniatures and a lot of complicated things; a lot of trucks and a lot of hardware. Not that [Guest's] bad at it, but I think he's more comfortable keeping it small. He told me, 'Joe — I'm going to try something next, and if this doesn't work, I don't know what I'm going to do.'"

That next thing turned out to be *Waiting for Guffman*, a return to the documentary-style, improvised comedy that *This Is Spinal Tap* pioneered successfully in the early 1980s. In this case, however, Guest made a modification.

"I decided to remove the interviewer from the film entirely, and so you never heard any questions, and it's more of a hybrid in the sense that it is a more conventional film in its style than *Spinal Tap* was,"[1] he told the Sundance Channel's Jack Tapper.

"Chris has been moving away from the stricter fealty to pure documentary-style, and going into a hybrid form," Harry Shearer explains. "It doesn't call for a storyteller on screen, or even an off-screen interviewer. You never really hear a question being asked. These people are talking to somebody off-screen, so it's more a conceit that helps the style, that helps tell these stories, than *Tap*, which was a specific parody. It's broadened from that now."

Although there was no Marty DiBergi — or even Marty Scorsese — to guide audiences through *Waiting for Guffman*, that didn't mean the documentary format need totally be sacrificed. In 1993's *Husbands and Wives*, Woody Allen also instructed actors to address the camera as if in one-on-one interviews, and though the narrator was heard, he was never seen.

Going back further, D.A. Pennebaker's Bob Dylan tribute *Don't Look Back* eschewed the role of the narrator totally and permitted audiences to make individual conclusions about the featured subject. *Gimme Shelter* was the same — no narrator present.

Even sans narrator, *Waiting for Guffman* would still adhere strictly to many of the tenets of the recent movement in documentary filmmaking called *direct cinema* — a concentration on impromptu interviews — a conscious informality in the (largely handheld) camera work, and an "attempt to break down the barriers between filmmaker and subject, to oversimplify the procedure to get at the whole truth and nothing but the truth and to catch events while they are happening."[2]

Actors improvising lines offered ample opportunity for stammers, pauses and other tics that reflect real life more than the polish of a traditional Hollywood narrative, and that's always what Guest seeks. The documentary style is also practical in many senses for a low-budget filmmaker. It involves fast setups and is cheap to shoot.

"There are no lengthy setups," actor Jim Piddock states. "You can have the camera moving herky-jerky, and it's okay."

"He obviously knew that his improv, kind of documentary-style thing was something he was good at," Garrity adds, "and he knew his friends were good at it. This is where they've all come from."

This time, Guest's humor, which he himself describes as "silliness-framed intelligence,"[3] was targeted not at the world of heavy-metal, rock 'n' roll pretensions, but small-town America, and in particular, community theater.

"Starting in theater in high school and having been on Broadway and playing Carnegie Hall and doing movies, there really is no difference other than you get paid more," Guest commented once. "It's all the same thing."[4] In other words, human egos, foibles, and pettiness are all on display backstage, regardless of the magnitude of the venue.

Guest also conceived his project not as something that would skewer or hurt people, but rather as a film that would depict — with some affection — the great enthusiasm and energy that people, even untalented ones, have for performing. "I have to entertain," Dr. Allan Pearl emphatically repeats in the film. "I *have* to entertain." He's so adamant about it that it almost sounds like a threat.

"Chris told me he originally came up with the idea for *Waiting for Guffman* when he went to see one of his kids' school plays, and they were putting on *Annie, Get Your Gun*," Deborah Theaker confides. "There were all these little kids with handlebar moustaches and he thought it was just hilarious and sweet at the same time, and wanted to translate that into a movie. That was the impetus."

On the DVD commentary for *Guffman*, Guest also likened the situation at the heart of Guffman to that of actors in a Broadway show learning that someone like Woody Allen is in the audience and concluding that he *must* be there to see them, and what's more, hire them. It is the "discovery" delusion of everyone who has ever dreamed of going to Hollywood; the belief that the right person will see you, discern your captivating abilities, and deliver you to fame and fortune.

THE LEVY CONNECTION

After Guest imagined the film's concept, he contacted Eugene Levy to collaborate on the film's dialogueless screenplay with him. "I live in Toronto, and Chris called me [from L.A.] and said he wanted me to write *Guffman* with him," Levy revealed to *Back Stage West*. "It wasn't until quite recently that I found out he called me because he liked my work on *SCTV*."[5]

In fact, Levy at first believed that Guest's call was a prank.[6] Fortunately, it wasn't, and Guest had selected both carefully and wisely. Not only was the Canadian Levy a brilliant actor, writer, and director in his own right, but he also had significant experience with the so-called mockumentary format, specifically the 1984 HBO special called *The Last Polka*, a parody of *The Last Waltz* and chronicle of the life and times of the Happy Wanderers, the Schmenge brothers (John Candy and Eugene Levy) — characters from the *SCTV* series.

Born in 1946 in Hamilton, Ontario, a small town some forty miles or so from Toronto, Eugene Levy lived a youth not that different from that of Guest. He always had a love of music and attended McMaster University in the late 1960s. He dropped out during his fourth year and worked as a coffee boy on the set of the 1971 Ivan Reitman movie *Foxy Lady*, a job that earned him only about sixty dollars a week.[7]

Soon thereafter, Levy began appearing in Toronto theater productions like *Godspell* in 1972, alongside co-stars including Paul Schaffer, Gilda Radner, and *Alias'* Victor Garber. Sometimes termed a "walking encyclopedia of show business,"[8] Levy then joined the Toronto branch of Second City in 1973.

By 1976, Levy was headlining in the legendary television series *SCTV* alongside Rick Moranis, Martin Short, John Candy, Andrea Martin, Dave Thomas, and eventually his Guest movies' co-star, Catherine O'Hara.

The series focused on the fictional SCTV studios, channel 109, and all the crazy characters who appeared on the air, in commercials, and behind-the-scenes at the network. Replete with several skits per show and a number of recurring characters, the syndicated, Canadian-produced, thirty-minute series expanded to fit a ninety-minute slot on NBC in America in the early 1980s, and aired from 12:30 to 2:00 AM on Friday nights.

Like Guest, Levy demonstrated a fondness for incorporating music into comedy routines and wrote many musical parodies for the series, including those involving a folk group called Five Neat Guys. Presaging the folk music comedy of *A Mighty Wind*, this skit involved a quintet of folksy serenaders (Levy, Candy, Moranis, Thomas, and Joe Flaherty) decked out in letterman sweaters, gold bow ties, and gold lamé pants. Levy also served as co-host alongside John Candy for the aforementioned Happy Wanderers, a polka-style, musical variety show. John Candy and Eugene Levy played brothers Yosh and Stan Schmenge.

Though *SCTV* earned a comedy-writing Emmy award for the 1982–83 season and also acquired a legion of devoted admirers, Levy didn't truly become a beloved part of the American pop-culture landscape until 1984, when he played the scheming villain in Ron Howard's mermaid comedy, *Splash*.

Over the years, Levy has been a solid character actor in mainstream comedies like *Father of the Bride* (1991) and *Multiplicity* (1993), but in 1999 he achieved everlasting fame as the kind-hearted, accepting father of Jason Biggs' pastry-screwing character in *American Pie*.

After appearing in two sequels, *American Pie 2* (2001) and *American Wedding* (2003), Levy again stole the show with his deliberately straight-laced delivery of hip-hop jargon in the Steve Martin–Queen Latifah comedy *Bringing Down the House* (2003).

Levy has also produced TV series such as Canada's *Maniac Mansion* (featuring Deb Theaker) and collaborated with Christopher Guest on a comedy pilot for HBO called *D.O.A.* (1999), which followed the comic misadventures at a talent agency. In 1998, after *Waiting for Guffman*, Levy appeared in the Guest-directed traditional narrative, *Almost Heroes*.

On *Waiting for Guffman*, the highly respected Levy not only co-wrote the screenplay, he portrayed Dr. Allan Pearl, the small town dentist with big time dreams of Broadway and beyond.

Michael Hitchcock still recalls his excitement the first time he met Levy in the flesh, during an interview with Guest in pre-production of *Waiting for Guffman*. "I remember, all of a sudden, Eugene Levy walked out of the door, and I was almost speechless. I said, 'Oh, that was Eugene Levy!' And Chris said, 'Yes, and Bob Hope is in that room, too,' very dryly. So that was my introduction to Eugene."

GETTING TO KNOW BLAINE

When the screenplay for *Waiting for Guffman* was completed, there was a sixteen page outline/script to show for Levy and Guest's efforts, and what emerged from their work was the story of Blaine (rhymes with plain) and its starry-eyed residents.

Some early touches were changed before filming, including a denouement that would have seen the town's stage destroyed before *Red, White and Blaine* could premiere. It was all part of a running joke related to *The Wizard of Oz* (1939). Blaine was originally a town in Kansas,[9] which explains the aforementioned tornado, and Corky owned a memorabilia shop called Over the Rainbow, where stills and posters from that film could be seen. But as the story developed, Blaine moved to Missouri, and the *Oz* references dwindled, or at least slid into the background.

Another mostly discarded concept involved the sprinkling throughout the film of several talking-head moments, featuring purportedly real Blainians. This was a funny allusion to a similar conceit in Warren Beatty's epic *Reds* (1981). In the end, only a confused UFO expert (David Cross) and blasé abductee (Paul Dooley) were shown.

Named after its hapless founder, Blaine Fabin, who mistook Missouri for California, the fictional town of Blaine became known, according to the film's screenplay, for its manufacturing of one marginally useful item: footstools.

Known as the Stool Capital of the World, Blaine proves to be a prodigious source of jokes for the film's creators, but in accordance with Guest's "comedy is reality plus one step further" theorem, the town is not too off the wall. Indeed, there are probably weirder towns in middle America. For instance, in North Carolina, a town called Bethune proudly heralds itself as "the home of the chicken strut."

At Blaine's center of gravity stood a very strange and singular individual, the colorful Off-Broadway exile named Corky St. Clair, who had relocated from the Big Apple to the film's primary setting. The fey Corky was a variation and evolution of characters that Guest had developed in other venues, including *Saturday Night Live* and some old cable TV specials.

As *Waiting for Guffman*'s screenplay was forged, talent from both sides of the camera came aboard the project. Karen Murphy produced *This Is Spinal Tap* and had made a name for herself in Hollywood with challenging material like David Byrne's *True Stories* (1986) and Gus Van Sant's *Drugstore Cowboy* (1989). She had worked with Guest before not only on *Tap*, but also in a series of Showtime specials called *Likely Stories* in the early 1980s. Also helpful was Murphy's experience with authentic documentaries, which she had produced for both PBS and the American Film Institute.

Another talent marshaled for the film was Guest's old supporter from *The Big Picture* and *Attack of the 50 Ft. Woman*, production designer Joseph Garrity. He still remembers his initial conversations about the project and its design. "The thought was that it's all very real. Nothing was going to be staged and nothing was going to be perfect.

"You have a character and you discuss him with Chris," Garrity describes. "Each character has a history and space he lives in. For Corky, he has a history of doing bad theater, and we had to come up with a lot of posters on the wall for these oddball plays. I always went to Chris and Eugene and asked them for the names of plays Corky had done. They would come up with weird names and I would put some insane images to them."

Among Corky's previous productions from off-off-off-Broadway were *We'll Dance 'til the Cows Come Home!* and *Cornelius McGillicutty and His Truly Amazing Flying Machine*. One of Corky's previous shows also had the distinction of opening at the East Side Recreation Hall/Annex, perhaps not a very well-known (or well-attended) venue.

In the casting department, a versatile group of performers, most of them boasting extensive improv experience, joined the team. Deborah Theaker, a graduate of Second City, and Michael Hitchcock, discovered by Guest during a performance of the Groundlings, were cast as town council member Gwen Fabin-Blunt and pharmacist Steve Sark, respectively.

"Though you never know exactly why you were picked with Chris, I think what got him interested in me is that I had done a lot of community theater growing up in the Chicago suburbs, at a place called the Theater of Western Springs," says Hitchcock, "and I was relaying some of my experiences with that. I guess something clicked, and I was asked to join the film."

Fred Willard signed on to play Ron Albertson. His domineering character was one half of the married acting team that Corky referred to grandly as the Lunts of Blaine. Ron's wife Sheila was played by Second City vet and *Home Alone* (1990) mom, Catherine O'Hara, sister of singer Mary Margaret O'Hara.

Willard recalls how he came to be involved with *Guffman*. "I watched a rerun of *Saturday Night Live* where Chris Guest and Martin Short were doing a sketch. Guest was doing an incredibly effeminate character — it was Corky St. Clair, but he had a different name — and there was this long scene where they were sitting at a restaurant, this agent and a manager.

"The next day I was doing a voice-over for a commercial and my manager called me frantically and said, 'I just got a call from Christopher Guest and he wants to talk to you about being in a movie. How soon can you get down there?' I said, 'What's the big rush?' and he said, 'You've just got to go talk to him.' So I went down there and talked to Christopher — and he's not very forthcoming. He's very quiet.

"So I said, 'Christopher, I saw you last night on *Saturday Night Live*, and you were doing this character. Was that all improvised?' And he said, 'Unfortunately, yes it was,' and I said, 'Well, it was the funniest thing,' and I spit all his lines back at him. Then he said, 'It's funny you mention it, because we're doing this [improvised] movie and we're calling it *Waiting for Guffman*.' I assumed it was a take off of *Waiting for Godot*, but they weren't sure that was going to be the title.

"My first thought as an actor was 'Wonderful, no lines to remember!' Then Chris said, 'You're going to play Catherine O'Hara's husband,' and I said, 'This is even more wonderful because she's one of my favorite actresses,'" Willard recalls. "So I said, 'Count me in!'"

Unfortunately, on a second meeting, Willard learned that Catherine O'Hara might actually drop out of the project, and Willard recommended Mary Gross for the role, since she had been in the same company with Guest on *Saturday Night Live*. In the end, O'Hara came aboard, and went on to become a beloved player in this repertory company.

Also cast in the film was Lewis Arquette, formerly of the 1960s political satire group the Committee, as well as Sills and Company. He would be playing Blaine's resident old fart, Clifford Wooley, who was responsible for narrating *Red, White and Blaine*.

Parker Posey, an actress well-known as Queen of the Indies for her roles in cutting-edge, independent cinema like *Party Girl* (1995), *Flirt* (1995), and *The Daytrippers* (1996), also met with Guest to discuss the role of the town's Dairy Queen employee-turned-actress, Libby Mae Brown.

A native of Laurel, Mississippi, and named after 1950s supermodel Suzy Parker,[10] Posey impressed Guest during their ten-minute meeting. "Parker is really able to spontaneously create a multi-dimensional character that is very rich," Guest noted of the SUNY-Purchase graduate after shooting *A Mighty Wind*. "She's very serious about her work, and I think that it shows ... It's why I keep working with her."[11]

Another young cast member was Matt Keeslar, fresh from appearances in *Renaissance Man* (1994) and *Quiz Show* (1995), and late of the Sci Fi Channel miniseries *Dune* (2000). Keeslar, who had once played Marlon Brando's role in a television version of *A Streetcar Named Desire* (1995), was perfect as Corky's secret object of desire, Johnny Savage.

Rounding out the cast was a team of veteran comedians and actors including Larry Miller, Don Lake, Scott Williamson, Brian Doyle-Murray, Linda Kash, and Frances Fisher (*Attack of the 50 Ft. Woman*), whose role as Johnny Savage's mother was subsequently cut from the film, despite her prominence in the film's trailer.

Bob Balaban joined the *Guffman* roster when Guest's pal and *Spinal Tap* collaborator Harry Shearer was not available to appear in the film to play Lloyd Miller, Blaine High School's music director and foil for Corky.

"I got a call out of the blue, and Christopher said, 'Would you like to be in *Waiting for Guffman*? This is what it is, and this is what we do,'" Balaban remembers. "I had the good sense not to ask too many questions and just say, 'Anything you want to do, let's do that.'"

However, as the film revolved around a musical revue, at least to some extent, Balaban had to prep for the part.

"When Christopher called about *Waiting for Guffman*, he said, 'Oh, by the way, you'd be playing the musical director. Do you play the piano? We might have you play at rehearsals.' I said, 'I don't really play too well.' I've taken a lot of piano lessons and if I've got the music all written out — note for note — months in advance, I could probably memorize it," Balaban says.

But by the time of the shoot, Balaban didn't feel comfortable playing piano, so Guest — in Balaban's words — "improvised," thus making Lloyd the orchestra's conductor and giving Miller a female assistant to tickle the ivories instead.

"Looking back on it, Christopher said to me, 'Isn't it great you couldn't play?'" Balaban says. "So I could go around ordering people about."

While Balaban trained to conduct the orchestra with musical director Jeffrey C.J. Vanston, the elements really started coming together. As *This Is Spinal Tap* had featured funny tunes such as "Big Bottom," "Sex Farm Woman" and "Hellhole," *Waiting for Guffman* would generate more than its fair share of bizarre theatrical numbers, including "Stool Boom" and "Nothing Ever Happens on Mars," both of which Guest co-wrote with Shearer. *Spinal Tap*'s David St. Hubbins, Michael McKean, co-wrote the music and lyrics to the 1845 set piece, "Covered Wagons, Open-Toed Shoes" and the romantic show-stopper, the ludicrous World War I era ballad "A Penny for Your Thoughts" (which Guest performed on stage with Parker Posey).

A LITTLE TOWN WITH A BIG HEART

In the early months of 1995, the cast and crew of *Waiting for Guffman* packed their bags and on a budget of just four million dollars, descended on Lockhart, Texas, for an intense twenty-nine-day shoot.

Nestled deep in Caldwell County and boasting a population of just over 11,000, Lockhart is approximately thirty miles south of Austin, and quickly proved the perfect site for the mythical town of Blaine. In the center of town stands the magnificent, and spired Caldwell County Courthouse, an imposing edifice built in 1893 that features a four-way Seth Thomas Clock. With this distinctive landmark dominating the town square, Lockhart could easily be Anywhere, U.S.A.

Billeted in a Sheraton Hotel in Austin, about an hour from Lockhart, the film company had access to a whole world outside of Hollywood, and Guest put the locale to good use.

A bustling community with its own outdoor festivals and local celebrations, Lockhart granted the *Waiting for Guffman* crew the opportunity to film authentic local color for their pseudo-documentary.

"The ceremonies that were happening in the park — where all the people are singing in the square? That was an actual event happening in town," Garrity explains. "They were having some kind of event that they do every year, so we got in there and made a banner for Blaine that we put in the foreground, and we shot this event as it was going on.

"We made it our event," Garrity laughs. "We just got in there with [the director of photography] Roberto Schaefer and Chris, and they got girls singing and all this other good stuff, and a few of those things made it into the movie. We got real close with that community. We linked with it, and we got to know people like the librarian. They were all wonderful people. We were a part of them and they knew we were around; that contributes to the reality of it, I think."

"It was such a great place. It was a funky little burg," Deborah Theaker agrees. "I do remember that one day Chris, Mike Hitchcock, and I cut out on craft services and went out for ribs. We went to a Texas barbecue place where they put a stack of white bread on the table and a big cube of cheese, and you get your rack of ribs. It was so good."

"Being on location was terrific," Hitchcock agrees. "It was my first time to Austin and that area, and we, as a cast, especially Deb and I and the other council members, would travel around the city and check out some of the nightlife. Lockhart itself is just a beautiful, sleepy town that apparently appears quite a bit in different motion pictures, television shows or commercials."

Garrity enjoyed finding original locations near Lockhart that were suitable domiciles for the film's dynamic characters. For instance, old Clifford Wooley — a retired taxidermist — had his own exceptional abode in the middle of nowhere.

"That was a field where we just brought in a little trailer," he remembers. "I love those kind of sets, because it's usually very cheap and you can bring things in from the junkyard. And Chris always finds the one element, like the paws of the deer on the rack, and flies with it. A lot of people ask me, 'Is it hard to know what to put there?' 'What the hell are [the actors] going to do?' Because it's just a paragraph that explains what happens in the scene."

Some Texan locals were also cast in the film in some small roles, appearing during Corky's auditions for *Red, White and Blaine*. A retired gentleman from Texas who also played the governor's chauffeur in the Burt Reynolds film *The Best Little Whorehouse in Texas* (1981), actor Jerry Turman, remembers how he became involved with *Guffman*.

"When they auditioned me, they were looking for a guy who would be uncomfortable with profanity, and I think my agent sees me as Mr. Cream Cheese, for some reason," Turman considers. He auditioned for Guest in February of 1995, learned he had won the part of the foul-mouthed Raging

Bull Auditioner on February 27, and shot his scene on March 16 at one of the high schools in Lockhart.

"I think I was the only one in the whole movie who was scripted," Turman reports. "They sent a package with the script from *Raging Bull* and some history of the hypothetical town and so forth."

As it turned out, his monologue from the Scorsese film was a heated and profanity-laced confrontation between the characters portrayed by Robert DeNiro and Joe Pesci. It was littered with a common four-letter expletive.

"I checked out *Raging Bull,* and I studied the scene over and over again, and there's no way that a guy from East Texas is going to do DeNiro or Pesci — either one," says Turman, "so I did it in my natural voice and told [Guest] and the casting director at the beginning of it, 'That's the only voice I have,' which is mostly east Texas, some central Texas. Everybody down here sounds like Willie Nelson. It's the pollen, I think."

But Turman found out that this offbeat line reading was precisely what the director had hoped for. "They wanted a bad audition for these guys, and I had a chance to work on it for several days," says Turman. "I knew it very well, and had to learn both parts because the responses were so strange to me. We don't talk that way here. So I had to learn it, and sure enough when I got in, he had me do both parts. So I was prepared.

"Catherine O'Hara was in the room," Turman adds. "She stood over in the corner and smiled at me, which helped. [The scene] took forty-five minutes and we did four takes."

What emerged was one of the most memorable moments in the film, as this southern gentleman spouted some very profane language in a straightforward manner.

"I didn't have any qualms about it," Turman laughs, "but I do have grandkids, and suddenly I'm aware that my grandkids are going to know about this. But I wasn't uncomfortable doing it. It was the first shot I had at a principal part in a feature film, so I was delighted, actually."

The only problem, as Turman learned, was that his part, filled as it was with such invective, could never see the light of broadcast TV. "My audition doesn't make it to television," he notes. "I can't imagine why."

Unlike Turman's audition, which was indeed scripted, the other auditions turned out to be something of a surprise to the director. It was Parker Posey's idea to revive the popular Doris Day tune "Teacher's Pet," and subsequently perform an expressive and sexually charged interpretation of it for Corky and Lloyd.

Fred Willard and Catherine O'Hara came up with a bizarre nightclub act that played like a Taster's Choice coffee commercial, drafting the lyrics of David Nichtern's hit, "Midnight at the Oasis." Notably, that song had also played in the background of a Hollywood party scene in Guest's 1989 film, *The Big Picture*.

Not to be left out, Eugene Levy performed a (deliberately) painful Stephen Foster medley that included snippets of "I Dream of Jeannie with the Light Brown Hair," "Swanee River," and "Camptown Races."

Turk Pipkin performed a near-fatal ping-pong-ball trick with his mouth and throat, and eagle-eyed viewers will notice comic Bob Odenkirk (*The Ben Stiller Show* [1992–93], *Mr. Show* [1995–98]) standing outside the audition room, dressed as a vampire, though his routine didn't make the final cut.

In his missing scenes, Odenkirk played the town minister of Blaine, a role originally assigned to Michael Hitchcock. The role of the priest was then cut out all together, but for a fleeting glimpse.

"He's still in it briefly," says Hitchcock, "but Bob had a scheduling conflict, and I became a councilman at the last minute. I knew before I arrived what I'd be."

Another auditioner, Jerry Turman recalled, was an eighty-year-old local woman who spoke with some excitement about her opportunity for stardom, but whose time on camera was not utilized in the final cut.

In all, the weeks spent in Lockhart are remembered by many among the cast and crew of *Waiting for Guffman* as a time of real bonding and creativity. The cast often got together to eat dinner and review the day's footage.

"They'd order some kind of dinner, sometimes Chinese food, and we'd be in the hotel and watch dailies practically every night," remembers Hitchcock. "It was the same with *Best in Show* [in Vancouver] as well."

MEET MR. ST. CLAIR

Although the characters were established, the locations scouted, and work commenced on *Waiting for Guffman* in the early months of 1995, nobody on the set was prepared when Guest first strode onto the set in the guise of his *Guffman* alter ego, Corky St. Clair.

"We didn't quite know what he was doing until the first day," Joseph Garrity reveals. "The first day, in his little apartment that we shot in Lockhart, he walked in with his band-leader uniform on, and we went, 'What's this?' We knew he was going to be a little flamboyant; we knew from the outline of the movie that he was probably a gay character — probably. But we didn't know what he was going to do, and it was hilarious. We all started leaving the room, because we couldn't keep our mouths shut. He was very funny."

"When I first came to Texas, they were already in the middle of shooting stuff in Corky's loft," Theaker recalls. "I had never seen Chris in that goofy little wig. He had on these Japanese sandals and white socks, and a kimono. I really didn't quite recognize him at first."

In fact, many performers had difficulty maintaining a straight face in the company of Monsieur St. Clair. "Your laugh restrainers break down a little,"[12] observed Bob Balaban.

"[With] *Waiting for Guffman*, things would happen, and I'd just crack up," Levy also reported, "I would work my way to the back of a crowd and literally drop to my hands and knees and crawl off the set."[13]

"I had no idea he would be so extreme," says Hitchcock. "I can remember when Corky said, 'I'm gonna bite my pillow,' I was biting my cheeks trying not to laugh. It was such an odd comment."

"I remember watching Chris do a scene," Fred Willard recalls. "He improvised with Matt Keeslar [playing Johnny Savage] and I watched him, and Christopher was just hilarious, at the height of his seductive gayness. He was drinking wine, and he invited Matt up to his apartment, and Matt says, 'Oh, would it be a problem?' Corky says, 'Oh no,' and he was drinking and looking at Matt as he said it. 'In fact it would be a bonus.' It was hilarious.

"When the scene was over, I rushed over to Matt and said, 'You did a wonderful job!' and he said, 'Thank you,' and I said, 'No, really, your impulse must have been to try to be funny, but if you had, the scene would have fallen apart.' He played the perfect straight guy. Matt was so straight, and if he had tried to be goofy, it wouldn't have worked."

Perhaps even more impressive, Christopher Guest not only had to stay in character as the dynamic (if ambiguous) Corky St. Clair, but also direct all the action and manage a fairly large crew.

"When he came in to do that scene in the Council Chambers, it was the end of a very long, taxing day," Theaker remembers. "Chris came in and did three or four, maybe more, completely different reactions, and in each one he was just as vehement, and he never dropped a line or fumbled, and he went for a different feel each time. It was amazing to me. I thought it was virtuoso given that not only was he in command of the crew and the big shoot, but he saved his close-ups and his shots until the end of the day, when he must have been most exhausted, and yet you could not tell.

"That's when I went, 'Oh my gosh, he's amazing,' because it's very hard when you're tired in the first place to do anything when it's scripted, let alone unscripted. Also, they weren't sure what emotion they were going to go with, or how they were going to have Corky react, so they tried it a bunch of different ways."

Of course, watching Guest direct (as Corky) had its funny side, too. "The hardest thing about this was Christopher in Corky-guise giving direction, because he would still be wearing the toupee and those outrageous out-fits, and he just looked so funny that it was hard not to be looking all over his body and that silly toupee while he was giving you notes," remembers Hitchcock.

DANCES WITH STUMPY

Although nearly every actor in the film has a deep background and experi-ence in the arcane art of improv, that doesn't always mean it is easy to get started, and on *Waiting for Guffman*, it took the performers a little time to get into the spirit of the thing.

Fred Willard remembers one occasion when he was worried there would be only dead air captured by the camera.

"Chris explained there's a scene in a Chinese restaurant where we would probably take some cameras and film for about two hours, and we'd just improv it," Willard says. "I thought, 'Oh my god, after five minutes, I'll run out of things to say.'"

Worse, the scene, a dinner date at the Chop Suey Chinese Kitchen be-tween the Pearls and the Albertsons, was scheduled for the end of a long day, and Willard feared that the promising scene had the chance of being lost if things didn't go well. "I thought, 'If we don't do it now, it either won't end up in the movie, or we'll have to do it first thing in the morning, so I hope we do it tonight.'"

To Willard's relief, they did do it that night, but there was still a lot of air time to fill with improvisation.

"We went [to the restaurant] and they set up the table, and well, you understand how Chris works. There was only one thing planned, and that was their idea that my character had this penis-reduction surgery," Willard recalls.

Then the camera rolled and ... *nothing*.

"Nobody said anything for about a minute," Willard recalls, "and the first thing that came out of my mouth was this thing about how in China they cut up a monkey at the table and eat his brains, and we got talking and it seemed to be going fine."

In fact, it went too well.

"[Guest] stopped the camera a couple of times to reload, and then said, 'That's it, we got it.' And I said, 'Wait a minute, we're just getting started!' Well, two hours had gone by so quickly." Willard remembers. "We could have gone on for another two hours."

The Chinese restaurant scene turned out beautifully, in no small part because Willard had another contribution to it, a succinct form of punctua-tion.

"In the trailer just before the scene, Christopher said to Linda Kash (Mrs. Pearl), 'What do you think you're going to do in this scene?' She said, 'I figure I'll just lay back and listen to the guys,' and I thought, 'This is the kind of actress I love to work with!' So in the scene, we were supposed to make the Pearls feel 'as comfortable as possible' by, of course, being as boorish as we could," Willard explains. "I said to Chris, 'I have an idea for something I want to do.' Chris said, 'I usually don't like to know what another actor is going to do in an improvised scene, but in your case I have trouble keeping a straight face, so please tell me what you're about to do.' So I said, 'I'd like to get up and drop my trousers to show Eugene my operation.' What could be more humiliating to someone?"

True to form, Willard stood up, went for his zipper, and approached the shocked Levy and Kash at the end of the scene. Naturally, they protested most vehemently (and amusingly) that they didn't care to see the results of his penis reduction surgery.

A SYMPHONY OF PROBING

Acting and improv legend Paul Dooley served as pinch-hitter on *Waiting for Guffman*. Christopher Guest had originally wanted the veteran actor to play the role of Blaine's mayor, the role eventually taken on by Larry Miller. But Dooley, a recurring presence on the ABC sitcom *Grace Under Fire* (1993 – 98) at the time, was unable to get out of his contract and head off to Texas for the duration of a four-week shoot.

"But then [Guest] called me up in the middle of it and asked me if I could come down on the weekend and shoot for a day," Dooley recalls. In particular, the director wanted Dooley to play one of the Blaine residents, a local fellow with a strangely blasé attitude about his close encounter of the third kind.

"I never really planned it," says Dooley of his memorable monologue about this most unusual — and penetrating — alien visitation. "I just went there and got in front of the camera and figured that it was better if it just comes to me. One of the reasons that people like it is that it seems very much like a real person talking. It's full of false starts and pauses, almost tripping over words.

"It was my symphony of probing," Dooley explains. "An elaboration of how many ways I could suggest probing. My handle on it was that I wanted to sound like a guy who didn't think it was strange. He was just reporting something like plowing. Actually, it *was* plowing in a funny way. It was a variation of 'They took me on, they gave me food, they took my fingerprints, and showed me a movie, and then I left. Except it was about... probing.

"So I went down there in one day, did my thing in two takes, got on the plane and left."

EVERYBODY DANCE!

Perhaps the most difficult components of *Waiting for Guffman* involved prepping and shooting the actual stage show that represented the picture's denouement, the stunning *Red, White and Blaine*.

"The stage we used had no room for all the scenery that was in this show," Garrity remembers. "It was just this little community basketball court/theater that was supposed to be in the high school."

It was there, at the Dorothy Miller Recreation Center on 11th Street in Austin, that the company spent the grueling last two weeks of shooting.[14]

"We built a lot of the scenery, and Chris even shot us building the scenery," Garrity explains. "Some of the people you saw putting paint down and sewing were the real people who did it.

"There was no wing space," Garrity continues, describing the venue. "There was very little space to bring scenery up, so that's why the cloud was hanging there [in 'Nothing Ever Happens on Mars']. There was a single cloud above the actors because we couldn't lift the spaceship high enough to hide it. We made this cloud quickly, and the spaceship came out from behind the cloud.

"In a way it was perfect, and Chris was fine with it too, because this is what might really happen. Nothing's precious. Nothing needs to be perfect, because most things aren't. And people laugh at these imperfections in people, like Eugene Levy without his glasses, stumbling off the horse."

There were, however other technical issues involved with putting on such an elaborate show.

"I find that a lot of movie people don't get theater," says Garrity. "They don't get what's involved. There's certain lighting, and how do you combine movie lighting with theater lighting? It's a lot more difficult than you might think. I come from theater, so I knew it was coming — and would be hard — but it worked out fine."

The *Red, White and Blaine* production represented the totality of the film's third and final act, so a significant amount of coverage was necessary to make certain it came off without a hitch. Actors had to perform live on stage, others in the cast had to be present in the auditorium as audience members, and cameras had to capture every detail.

"We were there for a long run of it," Hitchcock, one prominent audience member, reports. "When they went in for close-ups, they moved us out of the way. For me, as far as being in the audience goes, it was lucky that the first time we saw these numbers that the cameras were behind us, because I can definitely remember laughing out loud."

For many on the set during the show, two little words bring back a flood of memories: "Stool Boom."

It was a number that had to be performed over and over.

"It was really tedious," Deb Theaker remembers. "I thought if I heard 'Stool Boom' one more time, I would just snap like a twig in the wind. You don't love [the music] when you hear it day after day after endless day sitting in a chair. I thought I was going to lose my mind. They had to shoot it from all angles, and they'd do the same songs over and over.

"*A Mighty Wind* wears much better because the songs are so beautiful, but [in *Guffman*] the songs are musical theater songs, and definitely written for a specific genre," Theaker elaborates. "I found that hard to shoot. Is that rude? It was hilarious, but really difficult."

"The hardest part of that whole filming was that one number, 'Stool Boom,'" Fred Willard seconds. "Going in, all of us thought we would just play amateurs trying to dance and sing, and there was some discussion whether or not we'd lip-synch or sing live. Well, much to our surprise, they brought in a woman, a choreographer, and she put us through paces like we were going to do an Off-Broadway show. We were all taken back with all these steps they had us do.

"Saturday afternoons when we were off, we had to go over to a dance studio in Austin and for three or four hours go through this number. That was the toughest part, learning all that. I would watch Catherine, Eugene, and Parker Posey, and I realized they didn't know any more what they were doing than I did.

"Eugene injured his foot somehow, and was taking aspirins and wrapping his foot, so he was in pain during that," Willard recalls. "So the happiest moment of shooting was when we finished filming that number, and they said, 'Okay, cut, let's move on.'"

OVER THE RAINBOW

In *Waiting for Guffman*'s coda, Corky St. Clair escorts the camera on a tour of his odd memorabilia shop in New York City after his relocation to the Big Apple. Originally, all the sequences in the shop were meant to occur in Blaine.

"His store was in the town of Lockhart. Over the Rainbow, I think it was called, and it had this mural the size of a building with *Wizard of Oz* stuff on it," Joe Garrity remembers.

In fact, Corky's collectibles shop even had a local competitor. "I was his

107

chief rival," Deborah Theaker remembers. "I had Fantasia Gifts across the street. The kind of place where you'd buy a ceramic cheetah and stuff like that. So the props department had ads for my gift shop in the program for the show, but none of that ever entered into the movie, though we all knew about it."

"Between that store and the show at the end, those were the big things on the film," Garrity explains. The main problem facing the production designer concerned the legal issues surrounding Corky's unusual collectibles, including *Remains of the Day* (1993) lunch boxes, little figurines of the popular 1980s Brat-Packers, and *My Dinner with Andre* (1981) action figures.

"This was a big clearance and permission nightmare," Garrity sighs. "Easy to write — very funny stuff — but we had to reach all of these people and their representatives to get the okay to do this. People like Anthony Hopkins and Emma Thompson just laughed and said, 'Go for it.' It was those kids who were worried about how this was going to portray them: Andrew McCarthy, Anthony Michael Hall, Judd Nelson. They were a little hesitant, but they went for it in the end. And *My Dinner with Andre*? We had to contact those guys, too!"

In the end, everybody agreed to be in on the joke, and Garrity found a local woman in Austin who was a sculptor to produce the unusual action figures and other bizarre memorabilia.

In the final cut, Corky's shop was located in New York City, but Garrity says you can detect otherwise if you watch the film closely. "Although we didn't see much out the windows, if you look closely, there's diagonal parking with pickup trucks — and that wouldn't exist in New York City."

And Missouri license plates, too.

CUTTING UP

After a month shooting in Lockhart, the real job on *Waiting for Guffman* began in earnest: the editing process. In particular, more than fifty-eight hours of footage had to be vetted and assembled into a coherent, tight story lasting approximately ninety minutes.

"We had a lot of distracting, fun, good stuff, but our main focus was on the show in Blaine, Missouri,"[15] said producer Karen Murphy.

"Whatever didn't drive the story had to go,"[16] agreed Eugene Levy, and that edict translated into heavy cuts. In fact, one early version of the film is rumored to have all but removed the character of Corky St. Clair! Fortunately, that didn't happen, and this character remains the film's emotional heart and soul.

Still, a great number of deep cuts altered *Waiting for Guffman*'s final act.

The debut of the stage production *Red, White and Blaine* originally ran well over a half-hour, and Guest deemed it too long. As a result, two of the funniest — but lengthiest — bits disappeared all together, including "Nothing Ever Happens in Blaine," which featured Parker Posey and O'Hara performing spastic dance moves, and Guest doing a radical hip sway.

Another loss was the elaborate number entitled "This Bulging River." The song featured the whole ensemble, revived Willard's purposefully dreadful Henry Fonda imitation, and climaxed with Corky's expressive, operatic singing about Blaine's temperamental river being in his "bloo-oo-o-d."

"I miss that," Joe Garrity admits. "It's my favorite set." Thankfully, through the restorative magic of the DVD format, these numbers are now available for viewers to enjoy and have become an important part of the *Waiting for Guffman* experience.

Another missing scene is one that should be familiar to fans of Guest's work: the pre-show gathering. In *Best in Show*, there was a cocktail party where everybody got together, and in *A Mighty Wind*, it was the event at Steinbloom's apartment. In *Guffman,* the cast of *Red, White and Blaine* had a pre-show gathering in Corky's mauve apartment.

The lengthy editing process also revealed another issue. Some new shots had to be staged to clarify some elements of the storyline, and consequently there followed a period of reshoots in Los Angeles. "He puts these things together, and there are holes sometimes," Garrity explains, "and he doesn't know it until he edits. We did a few days of shoots in L.A. — we didn't go back to Lockhart."

In one circumstance, Corky needed to further explain the importance of Mort Guffman's impending visit to Blaine, as well as his determination to return to Broadway on his own terms. The scene was set in his brightly colored apartment. "That was a set that we built, a kitchen that we never saw in his real place," Garrity remembers. During Corky's one-on-one with the camera, he is seen cooking a tray of pigs in a blanket — even though he is the only person in his apartment. "It was a nervous thing," Garrity notes, "where he was cooking all those things." It was at this time that an alternate ending featuring Steve Sark and Corky living happily ever after in New York, was also devised and lensed.

In all, the editing process on *Waiting for Guffman* sprawled out across eighteen months. The time to edit a "normal" movie? Six weeks.

A RETURN TO FORM

In late August 1996, *Waiting for Guffman* was unveiled at the Boston Film Festival, a fact that explains why some databases list its year of release as 1996. The film didn't officially go to theaters until February of 1997, and upon its release, critics loudly cheered Guest's return to the so-called mockumentary format of *This Is Spinal Tap*.

The *New York Post*'s Michael Medved raved that the film contained "so many funny bits that you can share the best of them with friends without fear that you're spoiling the movie."[17] *Newsweek*'s David Ansen called it a "savvy satire of small-town boosterism and an affectionate salute to the performing spirit."[18]

In the *Chicago Sun-Times*, Roger Ebert reported that the film proceeded "with a certain comic relentlessness from setup to payoff, and its deliberation is part of the fun."[19] Writing for the *Village Voice*, critic Justine Elias considered *Waiting for Guffman* "clever but a bit cruel"[20] and *Entertainment Weekly*'s Owen Gleiberman raved that *Guffman* was a "madcap gem" and that it had transcended Guest's "usual teasing highs."[21]

By the vast majority, the reviews were positive, but business was not especially hot. After its initial release in only three theaters, the film didn't have the wide and highly publicized rollout of *Best in Show* or *A Mighty Wind*. In the end, the film grossed approximately three million dollars before shuffling off to the secondary market, where it promptly became a cult favorite. The DVD was released in August of 2001, following the success of *Best in Show*, and a whole new audience familiarized itself with Guest's first documentary-style comedy.

Despite the relative box-office disappointment, *Waiting for Guffman* was highly celebrated. Guest was nominated for an Independent Spirit Award for best director in 1997, though he lost to Kevin Smith for the New Jerseyite's *Chasing Amy*. *Waiting for Guffman*'s screenplay also picked up an Independent Spirit nomination, and Guest was among the five actors selected as a nominee for best lead actor for the creation of the unforgettable and indomitable Corky St. Clair.

"Somebody said that Winona Ryder had seen *Waiting for Guffman* fifteen times," Deb Theaker adds, testifying to the film's power, even among those who may have a vocation in common with Corky St. Clair.

GUEST SHOTS

SECRET INSPIRATIONS: Often, the actors in Christopher Guest's documentary-style comedies get to choose their own character names and occupations. "He asked me what I wanted to name my character, and I named her Gwen," Deb Theaker says. "I used the name Blunt because it was my friend's last name, and I thought she'd get a laugh when she went to see the movie. Everybody uses somebody's name."

And pharmacist Steve Sark? "He was a friend of mine from North-western," Michael Hitchcock explains. "Chris let us name ourselves in that movie, so I picked Steve Sark as a kind of goof to my friend."

Sometimes, real names don't get into the movies, but the actors' inspirations do. For instance, Fred Willard based Ron's relationship with Sheila on some people he actually knew.

"I modeled them after an acting couple I took lessons from when I first started in New York," he recalls. "It was a married couple, and I don't know that they'd ever worked professionally in their life, but they had this acting workshop ... and you could imagine their home life.

"I think I also modeled our relationship on some of my aunts and uncles from when I was little," Willard adds. "My aunts were always drinking, and my uncles were always saying, 'For god's sake, put that down,' and she'd pull away from him. Our relationship was based on that. She was drunk, and I'd say 'We need some coffee over here.'"

STOOL BOOM: One of the most enjoyable and silly production numbers in the *Red, White and Blaine* extravaganza is the incomparable "Stool Boom." Longtime Guest collaborator Harry Shearer co-wrote the song with Guest, and remembers how it came about.

"Chris came over and he said, 'There's this premise about the town of Blaine,' and that stools were 'the big thing.' So we were sitting at the bench of the piano in my house, and the phrase 'Stool Boom' came out. Chris had a melody already, which came out being the B part of the song. I was playing, and just sort of came up with the vamp, and a little magic stuff happened. You put yourself in the right mood and the song comes through you, even if it's a jokey song like that."

Joe Garrity remember his contribution to the production number, namely the giant gears spinning madly in the background, in part an homage to the Charlie Chaplin comedy about the dawn of the industrial age, *Modern Times* (1936).

"That was my idea," he laughs. "The gears were part of a factory churning out these stools. People had these little sticks and gears that we made out of cardboard."

FIVE LETTERS? David Cross' character, a deadly serious UFO expert examining crop circles in Blaine, bases his entire theory of extraterrestrial life on a notable fallacy. He claims that "Blaine" is an anagram for "Nebali," the hypothetical home world of distant aliens, and that the number five, the same number of letters in the word Blaine, has a special significance to these visitors.

The only oversight in this fascinating hypothesis? The word "Blaine" is composed of six letters, not five.

PRINCE OF TIDES: Michael Hitchcock's character, Steve Sark, draws an explicit comparison between Corky and Barbra Streisand during an intermission in the show

"The weird thing about these movies is that you don't really remember saying things," Hitchcock says. "When you watch them, you say, 'Oh my gosh, I can't believe I said that!' But I know my character was very enthralled with Corky, and I think that in my mind, my character knew a little more about show business than other people in Blaine might have known. So certainly he knew that Barbra was a triple threat, and obviously he thinks that Corky is, too. That's partly where that came from."

WE NEED A LITTLE COFFEE HERE: Catherine O'Hara does a great drunk, as she proves for the ages, during the memorable scene at the Chop Suey Chinese Kitchen. According to Fred Willard, the scene may have included less acting than the actress would have preferred.

"An interesting thing about that scene: Catherine was drinking wine and getting drunker and drunker — as the character — and at one point, Chris said, 'Keep drinking, drain the whole glass.' So she drank the whole glass, and he called, 'Cut.' Then she said, *'Christopher, that was real wine in there!'* Usually, they put apple juice in the glass, but he didn't know she was drinking real wine!"

UNDERSTANDING THE KENNEDYS: Another great moment in *Guffman* is Gwen Fabin-Blunt's admission that because of her famous name and heritage, she sympathizes with the concerns of a certain well-known Kennedy family. Theaker delivers that line with a beautifully effective deadpan, though the actress credits Guest with getting it out of her in the first place.

"That was such a far-ranging interview, and he constructed it to make it look like I earned that laugh," she says graciously, "but I know how long it took to get there."

IS HE OR ISN'T HE? There has been a great deal of speculation about Corky's sexual orientation. In the film, he supposedly has a wife named Bonnie, but she is never seen. For Guest, the matter is ultimately unimportant. "This isn't about Corky's sexuality," he told the *Advocate*. "The heart of the movie is about Corky as a person ... If I didn't like him and I was making fun of him, it wouldn't ring true."[22]

STAGECRAFT: In *This Is Spinal Tap*, a major set piece goes awry on stage during the performance of "Stonehenge." A little error (literally) by Nigel results in a Stonehenge replica standing just eighteen inches instead of eighteen feet, necessitating the employment of two dwarves. In *Waiting for Guffman*, a similar on-stage blunder evokes laughter.

"I broke up on stage," Willard remembers about this particular moment. "We were doing 'Covered Wagons,' and Eugene was supposed to ride out on a wooden horse, and we were re-creating the town's founding, and all of a sudden, Christopher Guest started to laugh and fell down on the floor. Everybody said, 'Chris, what's so funny?' and he said, 'I just realized Eugene is not going to be able to wear his glasses and he's going to come out, and the first line is going to be "What have your keen and perceptive eyes beheld?"' We all had a good laugh.

"So we got up on stage, and we were rolling cameras and I said, 'Whoa, I hear a horse,' and here comes Eugene dressed in buckskin with his eyes going different directions, and I looked at him and started to say, 'What have your keen and perceptive eyes beheld?' and I started to laugh. Chris said, 'Okay, cut, let's start again,' and I said, 'No, no, let me just stand here and look at Eugene.' I laughed and laughed and I actually went over and picked up my camera and told Eugene to sit on the horse, and I got a picture of him ... and he wouldn't crack up, either!

"I finally got all the laughter out of my system. That's the only time I ever cracked up."

PARKER POULTRY: One *Guffman* scene that never fails to elicit howls from viewers depicts a solitary Libby Mae Brown cooking a tiny piece of chicken on her grill. As she attempts to see the positive side of the show's cancellation, she notes — pitiably — that she's still welcome at the Dairy Queen.

"That was shot in the bad, rundown part of Lockhart, on the outskirts," Garrity remembers. "It was so pathetic to see this person with a ... lonely ... piece of chicken, just kind of kicking it over this grill. Her fat mother was in the background, hanging laundry. It's just sad — and very funny. That's the thing about [Guest's] films — some people find it very sad, and some people find it very funny. You root for these people."

THIS GOES UP TO ELEVEN: Longtime Guest aficionados will note that the green-hued alien visitor appearing in the production number "Nothing Ever Happens on Mars" has a relevant number emblazoned on his torso: eleven. This is an allusion to Nigel's famous conversation with director Marty DiBergi in *Spinal Tap,* and his conclusion that his amps are just a notch better than others.

Another possible allusion to *This Is Spinal Tap*: when Corky practices his cockney accent for an upcoming show, he mentions the word "hellhole." Of course, "Hellhole" is one of Tap's signature songs.

HAPPILY EVER AFTER? Viewers who note Steve Sark's enthusiastic appreciation of all things Corky might rightly wonder if there is more to the story of Monsieur St. Clair and Steve Sark than meets the eye. One alternate ending explored that possibility, at least briefly.

"In my favorite ending, they end up together," Theaker reveals. "The pharmacist and Corky end up living together in a loft in New York."

This ending was shot a few months after principal photography, during reshoots. Hitchcock describes the scene as he remembers it: "It started on a close-up of Corky talking," and then the camera pulled back and revealed that Steve was with him. "We were barbecuing on the roof, and we did a little limbo, so it was a little bizarre, but very funny."

"It's superlative," Theaker agrees. "They're sitting up on the deck of their loft, holding hands. I loved it. It was so sweet and touching that I thought it was the perfect ending for the movie."

"He pulled away from that," Garrity explains. "Sometimes he feels like he goes too far. He didn't have to answer that question [about Corky's sexuality], and that ending went away."

"From what I've heard from Chris, they just thought, 'Let the sexuality be.' It's obvious something is going on, that Corky is the way he is, and Steve is what he is, and we don't need to explore that any further, and I agree," says Hitchcock. "It's kind of nice to be left alone. It's a little more realistic. Steve probably stayed in Blaine with his family, and Corky moved on to New York."

BIG FISH: In the deleted musical extravaganza "This Bulging River," a cardboard fish jumps up between the tumultuous cardboard waves of the flooded river.

As Garrity remembers, there was a special helping hand behind the scenes. "That was the producer, Karen Murphy, I believe, who had a little roller thing — and she made the trout go up and down through the water. That was a lot of fun."

It is this attention to details, Michael Hitchcock notes, that makes these films so much fun to work on.

"I remember when we were in Corky's apartment, there was a coffee table that Joe had made that was a box that had the word 'puppets' on it. Corky [apparently] went out and bought this box, and nobody even saw that except us, but the detail with Joe is always just amazing. There's so much little detail that goes into his sets, it's incredible. His eye is fantastic, because he captures things so well."

NAME-DROPPER: Corky is a guy who thinks he knows a lot about theater and film (and dance), and his knowledge — or rather, half-knowledge — often emerges in a stream of strange allusions and inappropriate comparisons.

For instance, he calls Sheila and Ron Albertson "the Lunts" of Blaine, referring to Alfred Lunt and Lynn Fontanne, renowned as the greatest theater actors in American history. A slight exaggeration, perhaps.

Later, Corky describes an Alfred Hitchcock movie in which somebody gets put in a rubber bag and thrown in the trunk of a car. Corky may have been referring to 1972's *Frenzy*, the master of suspense's fifty-second film. *Frenzy* involves a psychotic grocer named Bob Rusk who, in one scene, hides one of his victims' corpses in a bag in the back of a potato truck.

Before *Guffman* is over, Corky has also misquoted Sir Arthur Conan Doyle's great detective, Sherlock Holmes, and his assistant Dr. Watson; referenced D'Artagnan; and also come up with his own strange Zen philosophy about the number of babies that fit in a tire.

These references may seem random, but they tell audiences a great deal about Corky's world, or more accurately, the world he would like to inhabit.

SENSE MEMORY

Christopher Guest's first documentary-style comedy as director, *Waiting for Guffman* is a textbook example of his theorem that comedy is reality plus that critical "one step further."

Though comedy is a notoriously difficult genre to assess and dissect because humor is often a subjective thing, *Waiting for Guffman* makes its funny points with effortless strides for two important reasons. First, it observes accurately and with clarity the universe of its characters, in this instance, middle-America's community theater companies, and secondly, because Guest's selection of the documentary format enhances the details of that chosen reality and generates in the audience a strong sense of sympathy and compassion for the starry-eyed *dramatis personae*.

In *Waiting for Guffman*, the filmmakers and actors have demonstrated special care in developing a world that is simultaneously believable and funny. Why is reality so vital in comedy? Well, simply stated, to laugh at a situation, viewers must identify with some aspect of it. There must be a vital connection between the viewer's life experience and that which he sees played out in the darkness of the theater, or it just isn't relatable.

Or, as author Gerald Mast notes in his treatise, *The Comic Mind: Comedy and the Movies*:

> A film (or gag, or line, or character) is truly funny when the audience is

> not conscious that it intends to be funny. As soon as one becomes aware
> of artifice and fakery ... comedy disintegrates into banal and obnoxious
> posturing. Although intellectual detachment is crucially related to the
> experience of successful comedy, when the detachment becomes so
> great that the mind is no longer amused and engaged, but notes the gap
> between intention and accomplishment, conception and execution, the
> comedy fails to amuse or entertain.[23]

In other words, a film's humor must be as closely tied to reality as possible, or it will be detected as artificial — a fakery. A film's humor must be genuine enough that viewers don't begin asking questions that will foster that dreaded sense of detachment, and could bring them back to an awareness of their surroundings.

Given Mast's observation, it seems that more comedies ought to follow Guest's lead and not take the construction of a plausible reality for granted.

Considering the importance of "reality," how does a comedy director foster it, and more important, how does he do so quickly and efficiently?

Well, Guest is a master at deploying archival footage such as photographs or newspaper headlines to instantly bolster his films' sense of reality. It is also important to note, that these archival documents usually arrive in the first third of his films — often in a flurry — when they are most useful. After all, archival footage in the last act arrives too late to do any good, doesn't it?

In short order, *Waiting for Guffman* provides persuasive documentation that these Blainians boast a history and background *outside* the confines of the silver screen. For instance, the camera focuses on the masthead and headlines from the local paper, the *Blaine Bugle*. Perfectly, its logo is that distinctive courthouse, the Lockhart Town Hall, which the audience has already seen and mentally connected with the town.

Similarly, the local historian, played by Don Lake, reveals a cluttered office filled with important town memorabilia, including a photograph of President McKinley, who stopped by on a whistle-stop tour in 1898, and a rough drawing of a UFO, which abducted town locals for a pot-luck dinner in 1946. He also has one other important item cementing Blaine's status as the Stool Capital of the World, a pennant that declares this dubious, double-edged honor.

Stills of Corky St. Clair's previous theatrical productions (*Barefoot in the Park* and *Backdraft*), and their inevitable fallout, also inform many of the film's earliest scenes, and these materials on the B-roll immediately enhance the feeling that we are peering into a real world, not merely being setup for a rat-a-tat-tat of punch lines.

116

As in *A Mighty Wind*, there is almost enough momentum in the beginning scenes that the film feels like sensory overload, as fact after fact, image after image, is presented to audiences about the world these characters inhabit. But it's all to the good. If the audience is distracted, concentrating and absorbing data at a very fast rate, it has no time to seek out fakery, does it?

Even personal histories are intricately laid out in *Waiting for Guffman*, as if each character has shared photographs from a personal album with the documentarian. For instance, audiences catch a glimpse of Dr. Allan Pearl's ancestor, the stage actor Hyam Pearlgut, who appeared in a "sardonically irreverent" musical revue generations back, in 1914.

We also see in other photos Pearl's dentist father, and Pearl himself, as a youth. All these archival materials hold center screen for seconds at a time, often with actor voice-overs conveying information on the sound-track, and they appear authentic enough to convince audiences that this material could be real rather than the artifice that Gerald Mast warned readers about.

Guest augments these many archival photographs, documents, and items with actual documentary footage of Lockhart's annual town celebra-tion, solidifying the belief that there are more folks living in this town than just those people who happen to be on the town council, or auditioning for *Red, White and Blaine*. By serendipity, the filmmakers captured a real-life event — an outdoor fair — and the authenticity of these locals further opens up the film's (relatively small) universe, granting a sense of a larger Blaine — again an essential facet if audiences are to believe that this could be a real documentary and not a put-on.

Waiting for Guffman also makes fine and notable use of the Lockhart and Austin locales, thus capturing the feeling and tone of middle America in the process. The Magic Carpet Travel Agency and the Chop Suey Chinese Kitchen feel not like Hollywood's glorified and romanticized renderings of suburbia, but the real Midwest, perhaps a bit shabby in places, perhaps a bit poor in corners, but very far indeed from either coast, and from that promised land, that city on the hill called *Hollywood*.

Given Guest's skill at vetting convincing archival materials and loca-tions, *Guffman* already goes a long way toward reaching its goal of estab-lishing a sense of reality. But then comes the next vital piece of the jigsaw puzzle — the actors themselves. They must inhabit this world as if they were born to it, and delightfully, they all contribute performances that come across as realistic rather than outrageous.

In fact, one of the big ironies of *Waiting for Guffman* is a self-reflexive one. This is a film about non-professional actors putting on a show, made by professional actors making a movie. This accomplished ensemble ren-ders the people of Blaine so colorfully and truthfully that viewers never feel an ounce of condescension either from the actors or the man directing them, and that's critical.

Instead, everybody behind the camera and in front of it really gets into the spirit of the show and into the heads of these quirky characters. The cast and crew has accomplished this task by modulating or tuning their talent level (some might say lowering it), to the level of the people they are depicting: enthusiastic amateurs with a flair for performing, but no real talent to speak of. This quality of zealous amateurism emerges in everything from the songs performed in *Red, White and Blaine* to the very stagecraft of the show itself, and it is all so charming and enthusiastic that it almost feels like admiration.

"We were trying to make ourselves laugh, but we were also trying not to write any better than they would have," composer Harry Shearer explains.

"The fun part of these projects is that you're never trying to write really bad stuff, but nor are you trying to write better than the characters are capable of. You're trying to write in character. That's part of your acting. You're trying to be in the heads of these people, so you're not judging them as you write. Instead, you inhabit them as you write."

"These are not professional people," Joseph Garrity stresses. "They live in an almost-hick town and they work with what they've got. I tend not to have a lot of money on these films, so I also work with what I've got. People put on shows in their community theater, so [in doing that] you become just like these people.

"How good are you?" Garrity asks. "If you are not very good, you are still doing the best you can. I think that's what [Guest's] films are all about: people doing the best they can."

Sometimes, the best that people can muster just really isn't that good, a fact Roberto Schaefer's probing camera notices with subtlety through-out the film. For instance, during Ron and Sheila's dreadful but amusing "Midnight at the Oasis" audition, O'Hara, as Sheila, visibly mouths all of Fred Willard's dialogue as she interacts with him, a typical amateur's mistake.

Yet the camera doesn't highlight this gaffe. There is no close-up of O'Hara, and no reaction shot featuring Lloyd or Corky or even the domineering Ron, realizing that Sheila is mouthing her husband's lines in an effort not to lose her place in the scene. Instead, in an all-encompassing master shot, Ron and Sheila simply do their thing, and O'Hara's deliberate but subtle gaffe represents one funny element of many in the scene. Because the joke isn't spotlighted, the audience feels rewarded when catching this minutiae, feeling it has discovered the punch line all on its own. Frankly, these laughs are always the best ones, when you realize the filmmaker isn't talking down to you, or spoon-feeding you the humor.

Indeed, audiences might miss the joke the first time around, but if they

Top: Heavy duty rock 'n' roll! From left to right, the brain trust of Spinal Tap: Derek Smalls (Harry Shearer), Nigel Tufnel (Christopher Guest), and David St. Hubbins (Michael McKean).

Bottom: The perfect accessory for those *Das Boot* and *My Dinner with Andre* action figures. Spinal Tap goes plastic!

The last temptation of Nick Chapman. Kevin
Bacon meets fetchin' Gretchen (Teri Hatcher) in
The Big Picture.

Top: Nick (Bacon) instructs his cinematographer, Emmet Sumner (McKean), on the set of that introspective classic, *Beach Nuts*. From *The Big Picture*.

Bottom: Nick (Bacon) reviews footage of a music video while his confidante, Lydia (Jennifer Jason Leigh), looks on. From *The Big Picture*.

Top: She's super sized! Nancy Archer (Daryl Hannah) one-ups Godzilla in Christopher Guest's HBO remake of *Attack of the* 50 *Ft. Woman*.

Bottom: Her hair isn't the only thing that's big! Our world is Nancy's dollhouse in *Attack of the* 50 *Ft. Woman*.

A study in intensity. Christopher Guest directs ...

sans funny haircut, wig, and marching band uniform.

Top: Not Lewis and Clark but an incredible simulation. From left to right: Jonah (Bokeem Woodbine), Leslie Edwards (Matthew Perry), and Bartholomew Hunt (Chris Farley) stand proud in *Almost Heroes*.

Bottom: Eggs over easy. Hunt (Farley) poaches breakfast from a very surly eagle in *Almost Heroes*.

Male bonding. Edwards (Perry) and Hunt (Farley)
get too close for comfort in *Almost Heroes*.

Nothing ever happens in Blaine ... except really bad community theater. From left to right: Ron Albertson (Fred Willard), Sheila Albertson (Catherine O'Hara), Corky St. Clair (Christopher Guest), Libby Mae Brown (Parker Posey), and Dr. Allan Pearl (Eugene Levy) put on a show in *Waiting for Guffman*.

The eternal optimist. Christopher Guest as the
indomitable Corky St. Clair in *Waiting for Guffman*.

The Albertsons go to Hollywood. Ron (Willard) and
Sheila (O'Hara) cowboy-up in *Waiting for Guffman*.

Top: The zealous pharmacist. Blaine's own Steve Sark (Michael Hitchcock) extols the (many) virtues of Corky in this scene from *Waiting for Guffman*.

Bottom: Audition competition: Corky and his arch nemesis, Lloyd Miller (Bob Balaban), rate the *Red, White and Blaine* auditions in *Waiting for Guffman*.

TOP: It's Mrs. Savage! Frances Fisher as a character cut from *Waiting for Guffman* (but still in the trailer...)

BOTTOM: Midnight at the Oasis. Ron and Sheila at their delightful best in *Waiting for Guffman*.

RON AND SHEILA ALBERTSON
Travel Agents

He *has* to entertain. He *has* to. Dr. Allan Pearl
(Eugene Levy) feels the love at the climax of *Waiting
for Guffman*.

Top: More than your average dog and pony show.
Christopher Guest—in the guise of southern
gentleman Harlan Pepper—directs *Best in Show*.

Bottom: Catalog people: Meg (Parker Posey) and
Hamilton Swan (Michael Hitchcock) debate the finer
points of Starbucks in *Best in Show*.

TOP: So much in common ... Leslie Cabot (Patrick Cranshaw) and his young bride, Sherri Ann Cabot (Jennifer Coolidge) pose with Rhapsody in White during *Best in Show*.

BOTTOM: The perfect couple. Stefan (McKean) and Scott (John Michael Higgins) with shi-tzus in *Best in Show*.

Top: The heart and soul of America: The Fleck family in *Best in Show*. Jerry (Levy), Cookie (O'Hara), and Winky.

Bottom: They understand the needs of lesbian purebred dog owners. Christy Cummings (Jane Lynch), Sherri Ann (Coolidge), and their poodle, Rhapsody in White.

TOP: There's a mighty wind a blowin'! From left to right, the music makers of *A Mighty Wind* take the stage: The New Main Street Singers, Mitch and Mickey, and the Folksmen.

BOTTOM: Catchphrase King: Mike LaFontaine (Fred Willard) tells us what happened in *A Mighty Wind*.

Top: Most of the abuse in their family was musical. Terry (Higgins) and Laurie Bohner (Lynch) in *A Mighty Wind*.

Bottom: Sharing a brain. Publicists Amber Cole (Coolidge) and Wally Fenton (Larry Miller) promote the Town Hall concert in a scene from *A Mighty Wind*.

TOP: They rock us. Mitch (Levy) and Mickey (O'Hara) together again in *A Mighty Wind*.

BOTTOM: Straight from the school of hard knocks comes Parker Posey's Sissy Knox, in *A Mighty Wind*.

THE LETTERMEN in CONCERT

HEY, LOOK ME OVER • WHEN I FALL IN LOVE • WHAT
KIND OF FOOL AM I? • WEST SIDE STORY MEDLEY
YOU'LL NEVER WALK ALONE • FAST FREIGHT • FOLK
MEDLEY • GROUPS ARE NOTHING NEW MEDLEY

Capitol
RECORDS

HIGH FIDELITY

THIS PAGE: Kissin' cousins. Top: Folk
musicians the Lettermen on the cover of
their concert album. Bottom: The Folksmen
on the cover of one of theirs.

OPPOSITE: What happened to "g"? The
covers of two more Folksmen albums from
A Mighty Wind.

Any resemblance is purely coincidental and completely unintentional. Above: The New Main Street Singers. Below: The Serendipity Singers.

Mitch (Levy) and Mickey (O'Hara) perform "A Kiss
at the End of the Rainbow" at the 2003 Academy
Awards.

Christopher Guest is accompanied by his wife
(and presenter), Jamie Lee Curtis, at the 2003
Academy Awards.

return to the film, they may notice it — and perhaps even things more interesting and funny, too. Like the best comedy directors, Guest works by setting the stage for his actors and then standing back. Even in the editing room, the director holds back sometimes and preserves the rhythms of his people by employing long shots and group shots.

Why? Because what's funny about this movie is seeing Willard and O'Hara act *together*. Or Levy, O'Hara, Guest, Willard, and Posey on stage all at once, playing and reacting with one another. The editing doesn't intrude on the space between these performers, and the magic of their chemistry is preserved. Part of the enjoyable "badness" of Ron, Sheila, Corky, Dr. Pearl, and Libby Mae is their total and utter inability to do any dance moves in synch, a factor that would be lost in close-ups or two-shots.

"It's a symphony of bad acting put on by incredibly terrific actors who make themselves look like amateurs," Paul Dooley describes with delight. "There's nobody better at that than Catherine O'Hara. She is just incredibly good in that."

"I think I was the baddest of the bad," O'Hara reported in an interview with journalist Bob Thompson. "I showed absolutely no potential."[24]

"So many actors have said, 'I've been in amateur groups just like that,'" says Willard, "and I've said, 'There are *professional* groups just like that!'"

In other words, these moments are not over-the-top or exaggerated, but finely hewn evocations of reality.

With all the documentary technique, including the one-on-one interviews, the handheld camera, the utilization of archival materials, and the finely crafted performances, *Waiting for Guffman* achieves the first half of its equation: it feels real. And because of Guest and Levy's sense of humor, and again, the fine acting of the cast, the jokes work and the film is funny. It goes "one step further" with Dr. Pearl's lazy eye, Corky's funky dance, and the auditions, and the results are big, but honest — and hard-earned — laughs.

When Corky must replace Johnny Savage in the show, substituting a mincing pioneer for a husky, hunky one, the film's humor comes to a boil. Watching the effeminate fellow discuss his burning love for Libby Mae Brown ("Oh, Emma ...") is a big joke, perhaps, but it is one that has been thoroughly earned at this juncture. It is honest, too, because no one other than Corky could replace Johnny Savage on a moment's notice and know the show's routines. But it is also utterly ridiculous, that final "one step further" moment that aficionados always cherish in the Guest canon.

It's interesting to note that many of the big laughs in *Waiting for Guffman* are the same way, elements that, taken one by one, aren't that funny, but in combination, seem hysterical.

"The richness and the vérité of all the minutiae of the strange little character quirks and idiosyncrasies just build up and create the whole," Deb

Theaker considers. "But those little moments, when you isolate and look at them, you see nothing is based on an easy joke, and nothing is based on a quick laugh."

"I like the little fun things that were never talked about," Hitchcock concurs. "I think what intrigues me about Steve is that he is kind of treated like shit. He really wanted to be in the play, and Corky told him he couldn't, because he missed the audition. But then, after the auditions, Corky is purposely going around to find other people, so he lied to Steve! Which Steve doesn't know. And he really has this little crush, and Corky doesn't care one way or another."

None of these moments are emphasized, they're just part of an interesting totality. "I can't read Chris and Eugene's minds, but I certainly don't think that on *Best in Show* they said, 'We're going to go after people who show dogs,' or in *Waiting for Guffman*, 'We're going to go after community theater,'" Hitchcock muses. "I think they're mostly just showing human nature in those settings. If you go to any business or community, you're going to find a myriad of people and see how they get along."

And while audiences indeed laugh at many of these moments, there remains something incredibly touching about this particular group of characters. The movie "hints at larger human dreams," writes *Salon*'s Sarah Vowell, "pinpointing the inherent sadness of yearning for talent, excellence, and escape. And that isn't mockery. That is actuality." [25]

Audiences root for Corky, Dr. Pearl, and the rest of the bunch because in these starry-eyed friends they can identify something of themselves, that irrational aspiration to achieve fame and success.

"In terms of *Guffman*, I think it was a ... sense of, well, some people can do it, and some people can *almost* do it. And here's a group of people who can almost do it," says Harry Shearer.

In fact, one of the most overlooked things in *Waiting for Guffman* is the recognition that the acting company actually succeeds, at least to some modest extent. Yes, their show is corny and amateurish, but who can deny that this group of actors really pleases the townspeople who attend the show?

When this author's mother watched the film, she sighed with relief when *Red, White and Blaine* ended, a feeling of tension released, because she had been afraid something really terrible was going to happen to the performers. In other words, she cared what happened to them.

In a mainstream Hollywood comedy, something terrible *would* have certainly happened in the last act. Maybe stage lights would have fallen from the ceiling and exploded during "A Penny for Your Thoughts," or an actor might have fallen over a set piece in "Covered Wagons" and broken an arm.

Maybe Ron Albertson could have inadvertently exposed his penis reduction surgery on stage in "Stool Boom," offering a moment of typical humiliation humor.

In most Hollywood comedies, that sort of outrageous thing, usually focusing on a character experiencing emotional or physical pain, is a seeming necessity, but the films of Christopher Guest don't play that game. They could be more outrageous, but they could hardly be more funny, or touching, and the fact of the matter is that everybody survives *Red, White and Blaine* relatively intact. Furthermore, the performance pleases the audience. Really, when you think about it, isn't that the ultimate goal, the ultimate success of any performer, on any stage? To make your audience happy? To elicit hoots of approval from the crowd seated before you?

The problem in *Guffman,* however, is that all the performers have become so obsessed with the dream of Mort whisking them away to Broadway, with making *Red, White and Blaine* the stepping stone (or footstool, in this case) to something bigger and better, that they can only parse their very positive experience as a failure because they haven't achieved what was unattainable in the first place. They put on a good, amateur show for their friends and neighbors — and made a group of Blainians feel proud and happy about their town, but to these guys, that success is lost because of Guffman's absence.

"One of the best sports books I ever read was called *The Professional,* I think," Willard explains. "It was about a sports reporter going to interview a fighter who had been up for the heavyweight championship of the world, and he followed him through training. [The boxer] was a clean-living, all-American, wonderful guy, and you were just rooting for this guy. He got into the fight, and he was doing well in the first round, but in the second round he slipped. Just a momentary slip, but the other fighter hit him and knocked him out, and he went into oblivion. And ten years later, the reporter went to interview the athlete again.

"There he was, one step away from being Rocky, and his foot slipped on a wet spot," Willard notes. "That's what happened to these people in *Guffman.* They believed they could have made it. It was really a show that the townspeople could have put together, and the townspeople loved it — it was a tribute, but the players were all crushed. We've all had failures [like that] in life."

"There's something ineffably sweet about an aspiration and belief that you can do anything," Deborah Theaker says, "and the reason that you feel let down as an audience is because we all clearly saw the show — and it wasn't a Broadway caliber show at all — but they played it with such commitment. I mean, even Chris doing splits in 'A Penny for Your Thoughts' at the end … it just destroys me. Because you know Corky is trying so hard to give these people their entertainment value, and it's all doomed to failure. There's no way he's going to be a leading man.

"I've read a lot of critical things that said he doesn't really like his small-town characters," Theaker continues, "and that he's making fun of them, but I don't think that's the case at all."

Willard agrees. The final coda, which returns to the characters some time after their failure to make it to Broadway, reveals a group of determined people who may be battered and bruised, but who aren't down for the count. At least not yet.

"They went on with their lives, though Catherine and I were still kind of delusional," Willard says. "One of my lines was, 'We're living in Los Angeles, and luckily in Los Angeles, you don't need to have a car.' But they were still trying."

And that's the overriding texture of *Waiting for Guffman* — that these people are *still* trying, still clinging to a dream. Mitigating factors that might have made the protagonists appear less appealing, like the fact that Allan Pearl has left his wife and baby in Blaine to pursue his hopeless dream of big-time success in Miami, have been excised from the film to foster the notion that these are really good, decent folk doing their best. The result is a movie that often seems like a paean to man's capacity to keep going for the gold, even when it is really, really far out of his grasp.

Oh William Hung, where art thou?

Considering the psychology of the wannabe, it is probably appropriate to end any discussion of this film with a notation about Corky. This "curiously endearing nincompoop,"[26] as *People* magazine described him, is one of modern cinematic comedy's truly great characters. Petulant, silly, pretentious, and all-together charming, Corky St. Clair may be the quintessential theater guy, but he is also much more. He symbolizes the dreamer in all of us, the fella who might get "slammed down" in one venue, but then pops right back up in another one, more optimistic and determined than ever.

It's no wonder that Steve Sark leaves *Red, White and Blaine* exuberantly shouting Corky's name. Gay or straight, married or single, a boob or a genius (there's a fine line), Corky represents something worthwhile in all humankind: the indomitable spirit of the dreamer. He never gives up, not in the face of "bastard people" or "ass faces," and that's why people love him so much.

"I love community-theater stories. I have a hankering for that, and I love that everybody is rooting for Corky to win," Michael Hitchcock says. "I love that so much."

Theaker agrees that Corky is memorable and funny not because of any lifestyle choice or sexual orientation, but because his character is universal, and very touching.

"How many people have you known like Corky throughout your life?" she asks. "I've had maybe five or six teachers in school who were that guy. You know, closeted — his mythical wife Bonnie that nobody's ever seen. He's just an irrepressible optimist, and that's what I think is so sweet and endearing. At the bottom of it all, he believes he can be a star."

And despite the mincing, he makes us believe it, too.

They all do.

4. DOIN' IT DOGGY STYLE

BEST IN SHOW (2000)

SOME PETS DESERVE A LITTLE MORE RESPECT THAN OTHERS.

CASTLE ROCK ENTERTAINMENT PRESENTS *BEST IN SHOW* (2000)

DIRECTED BY: Christopher Guest
WRITTEN BY: Christopher Guest and Eugene Levy
PRODUCED BY: Karen Murphy
EXECUTIVE PRODUCER: Gordon Mark
DIRECTOR OF PHOTOGRAPHY: Roberto Schaefer
PRODUCTION DESIGNER: Joseph T. Garrity
FILM EDITOR: Robert Leighton
COSTUME DESIGNER: Monique Prudhomme
UNIT PRODUCTION MANAGER: Stewart Bethune
FIRST ASSISTANT DIRECTOR: Jack Handy
SECOND ASSISTANT DIRECTOR: Mindy Heslin
ART DIRECTOR: Gary Myers
DOG SHOW COORDINATOR/CONSULTANT: Carol J. Carvin
ANIMAL WRANGLER: Mark Dumas.

"GOD LOVES A TERRIER" written by Eugene Levy; performed by Eugene Levy and Catherine O'Hara
"TERRIER STYLE" written by Eugene Levy; performed by Eugene Levy and Catherine O'Hara.

STARRING (IN ORDER OF APPEARANCE)

JAY BRAZEAU: Dr. Chuck Nelken

PARKER POSEY: Meg Swan

MICHAEL HITCHCOCK: Hamilton Swan

CATHERINE O'HARA: Cookie Fleck

EUGENE LEVY: Gerry Fleck

LEWIS ARQUETTE: Fern City Spectator

DANY CANINO: Fern City Show Judge

BOB BALABAN: Dr. Theodore W. Millbank III

WILL SASSO: Fishin' Hole Guy

STEVEN E. MILLER: Fishin' Hole Guy

CHRISTOPHER GUEST: Harlan Pepper

MICHAEL McKEAN: Stefan Vanderhoof

JOHN MICHAEL HIGGINS: Scott Donlan

JENNIFER COOLIDGE: Sherri Ann Cabot

DON LAKE: Graham Chissolm

PATRICK CRENSHAW: Leslie Ward Cabot

DEBORAH THEAKER: Winky's Party Guest

SCOTT WILLIAMSON: Winky's Party Guest

JANE LYNCH: Christy Cummings

LINDA KASH: Fay Berman

LARRY MILLER: Max Berman

CODY GREGG: Zach Berman

ED BEGLEY JR: Hotel Manager (Mark Schaefer)

FRED WILLARD: Buck Laughlin

JIM PIDDOCK: Trevor Beckwith

HIRO KANAGAWA: Pet Shop Owner

DON S. DAVIS: Mayflower Best in Show Judge

FILMED IN VANCOUVER, BC, AND LOS ANGELES, CALIFORNIA

127

DOG-UMENTARY

THE 125TH ANNUAL MAYFLOWER KENNEL CLUB DOG SHOW in Philadelphia is just days away, and proud dog owners from all over the country assemble for the major event.

From Fern City, Florida, Gerry and Cookie Fleck prepare their Norwich terrier, Winky. From Tribeca, New York City, a gay couple, Stefan Vanderhoof and Scott Donlan, groom their Shih Tzu, Miss Agnes, for victory. From Pine Nut, North Carolina, aspiring ventriloquist Harlan Pepper preps his blood-hound, Hubert, for the competition. Also putting on their game face is a rage-prone, upscale yuppie couple from Moordale, Illinois, Meg and Hamilton Swan, whose shell-shocked Weimaraner, Beatrice, seems as dangerously unstable as her owners. Fortunately, she's in therapy.

These competitors all have their eye on the prize, the "best in show" cup to be awarded by the Mayflower bigwig, humorless Dr. Theodore Millbank. But the enthusiastic owners also realize that their noble canines must unseat the reigning champion, a standard poodle called Rhapsody in White. Owned by millionaire senior citizen Leslie Cabot and his young wife,

Sherri Ann, and handled by the mannish Christy Cummings, Rhapsody in White is the odds-on favorite to take home the gold.

As the night of the show approaches and the owners and their dogs gather at the Taft Hotel, tempers flare between the Swans over a misplaced squeaky toy called Busy Bee, while the Flecks confront a financial disaster with the help of a kindly hotel manager, Mark Schaefer. All the while, Sherri's nerves about the pending show escalate, as do her feelings for Christy.

Finally, it's the night of the show, and many surprises are in store for the dogs and their handlers as co-hosts Buck Laughlin and Trevor Beckwith call the shots on national television.

MAN'S BEST FRIENDS

Christopher Guest is a thoughtful comedian who mines no comic gold before its time, and the genesis of *Best in Show*, originally known as *Dog Show*, reflects that characteristic. As early as 1994, well before the genesis of *Waiting for Guffman*, he pondered the unusual relationship between dog owners and pets.

One day he was out in a park with his wife, actress Jamie Lee Curtis, walking one of their dogs, Henry, a mutt that is part golden retriever and part lab. While there, the director began to detect a strange hierarchy at play in the dog world — at least by some owners' manner of thinking.

"If someone had a poodle, they would look at the person with the German shepherd in a way that was almost like religious discrimination,"[1] Guest recounted in one interview. In particular, one "incredibly patronizing woman" appeared shocked that a mix like Henry had been permitted in the park.[2]

This strange encounter soon had Guest's mental wheels spinning, and suddenly he had the kernel of a movie plot involving another unique ensemble of characters, and another kind of show — this time a competition like the Westminster Kennel Club show.

Known as America's "oldest organization dedicated to the sport of pure-bred dogs"[3] this so-called Super Bowl of dog shows was established in 1877. In fact, Westminster has a revered and much-storied history. It is the second-longest, continuously held sporting event in U.S. history (after the Kentucky Derby), and every year some 2,500 dogs compete for the title Best in Show before rapt, cheering crowds in New York's Madison Square Garden. Many breeds appear in the contest, as well as many kinds of handlers, so the story possibilities about the making of a dog show seemed endless.

There was just one problem: partner and co-writer Eugene Levy didn't think the notion of setting a film at a Westminster-like show was particularly funny, and required some heavy-duty convincing. The main problem, Levy perceived, was the third act. How can you make a dog show, a display that basically involves people walking their pets around a long loop in front of a somber judge, *funny*?

According to Christopher Guest on the movie's DVD commentary, the answer was simple. He would unleash his secret weapon: Fred Willard would host the dog show.

Satisfied, Levy joined Guest on the project, and they commenced work on the script/outline. As it had been on *Guffman* and *Tap*, it was now necessary to construct a base of knowledge about dogs and dog shows, so the collaborators began extensive research on the topic.

"I did spend a year going to dog shows and reading," Guest told the BBC's James Mottram. "I looked at a ton of material about the way a dog show was shot for television."[4] He also subscribed to the periodical *American Cooner* and became further enlightened about the world he intended to depict.[5]

In addition to the overall riff on the dynamic of and among dog owners, Guest also found opportunity to more deeply develop a note he had scribbled to himself some years earlier, simply the notion of "catalogue people," — yuppies who live their lives out of the pages of J. Crew catalogs and in Starbucks coffee shops.

In the film, these catalog people were high-strung Meg and Hamilton Swan, the victims, perhaps, of too much caffeine. At some point, Guest had become fascinated with the notion that there are Americans who have become so obsessed with brand-names and the consumer world that they couldn't live without it.[6]

"Hamilton and Meg developed organically," Michael Hitchcock explains. "That's what's so scary about doing these films, and so exhilarating at the same time. Hamilton was obviously very meticulous to a certain degree. He is obviously judgmental, as is Meg. Parker and I decided, I think, that these two people are pretty miserable, and about the only people they can stand to be around are each other, because they make so many people unhappy — including themselves.

"In an early discussion about the characters, Christopher said something like, 'Why don't you wear braces?' and it helped determine our characters in a very subtle way," says Hitchcock, "in the sense that here are two people who probably couldn't afford braces as kids and they got them as adults, and like everything in their lives, they're almost a fashion show. They're trying to fix themselves up on the outside to be as perfect as their dog. Everything in their life is a dog show. Parker picked out clothing on purpose that is very petable. She almost looked like our Weimaraner."

Hitchcock had a different model for Hamilton. "When I was doing my character, I was talking to the hair people — which is really great of Chris, that we get that kind of freedom — and I said, 'Hamilton fancies himself Matthew Perry,' even though obviously I look nothing like Matthew Perry. So we found pictures of Matthew Perry's hair and we copied it. We dyed it Matthew's color and cut it, and this is something that no one would notice except for me. I always wear turtlenecks in that movie — except for the dog show itself, just to keep Hamilton stiff — a little more foreboding."

Another character in *Best in Show*, an aspiring but very untalented ventriloquist, may have been inspired by a similar character Guest featured in a commercial he directed for Resorts Hotels and Casino in 1999, which depicted a ventriloquist/waiter with an argumentative dummy.[7] The same commercial also featured a trainer with two less-than-enthusiastic dogs.

When production designer Joseph Garrity got the call from Guest to report for duty and learned about the film's canine subject matter, he was a little surprised at first. "I don't have a dog, I don't know much about dogs, and I certainly knew nothing about dog shows — so that's how I got into this," he says.

"But Chris has some dogs [Henry and Lucy], and had the opportunity to go to some of these shows and was fascinated by how seriously everybody took this. This is very, very, very serious business to the people who love dogs and breed them and all that. He found humor in the seriousness of all this … so we got tapes of the Westminster Dog Show that he had gone to."

For Garrity, *Best in Show* offered another opportunity to accomplish the task that the best production designers thrive on. He was able to absorb all the details of a totally new realm.

"What's fascinating about art departments is that every show is different and you have to instantly become knowledgeable, and just dive into a whole profession or club and just get it very fast," he says. "That's what we do, so it was fascinating to get into this world and see these incredible dogs."

Garrity also had fun developing the world of those catalog people, Meg and Hamilton. "His sets are so detailed," Hitchcock comments. "The little details were just amazing, and every movie is like that. He goes out of his way to create all these little worlds that are terrific."

In this case, Garrity's production design echoed the consumerism of the Swans. This meant that there were many authentic catalog items, including some from the Sharper Image.

"In the background, you'll see things that came out of the catalogs," says Hitchcock. "So they talk about catalogs, and catalog shopping — and their whole life is that. They would go to a store and see a dressed mannequin — and then they'd get exactly that outfit. They'd see it in a catalog and buy it exactly that way. They'd furnish their home the way the catalog looked because they didn't have a lot of imagination, as far as we were concerned."

Cookie and Gerry's Fern City home also reflects the personalities of the owners. Garrity's production design included a funny mailbox in front of the home that resembled a Norwich terrier, and plenty of terrier kitsch in the living room, which can be seen behind Jerry and Cookie during their interviews.

KENNEL CLUB

Before long, friends and colleagues from *Waiting for Guffman* and *This Is Spinal Tap* received the call to appear in *Best in Show*. *Spinal Tap*'s Michael McKean joined up, though Harry Shearer was unable to appear because he was directing his first feature film, the comedy *Teddy Bears' Picnic*.[8]

Bob Balaban, Parker Posey, Catherine O'Hara, Fred Willard, Larry Miller, Linda Kash, Don Lake, Deb Theaker, Scott Williamson, and Michael Hitchcock were all ready for an encore to *Waiting for Guffman* and came aboard. They were joined by some new faces, including two dynamic blondes. The first was spacey Jennifer Coolidge, Levy's co-star in the *American Pie* movies.

An accomplished stage and film actress, as well as a graduate of improv groups such as Gotham City and the Groundlings, Coolidge is a performer with an edge, and a unique, some might even say bizarre, quality.

"I lack self-awareness," she told reporter Nicole LaPorte for *American Theatre*. "There can be something really wrong with me, and I won't know it for a long time. I think that makes people laugh."[9]

Indeed, Coolidge would prove to have exactly the qualities so important in depicting the flighty, somewhat confused poodle owner, Sherri Ann Cabot.

Another blond actress named Jane Lynch was Coolidge's perfect opposite. This Illinois native was already an acclaimed playwright and successful actress who had appeared in the film version of the 1960s TV series, *The Fugitive* (1993). Lynch had worked for Guest in a breakfast cereal commercial for Kellogg's Frosted Flakes that he directed prior to *Best in Show*, and possessed a serious, intense demeanor that was perfect for the part of the controlling, dominant handler of Rhapsody in White, Christy Cummings.

John Michael Higgins was another addition to the repertory company. A charismatic young actor of startling versatility, Higgins has a sense of real joy about himself that transmits well in every performance he gives. Higgins had starred as David Letterman in the TV movie *The Late Show* (1996), and in Guest's new film, his scenes would team him with Guest's long-time friend, Michael McKean. The duo would play flamboyantly gay, but very happy and loving, shih tzu owners.

Another new face belonged to English gentleman Jim Piddock, a writer and director in his own right who was busy toiling on his TV series, *Too Much Sun* (2000), for the BBC during the time *Best in Show* was shot. On the day of his interview for this book (December 20, 2003), a sizable earthquake rocked California and interrupted our long-distance conversation for a few minutes, but Piddock remained absolutely unflappable throughout (and on the line). He described the interview as the most "earth-shattering" one he had ever granted.

Piddock met Guest through Eugene Levy and soon learned that they were on the same page as far as his character, dog expert and TV co-host, Trevor Beckwith, was concerned. Once it was determined that Piddock could adjust his schedule to appear in the film, he had to deal with the fact that Trevor Beckwith was not merely a funny foil for his more boisterous on-screen companion, but he was the audience's go-to guy for authenticity about the world of dogs and dog shows.

"That was the hard part," says Piddock. "I did a lot of research, and Chris gave me a book called *The American Kennel Club*. When I was doing this show in England, every night I would sort of spend an hour reading it," he says. "It was not interesting reading."

Still, the book proved helpful. "I did learn quite a lot about dogs and dog shows, and I felt like I had to know more about dogs than anyone in the movie. I couldn't fake that. The thing that is fun about improvising is going where your subconscious takes you, and in this case I had to really have a foundation of knowledge or the character just wouldn't work."

Unlike Fred Willard's character, who was based on a specific person, at least loosely, Piddock did not base his character on any real personalities.

"I didn't have any specific person in mind," says Piddock. "I felt there were just a few things I had to make sure I got right. One was that you believed this guy was serious about dogs. Two, that he was a very amenable character — he was quite jolly and enthusiastic. And third, that he would try to keep things [on the telecast] going, and not get too thrown by whatever his co-host came up with. Those were my real sensitive areas."

While Piddock hit the books and became the authority on canines that his character needed to be, Willard also became involved with the movie and had a discussion with Christopher Guest about Beckwith's singular co-host, the inimitable Buck Laughlin.

"Chris told me when I did *Best in Show* that the less I know about dogs, the better, because Joe Garagiola has done nothing to prepare," Willard explains.

At the time of *Best in Show*, Garagiola had hosted the Westminster Dog Show for five years running on the USA Network, and the former professional baseball player (1946–1954) and one-time *Today Show* host had become infamous for his "obtuse quips" and his propensity to "work baseball into his commentary wherever possible, to head-shaking results."[10]

Modeled on such a colorful figure, Laughlin was a character that Willard, always a fan of Garagiola's sports achievements, could clearly sink his teeth into.

Still, when he received the *Best in Show* screenplay, Willard understood he had to be ready with something very special, or his character might just vanish from the movie altogether. "*Waiting for Guffman* was very funny. It was one of those things that we did and we all knew we were enjoying it," Willard says. "It took a long time for Chris to put it together and get it out. It got wonderful reviews and in the industry a lot of people recognized me, and I got a lot of stuff from it. But an awful lot of stuff was cut out, from everybody.

"So when I got this part in *Best in Show*, they sent me a fifteen-page outline and my character wasn't even listed in it. So they called me the next day and said, 'Did you get the outline?' I said, 'Yeah, Buck Laughlin isn't mentioned,' and they said, 'For heaven's sake, what a mistake.' So they sent it back and it said, 'Buck Laughlin narrates with his sidekick,' and I said, 'Oh boy, this is gonna end up as voice-over or on the cutting-room floor.' So I went in there with both guns blazing. If he's going to cut me, I'm going to give him everything I've ever thought about dogs and sports."

While Willard readied himself to unleash the hounds, as it were, on unsuspecting and studious Jim Piddock, the remainder of the *Best in Show* cast had a different assignment — they needed to grow comfortable with the film's other stars, the dogs. Training with professional handlers, including the film's technical advisor, Earlene Luke, the cast crammed an "eight-week training course into five intensive days."[11]

"That's what I love about Chris's movies," Michael Hitchcock reflects. "Even though you don't rehearse, per se, you do prepare for the character, so it all looks as real as possible. So I went to training here in Los Angeles, and we also trained extensively once we were in Vancouver to get to know the dogs. Our dog, Beatrice, was a movie dog. She used to be a show dog, but then she was trained for movies because she had to do bad behavior. And real show dogs, well, their owners, probably rightfully so, didn't want to teach their dogs that bad behavior, like attacking people."

Once again assuming the duties of producer, Karen Murphy bore an equally difficult task, auditioning some 150 canines who, along with their owners, hoped to appear in the film.

One dramatic hurdle that designer Joe Garrity had to face involved the production of the climactic dog show. The filmmakers' original intention had been to piggyback on top of a real dog show, perhaps even Westminster, using it as a backdrop for the movie much as the company had used a local fair and parade in Lockhart, Texas, during *Waiting for Guffman* to add to the sense of reality. When that plan fell through, it became clear that Garrity's services would be needed to design a dog show from the ground up.

"We went to some dog shows in Vancouver, and I started connecting with all the vendor people, because we wanted to have them come to our show and set up in the back area where they groom the dogs," Garrity explains. "So we started a whole relationship with the people up there and arranged for them to come [to the movie] just like they were coming and doing a real dog show."

Encouragingly, the film soon had corporate sponsorship to provide further verisimilitude. "Iams and Eukanaba sponsored it, and we had some product placement and their banners hanging. It looked legit; it looked very real," remembers Garrity. "The Westminster was our guide and we just became the Mayflower Kennel Club, and we had a similar logo, but we changed it enough [so] that it wasn't like theirs exactly. Their colors were gold and purple, I think, and ours were blue and gold."

DOG DAYS

Armed with a budget of six million dollars and manned with a crew of nearly 150 people, plus several dogs, the *Best in Show* production company moved north to Vancouver to commence principal photography on November 8, 1999.[12] The crew shot in the Lower Mainland, Belcarra, and at a veteran's hall in Mission.

"I'm a big fan of just going other places, getting new images, and not just using the same old stuff in Los Angeles. So I'm all for going anywhere," Garrity says.

"A lot of times, people are more fascinated by what you do, they're not jaded, and you need to go places where people aren't going to gouge you, thinking that you're an *Indiana Jones and the Temple of Doom*–type of shoot. We're not," he explains. "We had to befriend people, and I'm really good at coming into a place and getting to know the locals. They can help you — they loan you things. They tell you where to go, faster than you would figure it out for yourself.

"I had great people there," Garrity adds. "They worked very hard, and it was a beautiful part of the world too. I'm also into walking on the weekends, which you can't do here [in L.A.]"

One of the many behind-the-scenes challenges of *Best in Show* involved the re-creation of North Carolina in Canada, and Garrity found a perfect spot, a general store in Belcarra that could double as Harlan Pepper's Fishin' Hole. His team painted the colorful mural on the side of the building, and fortunately, he had on hand an expert on the topic of fishing to help him decorate the store's interior.

"We pulled out a lot of the stuff that was in the store and brought in bait and tackle things. Chris was particular about that because he loves fly-fishing," Garrity describes. "He brought me down to his house and had a little fly-fishing corner where he did all of his things. He brought me to the basement, where he ties his own flies, and showed me all kinds of equipment. That [material] was part of the store — all the fishing equipment, and he loved it. A lot of things that are in his films are things that he knows something about."

A second challenge was turning the Pacific Colosseum in Vancouver into the Mayflower Kennel Club. The edict was to stick as close to reality as possible. "[Westminster] put down Astroturf on the floor, and we put Astroturf down on the floor. They hung curtains, so we hung curtains," Garrity describes.

A larger problem, however, was filling the stadium with extras on such a small budget.

"There were a lot of cameras, and Chris gets very wide shots. We had a lot of cut-out [cardboard] people that you could put in the seats for the background, and put some real people in among them, some of the locals. But we couldn't afford to fill the stadium at all. We just had to fill portions of it. No digital here! No CGI shots here! So we had to fake it."

Though Hollywood legends warn actors to beware of working with children and animals, all quarters agree that the dogs on *Best in Show* were miraculously well-behaved.

"We worked with a lot of dogs and for the most part they were good," Garrity remembers. "Chris really loved his bloodhound. He just had a blast with him."

"They're like very expensive wigs running around the arena,"[13] Michael McKean joked about his shi tzus, and Guest told interviewer James Mottram, "Oh, the dogs were nothing. They were absolute professionals."[14]

"I have such respect for real dog trainers and for real dog handlers, because it's very hard to do correctly. In the scenes where we were actually doing the dog show, I was almost terrified of the woman who was in charge of training," says Michael Hitchcock. "She was very meticulous. You know, it's her reputation on the line, and she wanted to make sure we looked as real as possible. So I remember when I trotted out in front of all those extras in the stadium, I was thinking, 'Oh boy, I hope I'm doing this right, because she's watching.' She was playing one of the judges."

But while the actors and production team had to sell the illusion that the Mayflower Kennel Club was a real dog show, and even the dogs played along with the fantasy, Guest was forced to contend with some ornery folks who couldn't quite handle the notion that the contest was, in fact, an illusion. When one outraged owner learned that her poodle was not going to win the Best in Show cup at the climax, she pulled her dog from the film, and the company had to find a double within forty-eight hours.[15]

Another handler could not cope any better, and perhaps even held a grudge against Guest for the show's results.

"He told me this, and I thought it was funny," Theaker says. "Even when they were shooting it, he ran so close to reality with the way he was framing the shots that one of the women whose dog was in the show got upset that she didn't win. He had to explain to her, 'This is a movie, this isn't a dog show.'"

"There were a couple of people that got a little weird with us," Garrity remembers. "The thing about it was, we knew who was going to win!"

Another difficulty with the authentic dog show people was narrowly averted early on. The first day of shooting in the grooming and preparation area backstage involved a dramatic shouting match between the Swans over the missing dog toy, Busy Bee. It was quite intense, as Michael Hitchcock remembers, and no doubt caught some of the folks off guard.

"All the background people were actual dog show people, and so here we were, both screaming at the top of our lungs, and then I'm screaming at the dog," he says. "I think they were so surprised, because they had no idea what we would be doing, and I didn't know it would get quite that heated, either. It just kind of happens.

"We did the scene, and Parker said, 'Quit spitting at me!' and sooner or later they yelled, 'Cut,' and we all started to laugh, because I had no idea I really spit on her, and I love that she used that. It was very embarrassing, spitting all over her."

Before the scene was done, Hitchcock had crawled madly in and out of a dog cage, and he and Posey — in character — had made a spectacle of themselves.

"Afterward, the producer Karen Murphy was a little concerned that the dog people would walk," Hitchcock reveals. "Because the movie isn't about us, it isn't about mean, evil, dog people. So we went around and said, 'You know, listen, we lose. This isn't what the whole movie is about,' to reassure these people that they hadn't been tricked into some movie that just denigrates dog owners."

MUTT AND JEFF

Fred Willard and Jim Piddock play the hosts of the Mayflower Kennel Show, men of vastly different temperaments, and the contrast between them works well for the movie, propelling *Best in Show* through its final act with a bolt of comic lightning. Amazingly, the entire hosting sequence was filmed in one day, due to the fact that Piddock had so rigid a schedule on his TV series.

"We were so pushed for time because I had to get back to London, and we literally shot, just him and me, from dusk till dawn," Piddock remembers.

By the time they came into the arena to shoot their narration of the dog show, all of the footage with the dogs was already in the can, and Willard and Piddock had the opportunity to review it. "They got us into wardrobe and makeup and... they showed us some tapes of what they already filmed." Willard says. "We sat there for about four hours."

The next day, Guest got the two actors on the set, sat them behind their desk and very concisely set up the specifics of where the dogs and their handlers had been. "We were in the stadium, and you could imagine where [the competitors] were going," Piddock explains, "It wasn't too difficult — Chris was on top of that."

So shooting began and, according to Willard, he "came strong out of the chute," firing off a barrage of crazy questions and comments regarding the dogs, and in the process thoroughly antagonizing poor Trevor. "I thought, 'What would be some things Joe Garagiola would say about these dogs?'" Willard remembers. "I had prepared a joke about the shih tzu. On the first night when I got in, I had dinner with Chris and Eugene, and I said, 'I have a line planned, and I'm sure there have been a lot jokes about shih tzus,' and they said no. I couldn't believe it.

As all of Buck's crazy thoughts came rolling out, nearly stream of consciousness, put-upon Beckwith had a harder time staying chipper and upbeat. "There's a very gradual shift," Piddock remarks, "from being, you know, mildly amused at first, to getting quite irritated, and in the end finally making a remark that is pretty much a 'fuck you!'"

Piddock, for one, enjoyed his character's slow-burning arc.

Willard liked it, too. "When I watched it, I said, 'Jim is so wonderful.' He was so long-suffering. And he had one line there — I made some joke about my proctologist, and he says, 'Yes, yes, you said that last year,' which starts a whole other story that this wasn't our first year together, and he's had to sit there for years and suffer through this guy. That becomes a whole new subplot."

"It was hilarious," says Garrity. In fact, he wishes he could have stayed the whole day to watch the veteran actors do their thing. "I had to leave in the middle of that, to go back to L.A. and shoot all of the Fleck stuff."

The chemistry between Willard and Piddock was indeed magical and very funny, and after it was over, Willard sought some feedback from Guest.

"We would go for like ten minutes and we'd get done, and Chris says, 'Cut' and would walk up to me and I'd say, 'Was that funny, Chris?' And not even smiling, he'd say, 'Yes, yes, that was very funny. Now what I want to do is move on.'

"That's how he is," Willard says. "And now I try to be a thorn in his side. I'll keep saying, 'Is it funny, Chris?' 'Yes, Fred.' Then he'll call, 'Cut,' and I'll say, 'No, Chris, I wasn't done. Let me call cut. I'll call cut.' And he'll say, 'Yeah Fred, we've got to move on.' But I think I've kind of slowly gotten to Chris."

It might not be slowly, either. As it turns out, Karen Murphy saw Willard after his sequence with Piddock and let him in on a little secret. "I've got to tell you," she told Willard, "I've never seen Christopher laugh so hard [as he did] while you were doing your thing."

And Willard's response? "You're kidding!"

Despite such triumphs, Willard still has one suggestion for Guest regarding a revised ending of *Best in Show*. "The only thing that I missed that I would have liked to see, and several people have said it, is Jim Piddock and me walking out of the arena at the end of the show, getting into a cab ... kind of a final thing."

BEST IN SHOW? BEST OF YEAR!

After a shooting schedule of twenty-six days, the requisite period of intense editing (some eight months) — this time with Robert Leighton rather than Andy Blumenthal — Christopher Guest's second documentary-style comedy, *Best in Show*, went from being an in-the-raw accumulation of sixty hours of footage, to a lean eighty-four minutes.

Many of the cuts concerned Guest's own character, Harlan Pepper, and his strange obsession with collecting beach balls. Another trimmed sequence saw Harlan describing for the camera a stretch of highway in rural North Carolina called Phantom Hill, where there was neither a phantom nor a hill. Cookie and Jerry's "six months later" clip was also changed to include the ditty "God Loves a Terrier" rather than feature product promotion for Fleck's now-popular brand of shoes (with two left feet per set).

Another cut involved one of Meg Hamilton's predilections: smoking weed. "Parker's character smoked pot here and there throughout the movie, including right before we go to meet everybody at the hotel for the cocktail reception," Hitchcock recalls. "It was deemed afterward that this would have given the movie either an R rating or a PG-13 rating, and they didn't want to do that, so the part was cut out. But that was partly why I would be uptight around her, because my character didn't like her smoking so much pot."

Best in Show premiered at the Toronto Film Festival, opened on thirteen screens, and then went wide, hitting 497 screens nationwide at the beginning of October 2000. The film immediately drew the accolades of America's critics, who were bowled over. Roger Ebert called *Best in Show* "wickedly funny" and noted that it sometimes ascended to a kind of "crazed genius."[16]

Writing for the *Detroit News*, Susan Stark declared it "even-handed, sly, and true,"[17] and the *New York Post*'s Lou Lumenick raved, "I was laughing so hard, tears were streaming down my cheeks."[18]

Writing for *Slate*, David Edelstein commented that "what nails it is that Guest and his cast ... have done their research."[19] In *Variety*, Eddie Cockrell praised Guest and Levy for their interest in "character quirks" and noted that the documentary style offered a situation that allowed the improvisers to "peel back layers ... and score points about people who just happen to lavish large amounts of time and money on this particular obsession."[20]

Among those who didn't enjoy the film as much as *Waiting for Guffman*, the consensus seemed to be that there was no central character as strong as Corky. In the words of *Washington Post* critic Rita Kempley, the film needed a "strong protagonist" because moviegoers, "like dogs, need somebody to bond with."[21]

Many reviewers took individual notice of Willard's dynamic show-stealer and Michael Wilmington wrote in the *Chicago Tribune* that the film created "one comic character for the ages ... Willard as addled, veteran, loose-lipped, sex-obsessed sports TV commentator, Buck Laughlin."[22] Willard was not alone in pleasing the critics, and the *San Francisco Chronicle* enthused that John Michael Higgins was "sensational."[23]

By the end of the year, *Best in Show* had landed on several top-ten lists for 2000, including those of *Time* magazine and *Rolling Stone*. It also racked up a large number of awards and nominations. Fred Willard and Catherine O'Hara won the American Comedy Awards for best actor and best actress, respectively, and Willard repeated his victory with a nod from the Boston Society of Film Critics. The film took home a British Comedy Award for best comedy film, and garnered a nomination for best screenplay from the Writer's Guild of America.

Best in Show was nominated for a Golden Globe for best motion picture (comedy/musical) and earned for Guest a best director nomination at the Independent Spirit Awards.

But unlike *Waiting for Guffman*, *Best in Show* proved an immediate success at the box office. The film earned ten million dollars by early November, just a month into release, tripling *Guffman*'s total box-office take in record time. By the end of its box-office run, the film had grossed well over seventeen million dollars, making it a bonafide hit on its budget of six million.

"I think what happened was a combination of several things," says Willard. "The basic, core audience was ready for Christopher Guest's next movie, Warner Brothers really got behind it and gave it a big push, and a lot of people might not have been into amateur theatrics, but everybody owns a dog, or knows someone who does, or watches the Westminster Dog Show, and it just struck a note with people. So it was a snowball effect — 'Oh, this is Christopher Guest's *next* movie.'"

Still, Willard is amazed and gratified by the attention the movie continues to bring him. "I still get people coming up and saying, 'I loved you in *Best in Show*,' and that's three years back. I was very lucky," he considers.

"Very modestly, I came in at a point in the movie where the plot had kind of settled, and all of a sudden there's the excitement of 'Live from Philadelphia, it's the Mayflower Kennel Show!' We were shot out of the cannon, and it was a whole, fresh thing. Watching it, I thought, 'I'm almost getting tired of myself.' I thought Christopher had just enough [of Buck]."

Director Guest's avid following just grew and grew following *Best in Show*, which rapidly became an enormous hit on video and DVD during its release in 2001. The time was ripe, and the audience was primed for a third documentary-style comedy, one that would return Christopher Guest to his musical roots.

GUEST SHOTS

CORKY WOULD BE PROUD: Blaine's own Corky St. Clair, owner of Over the Rainbow Collectibles, might very well order the strange movie calendar produced by Stephan and Scott in *Best in Show*'s finale. These calendars feature shih tzus staged in re-enactments of scenes from famous Hollywood movies, including *Gone with the Wind* (1939) and *Casablanca* (1946).

"We did the old movies," Joe Garrity remembers. "We got stills from them. On *Casablanca*, we found a miniature plane that was very similar to the one [in the film]. We set that up in a black void and had fog, and put little pin lights as landing lights. The costumes were hilarious. Putting those dogs in them was a lot of fun. We just had to get them in the outfits, and they'd kind of slump down — it really worked out.

"*Gone with the Wind* was hilarious," Garrity adds. "We got stills of the movie and created these cut-out buildings and had fans blowing the fire. There was a little piece of wagon and we had to get these little dogs into it"

But the last calendar page — *McMillan and Wife* (1971–1977)? Why select a clip from that TV police drama starring Rock Hudson and Susan Saint James? What's that about?

"That was Chris," Garrity laughs. "He puts the strangest combination of movie titles together, and that's funny to him. You might notice a lot of Chris's films have theater marquees. Like [in *Attack of the* 50 *Ft. Woman*]: *Milo and Otis* (1986) and *Yentl* (1983). They're two real movies, but the funny thing is that they're together. He always comes up with two oddball films that should never be in the same building."

BACKSTORY: Deborah Theaker and Scott Williamson played friends of the Flecks in *Best in Show*, Fern City suburbanites who were mostly background characters in the final film. But that doesn't mean that these characters didn't have their own story to tell.

"What Scott Williamson and I came up with was that I was very, very competitive with Catherine, and while she's away, I basically roll around in her scent, we have sex in her bed, and I take over her life," Theaker says.

"The other backstory involved my own dog, who wasn't a purebred. I talked originally with Chris about whether I could bring my own dog into it, because I wanted to be jealous of Catherine, of the fact that she had a purebred," Theaker remembers. "You know how everything is relative — to me, Scott and I wanted to be Cookie and Jerry so badly because they were so unbelievably cool in relation to our context. None of it ended up being used or needed. It was extraneous, and you feel that it is extraneous as the scenes are happening and that Chris won't need to draw on that."

HOBBY DU JOUR: In some manner, all of Guest's films gaze directly at the notions of hobbies, or obsessions. In *Spinal Tap*, Nigel, like Guest, collects guitars — some of which he can't even touch or look at, let alone play.

In *Waiting for Guffman*, Corky's store is filled with odd memorabilia and movie collectibles, and in *A Mighty Wind*, Leonard Crabbe is a model-train enthusiast.

Best in Show may exemplify this thematic strand in the strongest manner. Harlan works hard to make his hobby, ventriloquism, a (poor-paying) vocation, and all the owners, to one extent or another, are responsible for turning a hobby (a love of dogs), into what William Shatner (addressing Trekkies on *Saturday Night Live*) called "a colossal waste of time."

"You can pick almost any field and there's going to be weird people,"[24] Guest has said. "I guess I'm obsessed, or at least fascinated, by those things, by going to a convention where people do a very under-the-radar hobby, a pursuit that is approached with that kind of obsession...I think that's fascinating."[25]

Based on Guest's love of music (*A Mighty Wind*) and dogs (*Best in Show*), his next documentary-style comedy just might concern fly-fishing.

BREAKFAST OF CHAMPIONS: Fred Willard remembers an early-morning surprise in Vancouver during the shooting of *Best in Show*. He was at the hotel's breakfast room when he heard a familiar voice.

"I'm sitting there, and a group of guys walk in, and I hear one of them doing a bad Arnold Schwarzenneger impersonation, and I think, 'Oh god, who is this?' Well, I looked up and it was Arnold Schwarzenegger, with six or seven guys around him. They were filming a movie in town at the time and staying at our hotel, and I could eavesdrop. And they were all doing bad body-building jokes. 'Jake here bought a stationary bike...and it's *still* stationary!' Karen Murphy, the producer, walked in and heard that line and looked at me and rolled her eyes like 'How corny,' and I thought it was great."

DOGGY STYLE? In one scene that didn't make *Best in Show*'s final cut, Trevor Beckwith turned the tables on his Mayflower co-host, Buck Laughlin.

"I had one long speech that was apropos of nothing, about canine anal sex," Jim Piddock reveals. "It was ridiculously graphic and very technical and very straight-faced. I was quite proud of the speech, but it was kind of wrong because it was me shocking [Willard]. It was the wrong dynamic, but I was able to use more of that type of stuff in *A Mighty Wind*."

NO BARK, NO BITE: While prepping *Best in Show*, Bob Balaban made a decision about what dog breed his character, Dr. Millbank, should own. "I actually requested a Dandie Dinmont since I knew one when I was a little boy, when I was three years old," Balaban explains.

Although Balaban had fond memories of the terrier breed, and the Dandie Dinmont is renowned as an energetic and bold animal, that didn't turn out to be the case with the dog cast in the film.

"Knowing what I know now, I probably wouldn't have requested one," the actor says. "The dog was very docile...he just kind of sat there. He was sort of sleepy. He wasn't a terribly engaging animal, although my character liked him very much. But he really didn't do too much."

FULL CIRCLE: Fred Willard was unprepared, though quite pleased by the critical attention and accolades that followed his performance as Buck Laughlin in *Best in Show*.

"One of my first heroes is Albert Finney," he explains. "He's the most naturalistic actor I've ever seen, and I've been a huge fan of his. The year after *Best in Show* came out, we were both up for an award from the Boston Film Critics and I won, and he came in second. When my wife told me, I laughed, because I knew I couldn't hold a candle to Albert Finney, but it was just like a full circle had come around. The guy had inspired me — and now I came in first for *Best in Show* — doing a bunch of jokes and being a wise guy."

THE MAJOR LEAGUERS: Deb Theaker loves working with the other performers in the Guest repertory company and joined up for *Best in Show*, even though she hadn't been envisioned for any of the central roles. She calls the documentary-style comedies "the major leagues for comedians," and notes that "you love being around that group of people, and even lunch hour is so entertaining. They're all *raconteurs par excellence* and such interesting people that I was more concerned that I would not be able to hang out with them than anything else. Just the experience of doing it and being in that company is enough."

METHOD ACTING: "Even though it was a comedy, I think Parker and I got into such an intense space that it was hard to shake the character off at night, to just kind of go have fun sometimes, because they were very intense people. It took a little while to get out of that character," Michael Hitchcock considers.

"At times, with the braces, I was very self-conscious. I had braces in high school and it was very strange to have them back on again, because you remember how they felt, and I noticed after seeing the film that most of the time I don't show my teeth, because, I think, subconsciously, I was trying to hide them. It worked for me in that sense, because my guy thinks he's Matthew Perry and very handsome, and he probably would be very embarrassed wearing braces."

SHOOTING FISH IN A BARREL: One of Willard's favorite scenes in *Best in Show* involved Buck Laughlin's interview with the senile Leslie Cabot and his lovely nurse. "The scene was shot at four in the morning, and it ended up as a monologue directed at this pretty nurse," he describes.

"It included a lot of medical jokes, including observations on rectal thermometers ... The fact that she was pretty and non-speaking made it a comic actor's dream."[26]

SAY IT AIN'T SO, JOE! There was at least one moviegoer who didn't think *Best in Show* was all that, former Westminster Kennel Club TV host Joe Garagiola himself. During an interview with CNN's Daryn Kagan in 2001, he told her he wasn't bowled over by the effort.

"I think Fred was playing me. I think he used some lines I wouldn't use, but he's a funny guy, and, hey, we all have our tastes. I didn't particularly like the show. I thought the satire went over the top."[27]

Still, *Sports Illustrated* ran a note-for-note comparison between Garagiola and Laughlin in October of 2000, and matched up their dog commentary in categories like odd backgrounds, exuberance, team players, handling with care, and why — ahem — size matters.

On exuberance, for instance, Laughlin noted that Beatrice went after a judge just like the woman was "made of ham." Garagiola's "exuberance" comment could have come straight from the same play book: "Every dog that's walked out there, you want to stick a jumper cable on them."[28]

TOP DOG

Best in Show could have been titled *Love Me, Love My Dog*, because it is a film that, in a very strange way, concerns class warfare. Not between pet and man, mind you, but among dog owners. The impetus for the film was that famous trip to the park, and Guest's observation that dog owners of "preferred" breeds looked down their noses at regular Joes like his mutt, Henry. Not surprisingly, given that light, many of the characters in the film use their dogs to further their own ends, enhance their image, or retain their social status.

Best in Show's tag line, "Some pets deserve a little more respect than others," is actually a perfect metaphor for people in general, and the characters populating this film, specifically. For each set of owners in the movie has chosen a dog that in some way mirrors their own personal issues and values.

"It was all about the people, of course," Guest explained. "The dogs were an extension, in a way, of their personalities."[29]

Let's begin with a study of Cookie and Jerry Fleck. They are good, average Americans with a few quirks, like Jerry's foot condition and Cookie's extensive past sexual experience. But they work hard, own their own house, and are nettled by some pesky money problems. They are nonetheless endearing and happy, and their dog Winky reflects all of these characteristics.

Winky is a Norwich terrier, a good-natured little guy who is a working terrier to go side-by-side with these working-class people. Norwich terriers are known to be loveable, and they generally play well with others. When

Winky and the Flecks win the show during the movie's climax, it is a startling upset not just to the more wealthy owners (like the millionaire Cabots and the upwardly mobile Swans), but to the more aristocratic dogs, as well. Winky's victory is the victory of every man, er, every dog.

Sherri Ann and Christy Cummings show a beautiful standard poodle, Rhapsody in White, at the Mayflower. This dog's breed is characterized as dignified, proud, and very elegant — perhaps even haughty. It is an upper-class aristocratic dog by its noble bearing, and the observant eye will notice that Sherri Ann is the trophy bride of a millionaire who lives in a grand old mansion, a kind of standard poodle of her own breed, the sort most famously represented by Anna Nicole Smith.

Handler Christy Cummings is confident about this dog to the point of arrogance, convinced that it will win Best in Show because it has done so in the past, during the last two contests. In fact, the dog actually wears a tiara to the pre-show party (as does Sherri Ann, by the way), projecting its status as canine royalty and the rightful recipient of the prize.

Looking at it objectively, this is a dog that has had all the privileges of life and is *expected* to do well, so Christy therefore looks down her nose at the other competitors, including Winky and Hubert, because they do not have the bearing, breeding, or background of Rhapsody in White.

The Swans are an interesting case. They have selected a Weimaraner as their dog, a particularly willful animal, but one also with aristocratic bearing. Why did they pick this particular animal? Probably because poor Beatrice's shiny gray coat blends well with Hamilton's merlot sweater. Or maybe, as Guest has suggested, because they saw a Weimaraner standing beside a model in a Ralph Lauren advertisement.[30]

The point is that Meg and Hamilton have cherry-picked a pet that, they believe, will reflect well on them, and therefore enhance their image in the world (like their Mac laptops, their braces, etc.).

Though they have trouble relating courteously to people, and treat others as servants, including the Taft Hotel maid and the hotel manager played by Ed Begley Jr., the Swans have no problems understanding how they would *like* to be perceived by others. When Beatrice blows that image by going after one of the judges as if the woman is a ham, they promptly rid themselves of Beatrice and choose a different animal.

Harlan's dog Hubert is a bloodhound (or a St. Hubert Hound), and these dogs are known as powerful, jowly, agreeable sorts. With their floppy ears, and hangdog expression, the bloodhounds look a little lonely, a little downcast, a little like Winnie the Pooh's sad-sack friend, Eyeore.

Now look at Harlan himself. Of all the dog handlers depicted in the film, he is the only one who attends the Mayflower alone, making him the human echo of the lonesome-seeming bloodhound. Harlan's red hair is not too different in shading from Hubert's coppery coat, and his face reflects several of the dog's most notable characteristics. Harlan and Hubert both have names that begin with the letter *H* and are unassuming, adrift kind of personalities. They don't seem quite sure what they want to do in life, but find true kinship only with one another. Harlan anthropomorphizes Hubert, certain that the dog understands his jokes about nuts, and is barking back relevant responses. He calls it telepathy.

Finally, let's not forget the delightful Stephan and Scott. They own a charming little shih tzu, Miss Agnes. These dogs are known to be alert, slightly arrogant, but with loads of character and charm. They can get snappish sometimes, and they require extensive daily grooming.

With his loud kimonos, strange suits, and litany of suggestive one-liners, all the same qualities could be ascribed to youthful Scott. Thus, Miss Agnes is a perfect reflection of this cocksure young man, a little overdone with the ubiquitous bow in her hair, always demanding attention, but in the end proving utterly charming.

This couple showers their dogs in true love, pampers them (telephoning Tyrone when they're out of town) and generally treating their dogs like children, which is probably how most Americans see their pets.

Considering how the choice of dog breed reflects the personalities of the owners, what one might conclude about *Best in Show* is that the Mayflower Show represents the perfect microcosm for diverse, economically divided America, because it brings all breeds together for a common purpose. There's the upper class (the poodles and the yuppies), the indulged but much-loved middle class (the shih tzus), and finally, the working class terrier and his kin. For vastly different reasons, each one of these subsets of American culture wants to win the show.

For modest Cookie and Jerry, who drive to Philadelphia in a van filled with snack food, and who max out their credit cards on the way, it would be a great boon to return to Fern City with such an honor, and indeed, they become local celebrities for doing so.

For Sherri Ann and Christy Cummings, the show seems to be about upholding tradition and standards ("rigid standards," as Dr. Millbank might remind us at this juncture). There's a legacy to maintain.

For the Swans, winning the dog show is an outside validation of their showy but ultimately empty lifestyle. The trophy is something they could set down on their fancy furniture and use to really offset the exercise machine and the futon.

Why are Harlan and Stefan and Scott involved in the Mayflower Kennel Club? That's a thornier issue, and one the movie dodges a bit. My guess is that Harlan boasts a genuine love of dogs, and has done so for all of his life, so he is legitimately in the lifestyle. Scott and Stefan seem so happy and fun-loving, and the dog show just seems like an interesting avenue they can pursue together, one that includes spending time with their "children." Just like the dog calendar they create and sell.

The point to all this speculation, one supposes, is that Guest has given the world yet another group of starry-eyed dreamers who believe that if they can just do one big thing (in this case, win Best in Show), their lives will change, and all for the better. As always in the Guest oeuvre, the coda set "six months later" reveals how the big show (whether won or lost) has a transforming effect on the participants.

The winners — the Flecks — have become hometown heroes and the fulcrum of a (small) cottage industry about Norwich terriers. By losing, Harlan has been freed to find himself. He takes a flight to Israel and on the kibbutz reassesses his priorities. He decides to pursue ventriloquism more seriously, a hobby that may not be accepted as freely in a region like the South, where raising dogs was a family tradition and probably the norm.

Freed from the prison of expectations and tradition, Christy and Sherri Ann have come out to the world and are pursuing their interests in a more open way six months after Mayflower. For the first time, they discuss openly their romantic involvement, and their confidence has given rise to a new joint venture, *American Bitch* magazine.

Scott and Stephan also go on to something else, the production of dog calendars, but their *joie de vivre* remains intact. No matter what aspect of the dog world they devote themselves to, they remain the same: happy, stable, and loving.

Finally, the Swans have traded Beatrice for a new dog, a better model. In other words, they are doing the same thing all over again, investing their self worth and image in a trendy thing (a dog) and hoping to achieve a different result. This happens to be the definition of insanity, by the way.

Best in Show is an entertaining and insightful comedy not merely because it reveals this world of "class warfare," or more accurately, class distinctions, where different dog breeds represent the various characteristics of their owners, but because, like *Waiting for Guffman* before it, it succeeds in making exemplary use of the documentary format. In fact, *Best in Show* is probably superior in that regard.

Though *Waiting for Guffman* may arguably be a funnier film, pound for pound, minute for minute, *Best in Show* achieves the distinction of being, in some manner, more realistic. Or perhaps more accurately stated, the dog show is a more appropriate and believable venue in which to set a documentary. It is easy to believe that an intrepid documentarian would choose to follow a variety of dog owners to the "Super Bowl" Mayflower Show; less so, perhaps that a filmmaker would be interested in the preparations for a sesquicentennial show in tiny Blaine, Missouri.

Unless one of the cast members happened to be a Friedman.

Appropriately, as the stalwart documentarian, Guest covers all the bases here, and one gets the sense while watching *Best in Show* that it concerns not just the dogs or the actual show, but the whole dog show lifestyle, and as such, is rather compelling as a universe that has not been illuminated in cinema before.

There are visits to the venue as it is prepared, with Don Lake as our guide; there is a survey of the hotel with Begley's kindly manager providing history and commentary, and together these background details cover the story from every conceivable angle, just like a good journalist should.

It's also important to highlight the fact that everything from the inclusion of real dog show judges in the film, to the very camera angles Guest adopts, accurately reflects the reality of this world. *Best in Show* is as close to true as possible because Guest is a director who always does his homework. A strong sense of reality must precede that delightful "one step further" of comedy. Probably the highest compliment that can be paid *Best in Show* is that it looks and feels just right, even to many of those in the industry.

"It's a bit of an exaggeration, but that's pretty much it," reported Mary Manning, event coordinator for the Tampa Bay Kennel Club Dog Show in 2001. "There really are people who think of the dogs as their children."[31]

Furthermore, the owners — with all their strange quirks — nicely and truthfully reflect the characteristics of some real-life dog owners and handlers. Sometime after *Best in Show* premiered, the *Pet World* Web site described a series of strange dog-handler stories, including one attention-grabbing handler who wore "a sequined electric-blue tuxedo"[32] in order to stand out to judges. That sounds like Scott and his bizarre hotel doorman-style outfit, doesn't it?

In a similar vein, *USA Today* reported that some handlers are afraid to wear armbands with the unlucky number thirteen emblazoned on their sleeves, and that one handler at the 2004 Westminister Dog Show would not wear any clothes in a color determined to be second-place red.[33]

One can see why Guest, with his obsession on unique hobbies, finds these people interesting and worthy of closer observation.

"We met a lot of dog-show people when we did *Best in Show*," Jane Lynch told a reporter once. "The movie just barely scratched the surface."[34]

Indeed.

The inclusion of Fred Willard as a Joe Garagiola-type commentator also heightens the reality of *Best in Show*, as do Jim Piddock's accurate and well-researched observations about the sport, the breeds, and the competitors. The inclusion of the requisite archival materials (including one hilarious hieroglyph, perhaps the earliest known example of ventriloquism) on the B-roll are not only funny, but further add to the veneer of reality.

Most accurate and carefully crafted, however, are the details and look of the show itself. Interestingly, there is even a real-life precedent for Winky's upset victory over the more regal standard poodle, as a Norwich terrier took the Best in Show title at the Westminster in 1994.

All in all, *Best in Show* is a carefully crafted, accurate, believable, and amusing portrayal of the dog show world, and it is no wonder that dog owners worldwide have flocked to it. In fact, dog show ratings have gone up considerably in the years since the premiere of *Best in Show*, because the film popularized the sport.[35]

Joe Garagiola may be retired (replaced by David Frei), but the bark of *Best in Show* still hasn't lost its bite, proving that every dog has his or her day.

5. A KISS AT THE END OF THE RAINBOW

A MIGHTY WIND (2003)

BACK TOGETHER AGAIN ...
FOR THE FIRST TIME

DIRECTED BY: Christopher Guest

WRITTEN BY: Christopher Guest and Eugene Levy

PRODUCED BY: Karen Murphy

DIRECTOR OF PHOTOGRAPHY: Arlene Donnelly Nelson

PRODUCTION DESIGNER: Joseph T. Garrity

FILM EDITOR: Robert Leighton

COSTUME DESIGNER: Durinda Wood

MUSIC PRODUCED BY: Jeffery C.J. Vanston

ART DIRECTOR: Pat Tagliaferro

ALBUM COVERS AND VINTAGE STILLS: Joe Pugliese

"**Old Joe's Place**" written by Christopher Guest, Harry Shearer, and Michael McKean; performed by the Folksmen; "**The Good Book Song**" written by Michael McKean and Harry Shearer; performed by the New Main Street Singers; "**When You're Next to Me**" written by Eugene Levy; performed by Mitch and Mickey; "**Kiss at the End of the Rainbow**" written by Michael McKean and Annette O'Toole; performed by Mitch and Mickey; "**One More Time**" written by Catherine O'Hara and Eugene Levy; performed by Mitch and Mickey; "**Just that Kind of Day**" written by Christopher Guest and Michael McKean; performed by the New Main Street Singers; "**Never Did No Wanderin'**" written by Michael McKean and Harry Shearer; performed by the Folksmen; "**Main Street Rag**" written by John Michael Higgins; performed by the New Main Street Singers; "**Barnyard Symphony**" written by Christopher Guest; performed by the Folksmen; "**Skeletons of Quinto**" written by Christopher Guest; performed by the Folksmen; "**Loco Man**" written by Harry Shearer; performed by the Folksmen; "**Fare Away**" written by C.J. Vanston, Michael McKean, and Annette O'Toole; performed by the New Main Street Singers; "**Potato's in the Paddy Wagon**" written by Michael McKean and Annette O'Toole; performed by the New Main Street Singers; "**Being Mitch**" written by C.J. Vanston; performed by Mitch Cohen; "**A Mighty Wind**" written by Eugene Levy, Christopher Guest, and Michael McKean; performed by the Folksmen, Mitch and Mickey, and the New Main Street Singers; "**The Catheter Song**" written by Catherine O'Hara, performed by Mickey Crabbe.

STARRING (IN ORDER OF APPEARANCE)

Harry Shearer: Mark Shubb
Michael McKean: Jerry Palter
Christopher Guest: Alan Barrows
Eugene Levy: Mitch Cohen
Catherine O'Hara: Mickey Crabbe
Bob Balaban: Jonathan Steinbloom
Paul Dooley: George Menschell
Paul Benedict: Martin Berg
Jane Lynch: Laurie Bohner
John Michael Higgins: Terry Bohner
Parker Posey: Sissy Knox
Jim Piddock: Leonard Crabbe
Don Lake: Elliott Steinbloom
Deborah Theaker: Naomi Steinbloom
Fred Willard: Mike LaFontaine
Ed Begley Jr.: Lars Olfen
Michael Hitchcock: Laurence E. Turpin
Larry Miller: Wally Fenton
Jennifer Coolidge: Amber Cole

THE OLD GANG RETURNS

LEGENDARY FOLK-MUSIC PROMOTER AND PRODUCER IRVING STEINBLOOM has passed away at the age of eighty-three in New York, and his children, Jonathan, Elliott and Naomi, want to stage a performance in their father's memory celebrating his life. In just two short weeks, at the Big Apple's Town Hall, folk music — the sound that inspired a generation — will be heard again.

Jonathan Steinbloom sets out to bring back the (semi) famous acts that his father was famous for signing a generation earlier. These include a trio called the Folksmen (Mark Shubb, Jerry Palter, and Alan Barrows), a creepily cheery "neuftet," the New Main Street Singers, and the romantic duo for the ages, the sweet Mitch and Mickey. The only problem with Jonathan's plan to assemble the old gang is that Mitch has suffered a nervous breakdown and hasn't performed with Mickey since the seventies.

While Jonathan works to bring Mitch back into the fold, the Folksmen experience difficulty determining which song they should perform at the tribute, unable to decide between their one-time hit, "Old Joe's Place," or Alan's pretentious ditty about the Spanish Civil War, "Skeletons of Quinto."

While the culty New Main Street Singers, led by Laurie and Terry

Bohner, practice for the big event and contend with their obnoxious manager, former TV sitcom star Mike LaFontaine, Mitch and Mickey meet for the first time in years, and attempt to recapture the innocent spirit of their music. One problem: their most popular song, "A Kiss at the End of the Rainbow," always spawned a kiss onstage, but now Mickey is married to a catheter salesman and model train enthusiast, Leonard Crabbe.

Thanks to the auspices of PBN (read: PBS) and folk-friendly TV executive Lars Olfen, the "Ode to Irving" concert will be transmitted live on TV, which causes further complications.

On the night of the show, it's high drama as Mitch disappears from the venue, the New Main Street Singers perform the Folksmen's chosen tune, and Jonathan, an obsessive-compulsive, has tremendous difficulties with the concert's stagecraft.

STARTING TO REMEMBER SOME THINGS

After the spectacular success of *Best in Show* with critics and audiences, a third documentary-style comedy from director Christopher Guest was a *fait accompli*. What wasn't so expected, however, was that Guest's newest project would delve not merely into the comedic format audiences had now come to anticipate, but take a dramatic left turn into deep, poignant emotions as well. The result was 2003's *A Mighty Wind*, one of the most celebrated films of the year, and a film filled with great music, funny moments, and a heart-wrenching love story.

In March of 2002, *Billboard* magazine announced the commencement of production on Christopher Guest and Eugene Levy's latest collaboration, a still-untitled "mockumentary film about folk music for Castle Rock."[1] As before, there was a kernel of a story, in this case, the desire to create something musical.[2]

From that basic idea, the skeleton of a story was developed, a skeleton featuring over a hundred specific scenes. Guest explained the concept succinctly to the *Hollywood Reporter*: "It deals with three folk acts that get together for a memorial concert at Carnegie Hall because a famous folk manager has died. These acts were active in the 1960s but have been out of the business since the early 1970s."[3]

Although a few details would change from this early synopsis to final product, most notably the location of the memorial show, much stayed the same. The film was a second chance for Guest and his cohorts, after *This Is Spinal Tap*, to explore the world of musicians, this time folk musicians, which Guest had grown up playing in the sixties.

Once the idea for *A Mighty Wind* was developed, it was time to build that all-important base of knowledge for the film, developing the backstory of the characters and their world. Performing their due diligence, Levy and Guest listened to hundreds of folk-music records in preparation for this attempt to document the world of the late 1950s and early 1960s folk explosion.

"We did elaborate histories for each character, where they came from, who played with whom," Levy told the *New York Times*. "None of that ends up in the movie, but it adds depth."[4]

Some of these details, including the history of a band called the New Main Street Singers, stretched on for five pages at a clip.

"Chris wanted all that laid out in voice-over in some cases, and with me as a talking head in some cases," remembers Paul Dooley, voice of the Main Street Singers as co-founder George Menschell. "He gave me a paragraph so that I could mention how we became the Village Folk, and became this and that. But other than the names I said in the progression of it, I could word it my own way. He did write out how we went from being a duo to a trio to a 'neuftet,' which, by the way, was Chris's line. Chris wrote that. A lot of the stuff I had in that close-up in the beginning was prepared by Chris."

"Chris and Eugene were very specific about the bands that we chose to do in the movie," adds Shearer, who was returning to the "mockumentary" fold on-screen for the first time since *This Is Spinal Tap*, playing one of Guest's bandmates, Mark Shubb, in the fictional group, the Folksmen.

"Some of the critics, I guess, missed the point and thought it should be more encyclopedic, and that every aspect of folk music should be represented. 'Where's the Dylan guy? Where's this? Where's that?' But they were very specific that these were three groups from the era where folk music appeared to be the next pop music, and people were sitting in New York offices writing faux folk songs designed to hit the pop charts," Shearer describes.

"They were mimicking some of the aspects of folk music, but they took the politics and the really horrible bloody stuff out. Most real folk songs are about some horrible form of death as a sort of cautionary tale, or a protest against some horrible set of injustices. But the commercial folk music of the early 1960s sanitized all that. So these three groups were partaking of that era and that aspect of momentarily commercial folk music. That's very different from the performers you find in the folk bins these days, many of whom I love. Richard Thompson, June Taybor, Paul Brady. I think that what's similar is the stylistic elements, but the impulses behind the music are totally different, and that's what we were making fun of."

Or, as Parker Posey put it, the groups were "folk before folk became political. There's an Up with People vibe."[5]

For Guest, the backdrop of folk music not only permitted him to strut his considerable skills as a musician, but to shine a light on yet another microcosm of somewhat strange people.

"I think any backdrop where people take themselves seriously ... is going to work," he explained. "Truthfully, we happen to like music and it's fun to play this kind of music, and because they take themselves so seriously, it immediately lends itself to this kind of comedy."[6]

As Eugene Levy and Christopher Guest developed the film's characters and story, they reached back into the past for inspiration, and pulled on a previous incarnation of Guest's, the Folksmen, a triumvirate that had appeared on *Saturday Night Live* in 1984 to sing "Old Joe's Place."

In 1992, the Folksmen also appeared in the concert video entitled *The Return of Spinal Tap* during the opening scenes, practicing in their dressing room to the tune of "Blood on the Coal," which concerned a late nineteenth-century disaster involving a train and Kentucky miners.

The Folksmen also appeared at a UCLA folk festival in the 1990s, and more amusingly, had been the (unpopular) opening act for Spinal Tap for some years, as recently as 2001.

This tuneful trio, Jerry Palter (Michael McKean), Mark Shubb (Harry Shearer) and Alan Barrows (Christopher Guest) had originated during a photo shoot with *Rolling Stone* magazine to publicize *This Is Spinal Tap* in the mid-1980s. The three men appeared for the shoot sans makeup and wigs, looking a bit older, a bit more sedate, and perhaps a bit strange. Perfect over-the-hill folkers, in other words.[7]

In real life, the Folksmen could have been any number of groups, from the Kingston Trio to the Limelighters to the Chad Mitchell Trio to the Tripjacks.

The Folksmen also had a major schism in their group in order to foster some tension, with Alan and Mark more interested in creating quality, thoughtful music, and McKean's Jerry in it simply for the fame and money.

"My character is the guy who was always in it for the money," McKean reported. "When the money ran out, he found something that ... paid him even less. But it was steady ... for thirty years."[8]

After the Folksmen, the second group featured in *A Mighty Wind* was the New Main Street Singers, a cheerful neuftet that seemed reminiscent of the New Christy Minstrels, a group begun by Randy Sparks that first appeared nationally on *The Andy Williams Show* in 1962. Popular for songs such as "This Land Is Your Land" and "Chim Chim Cher-ee," the group landed its own TV show on NBC in 1964 called *Ford Presents the New Christy Minstrels*. The group became so popular that it played at the White House during Lyndon B. Johnson's presidential term.

And, like the New Main Street Singers, the New Christy Minstrels became known for rapid turnover among its ranks. Lead singer Barry McGuire left in

1965, and the group had a revolving door of members for the next twenty-eight years that included Karen Black, Kenny Rogers, and John Denver. The New Main Street Singers in the film had only one original member, the sullen George Menschell.

The third and final act in *A Mighty Wind* is Mitch and Mickey, a romantic duo that many critics have compared to Ian Tyson and Sylvia Fricker, though others have suggested sources as diverse as Captain and Tenille, and Peter, Paul, and Mary.

"There were a lot of folk duos in that period," Guest told reporters. "It's too simple to just view them as an Ian and Sylvia act, and it's not really fair to us. That's too easy, that's a sketch, and we're not doing a sketch."9

In fact, Guest wanted it clear that his characters were an amalgam of the whole folk world, the whole movement from the early 1960s, not an attempt to skewer or parody one particular act.

"These are characters we originated, odd people we've put in our film. It was the same with *Spinal Tap*. That's not every rock musician, it's just three odd people,"10 he insisted. As in all his endeavors, Guest took this work very seriously, as an exercise in character building, not some one-note joke or sketch, as he put it.

To the director's delight, all the scheduling with his cast could be arranged, and every member of his informal repertory company returned, including McKean, Shearer, Catherine O'Hara, Fred Willard, Parker Posey, Jennifer Coolidge, Ed Begley Jr., Larry Miller, Michael Hitchcock, Jane Lynch, Bob Balaban, Deb Theaker, Scott Williamson, Don Lake, Paul Dooley, Jim Piddock, and John Michael Higgins. New to the team was young Chris Moynihan, who would be playing a novice among the cult-like New Main Street Singers.

Even with such a great team in place, there was a tremendous amount of material to prepare before the film, budgeted at nine million dollars. Many of the actors would need to learn to play instruments and actually sing, because Guest wanted to perform the concert portion of the film live.

Also, some two dozen songs needed to be written and rehearsed.

"There was a lot more involvement than usual because of the songwriting," McKean reported. "I did a lot of songwriting in this film with Christopher, Harry and C.J. Vanston, our musical director."11

"The idea, indeed, was to write very catchy, very memorable songs," Shearer says. "One of the things about that era was that those songs were very catchy. They were certainly more musically sophisticated than actual folk music, that's a part of the joke with the New Main Street Singers. They have all these harmonies that have nothing to do with folk music, but are fun to sing and fun to hear."

"Harry and I got together and wrote [some of the] songs in one afternoon. We wrote 'Wanderin'' and 'The Good Book Song,'" McKean says. "My wife, Annette [O'Toole], and I wrote three of the songs in there."[12]

These titles included a strange sea chanty by the New Main Street Singers ("Fare Away") — a collaboration with Vanston — and the delightful "Potato's in the Paddy Wagon," which O'Toole and McKean conceived on a road trip together to Vancouver, where her series, *Smallville*, shoots. Their final collaboration was the celebrated Mitch and Mickey tune, "A Kiss at the End of the Rainbow."

The latter was especially meaningful to the two actors, as they felt it was not just about Mitch and Mickey, but their own relationship as well. In the film, the song set the stage for the very important "will they or won't they" dynamic regarding a special kiss.

"Their whole relationship is really based around that song," O'Toole noted. "I was in tears at the end, thinking I was part of something that was so wonderful."[13]

Ironically, this beloved song almost didn't make the cut. When McKean originally brought it to Guest, the director said it was "too serious," and had to be convinced by his wife, Jamie Lee Curtis, that it was the right song for the movie.[14]

Many of the songs were designed to evoke certain trends in folk music history. "A Kiss at the End of the Rainbow" was designed by McKean and O'Toole to sound as though it "could have been written by [Stephen Foster] or one of his imitators from 150 years ago,"[15] said McKean. The Folksmen songs were reminiscent of calypso music ("Loco Man"). The (eventually cut) song "Killington Hill," by Mitch and Mickey, was a violent tale about bloodshed, mutilation, and death.

"There's one that's not on the album that we do in the live show," Shearer says. "It's called 'Corn Wine.' It's a form that was very familiar in commercial folk music like the Brothers Four. These groups all had songs like this, which is 'Here's how it is for a young man;' 'Here's how it is for a middle-aged man;' 'Here's how it is for an old man.' The ages-of-man conceit, done in a folk song."

Once the songs were written, they needed to be learned, and rehearsed well. Catherine O'Hara took lessons on an Autoharp because Sylvia Tyson and Mimi Farina had both played them; Eugene Levy boned up on his guitar, and so it went.

"This meant tons of rehearsals and pre-production," musical director C.J. Vanston explains. "These actors sang and played from a very deep place."[16]

"Parker Posey learned the mandolin to be in that group!" Fred Willard says with admiration.

"John Michael Higgins rehearsed [the New Main Street Singers] and structured the songs, and I went out to his house one night to hear them rehearse. I listened to them and I said, 'Michael, is that a real song?' I thought I was back thirty years ago listening to a real folk song. There were many, many worse folk singing groups than this. He was just wonderful," says Willard.

Indeed, Guest had cast wisely: Higgins was actually an accomplished vocal arranger and also an obsessive fan about the very brand of cheery music his alter ego, the New Main Street Singers' Terry Bohner, performed.

Why go the trouble of singing these two dozen or so carefully prepared songs live? It is something Guest feels very deeply about; that the public is being denied the live element in the contemporary music industry.

"Chris feels strongly about it, about how that experience has just been so decimated," said C.J. Vanston. "That's why I was so happy about Norah Jones' [Grammy success]. It's so timely — musicians sitting there capturing a moment, not months of moments!"[17]

Paul Dooley was one of the few actors featured in the film who didn't actually play an instrument, and so that became part of the joke about his character, George Menschell.

"I went to see Chris in his office as the movie was being cast, and he said to me, 'We have to find something for you to do in this new film. It's going to be about folk singing, do you play an instrument?' I said, 'No,' and he said, 'Do you sing?' I said, 'With two or three other people, it's possible,' and he said, 'Well, I don't care, you're funny, and I want you to be in the movie, we'll figure something out.'"

And indeed they did. Keen-eyed viewers will notice that George Menschell never actually plays his guitar, in part, perhaps because he spilled spaghetti sauce on his one-and-only uniform top, and now has to hide the stain by holding up his guitar.

"Then it just kind of caught on and became my trademark," Dooley recalls "... not playing."

In fact, Menschell's whole persona became one of total disinterest. "He's actually gotten tired of it, he's gotten jaded," Dooley describes. "He's the only living member of the original group. Maybe the guy who had the porn shop, Chuck Wiseman, is still alive, but he is the only one from the original group, the only charter member. He doesn't want to do the hard work of running the group anymore, and probably secretly he doesn't like [the Bohners] because they've taken over."

George's lack of interest in this enterprise generated a number of subtle jokes in the film and later in the live concerts. "Between numbers in front of the audience, the group would tune up, and I would tune up my guitar, and put my ear down to the strings. But I would never even touch the guitar."

THE TIMES THEY ARE A CHANGIN' — BACK!

While the songs were written and the actors prepped for their perform-ances, production designer Joe Garrity rejoined the team, and began con-ducting research about the folk music world of the early 1960s. For the documentary style to seem authentic, all of the archival materials such as record albums and live performances (on 1960s TV shows like *Hoot Nite*) had to appear genuine.

"We started getting this old footage from these old hootenany shows. We went to old record stores and started pulling tons of these albums," he remembers. "There were some staged, wacky covers, and one of our big jobs was to re-create those covers.

"It was a lot of fun," he laughs. "With the computer, we started putting things together roughly, and Chris approved them. Some covers were his idea and some were my idea. *Sunny Side Up* was my idea, with the heads [of the New Main Street Singers] in the egg yolks in the cooking pan. There was *Pickin'* on the back of a pickup truck, and *Wishin'* with a wishing well."

One of the challenges re-creating the album covers of the 1960s involved the actors' appearances. They needed to be in their twenties again, when most of the performers were a good two-and-a-half decades beyond that age. "We used a company called Digital Fusion that helped us with aging them correctly," Garrity explains. "We got old photographs of when all these guys and gals were younger. There was a lot of digital work to make them look younger and thinner. We did as much as we could with makeup and putting wigs on them.

"There was a lot of stuff to do, and it was all done in the first few days before we actually started shooting the movie," notes Garrity. "There was a lot of stuff; a lot of documentary footage of the groups in clubs and at fes-tivals like the Newport Festival. We did those in parking lots with platforms and banners, and we built little mini–Greenwich Village clubs, and little sets where they were signing their contracts with Steinbloom.

"All of these sets were in a little stage area," Garrity remembers. "There was a soundproof booth where the Folksmen were singing away, with the microphone hanging ('Singin"). Then we moved over and did the little graveyard set for Mitch Cohen's album (*Calling It Quits*). We had a little padded room set, with a fish-eyed lens to look down at him.

"The set with Mitch and Mickey — with the heart floating behind them, and they were in the clouds — was done with chicken wire and a rented sky prop. All of these things were lined up and we slam-bammed through them, and it was a lot of fun. We were all hoping it was going to work, and it did. It was very surreal, but everybody was ready for it."

The photos of album covers for the film were designed to evoke memories of certain signature albums of the age. "Some of them were almost rip-offs," Garrity laughs. "*The Serendipity Singers* were the basis for [*The New Main Street Singers*.] *Meet Mitch and Mickey* was, of course, *Meet the Beatles*. We had a great photographer, Joe Pugliese ... and Chris just loved him."

MIGHTY SERIOUS

A Mighty Wind began principal photography on May 21, 2002, and commenced its twenty-three-day shooting schedule. Though the film's events were supposed to occur in New York, the majority of filming was completed in Los Angeles. Many of the actors were a little out of their element, never having sung or played instruments on camera before, but one performer was probably a bit more concerned than the rest, Eugene Levy.

His character, the sympathetic but whacked out Mitch, is a troubled sort; a former folk god. Mitch has been in and out of a mental institution for the past two decades, never holding on to a job other than at a flower shop. He is a serious guy who takes serious medication, and his arc is a serious one.

"This was a big move into emotions, more than the others," Garrity considers. "Eugene was worried about his character and what he was doing."

"I know we venture into an area in this film that we didn't go to in other movies certainly with the storyline with me and Catherine,"[18] Levy informed Erin Cullin in an interview for *Empire Movies*.

Adding to the stress level, Levy developed an unusual, stop-and-go, almost sputtering dialect for the perpetually out-of-it, presumably heavily drugged Mitch. He denied rumors that the character was based either on the Prince of Darkness, Ozzy Osbourne, or the Beach Boys' Brian Wilson. Instead, Levy said, he found some inspiration in an "unbelievably intense and waaay over the top"[19] artist he observed at an L.A. art gallery.

"People just didn't know how to react," Levy told *MacLean's* about the unusual Mitch's stammering speech and strange mannerisms. "I said to Chris, 'Boy I feel like I've created a cliff that might be too high to jump off.' He said, 'Well, it's a brave choice.'"[20]

But Levy need not have worried. His characterization of the troubled Mitch impressed — and touched — just about everybody who saw his work. "There's a sweetness attached to his work that I think people get," Deborah Divine, his wife of twenty-six years, told *People*.[21]

"I've always been Eugene's biggest fan," adds Willard. "He can't help but be funny. I just worship Eugene."

When the film premiered, critics felt the same way, and Levy won a New

York Film Critics Circle award for best supporting actor and was nominated (alongside O'Hara) for a Golden Satellite award for best supporting role in a comedy or musical.

STAGECRAFT 101

Early on, it was decided that the interior of the Orpheum Theater in Los Angeles would double as New York City's Town Hall in *A Mighty Wind*. It was there, on the Orpheum's stage, that the three folk acts from the 1960s would make their comeback of sorts. But before that could happen, the venue had to be carefully vetted by organizer Jonathan Steinbloom, the obsessive-compulsive played with glee by returning repertory member Bob Balaban.

In one memorable scene, Balaban was joined by Michael Hitchcock, who played Larry E. Turpin, the put-upon event coordinator at Town Hall. Walking side by side, the two characters had some quality time together, strolling through the location and going over virtually every detail of the arena, from a floral arrangement with apple blossoms to the stage, where Steinbloom weighed whether the props on the stage looked adequately three-dimensional from the perspective of the audience.

"When I got to the theater, it was this kind of dichotomy of somebody who was in charge of something they knew absolutely nothing about, and yet was very controlling, probably based on fear, given his fearful background," Balaban explains.

"Bob is a genius," says Hitchcock. "I had no idea Bob's character was going to be so picky. I had no idea. We shot those scenes in order, so the very first time I found out that Bob was going to be picky was when we were in the scene with the truck being unloaded. I was trying to make a conscious choice as an actor not to be overly negative, because Hamilton was that way, and I was trying to play a guy who was helpful. He wasn't particularly enamored of folk music, but wasn't against it, either. It was just one of many concerts at Town Hall."

Inevitably, the scene continued, taking Balaban and Hitchcock to that floral arrangement that so vexed John Steinbloom.

"So I didn't really plan anything," Balaban continues, "but I looked at that plant and thought, 'What can I say about that plant?' It occurred to me that it was dangerous, so I went down that path with poor Michael Hitchcock."

"When Bob started doing that, I thought, 'Oh boy, this is something!'" Hitchcock exclaims. "As an improvisor, what a wonderful gift to be given.

Here he is, this annoying character, and it gives me something to play, something to react to. As an improvisor, you can't ask for a better gift. To me, the most ridiculous scene was him talking about the flowers that could be dangerous because you might trip on the stems. There was so much going on with him that it made my reactions easy."

"He made the plants out to be these dangerous things to stay away from that would stick you and kill you," laughs Garrity, "but that's not something that we knew was going to happen. That's what is funny about these movies. These are talented actors who see something around them, it sparks them, and they go with it. I don't know how they do it."

"We had a couple of locations that were not used in the film," Balaban continues. "We had to discuss the selling of the tickets and the holding back of certain press seats, and it was really interesting, because Hitchcock did start to be driven mad by me. At some point, he just stormed up the stairs carrying the entire floral arrangement. I don't remember if that made it into the movie or not, but I do know that when we finally made it onstage, it was a total surprise to me that I drove him crazy to the point where he would actually hit me."

"By that time," explains Hitchcock, "it had been about two days of Bob haranguing me, and I think I'd just had it. I didn't have anything else to say. What was I going to do? So I just gave him a good whack on the head, and the crew started to laugh, and Christopher started to laugh."

"We were all there, and it was absolutely hilarious, and nobody knew it was coming," Garrity remembers. "Everybody just exploded into laughs for about a minute. That combination of two people was just hilarious."

"I honestly thought it would be cut, because they laughed fairly quickly," Hitchcock remembers. "It was pretty immediate ... but Bob screamed pretty loudly, and I stayed in character, and then they yelled, 'cut,' everybody laughed, and it was such a strange thing."

"I don't think that Hitchcock necessarily planned to do something like that," Balaban points out. "I just think that there came a point where there was nothing he was saying that was affecting me in any way, and the only thing he could do to make me stop was hit me, so this thing emerged. It wasn't a decision by anybody, necessarily. It had to happen.

"I think that some of the best moments in these movies are when you set two people out with each other and something happens that nobody decided was going to happen," Balaban muses. "It becomes like life — you can't point a finger at someone and say, 'He started it; she started it.' It just happens because we were on a path and we believed in our path and Christopher allowed this to happen."

Regardless of how the scene emerged, Hitchcock's spontaneous tap on Balaban's noggin became one of the laugh-out-loud funny moments in A Mighty Wind, and was highlighted often in trailers and commercials.

THE LAST TRAIN TO CRABBEVILLE

Another moment in *A Mighty Wind*, Mitch Cohen's visit to Leonard Crabbe's model train haven in the basement of his home in Albany, dubbed Crabbeville, was "probably one of the worst moments" of the whole shoot, according to production designer Joe Garrity. "This was a day where you assumed something was going to happen ... and it didn't.

"We didn't have the budget to do our own gigantic set-up ... and we went to a couple of places ... [until] we found this wonderful and weird house in the valley," says Garrity. "The owner was a wealthy man with a movie theater in his house and a train room, and this [what you see on screen] was his train room. We went there, and we loved it, but nobody was ever there to make the trains work. Chris said, 'This is great ... as long as the trains work.'"

Well, fast-forward to the day of the shoot, when Garrity met up with the location people at the house to determine if the miniature trains were working. They assured him the vehicles would operate, but when Garrity probed deeper, he learned that though some trains were indeed working just fine, these were not actually the ones he needed for the shot.

After some toil, it was established that the trains the company had selected were *not* going to run, no matter how hard they tried.

"So everybody comes [to the house] and I had to go to Chris and say [there's been a] 'Fuck up!'" Garrity explains. "He was bummed out, but we made it work. We used monofilament and pulled that little train through, but it was the one time on all the films that I've worked on with him that something didn't work right, but it was a funny scene anyway.

"I went underneath [the display] and showed him where he could put the actors, so it looked like *Land of the Giant* (1968–1970), and he used that. And they [Piddock and Levy] were hilarious. The train was a little pathetic, but we showed enough of it to see that it was quite an elaborate situation there. But if you notice, there are not a lot of trains running around.

"We felt betrayed by how the location was represented, and disappointed, but in the end nobody knew about that," Garrity reports. "It worked out fine. So that was Crabbeville."

WHA' HAPPENED? FRED HAPPENED!

Fred Willard joined the cast of *A Mighty Wind*, and learned that his character,

Mike LaFontaine, would not be one of the performers, but the overbearing manager of the New Main Street Singers instead. He remembers his initial conversations with Guest about the role.

"Chris told me that I was a former comedy club owner, and I said, 'Why don't we take this a step further — that he was on a sitcom once that ran for a year and then it failed?' You know how these guys are, the next thing you know, they become agents or producers or managers, particularly in music. They're a big rock group for one year and now they have a recording studio.

"So I came up with some catchphrases that he might have had, like they all do," Willard explains. "I thought it was funny that this guy was like, 'Let's get this out of the way — I know what you want to hear — the old catchphrase.' And of course, nobody remembers [my] series."

Playing such a colorful role, Willard wanted to alter his appearance somewhat, but wasn't sure how to do so, until he struck upon the idea of dyeing his hair blond.

"It was actually my wife's idea," reveals Willard. "She showed me a picture of a group, I think it was Aerosmith. She said, 'What you want to be is this aging rocker trying to look young with blond spiked hair and black roots.' I said, 'Gee that's great, I'd like to top what I did in *Best in Show*, and I'm up against these guys that are singing and doing their own music."

From there, it was a matter of settling on a suitably flashy wardrobe. "I was walking down Hollywood Boulevard one day, and there was a clothing store with very loud clothes and there was a very loud white/yellow zoot suit, and I thought, 'God, I wish there was some place I could wear a suit like that.' I said 'Wait a minute, I think I could wear that as my character in the movie!' So I walked in and it was eighty dollars and I bought it," says Willard. "Then a few weeks later, I was in Cleveland and saw a downtown store with a bright electric-blue suit."

The moment of truth, however, was to present this new appearance to the film's director.

"I went in, and the wardrobe people loved the suits," Willard remembers. "And I had an earring, a dangling earring with a little cross — like Barry Bonds. Christopher Guest did not know I had dyed my hair blond, and he walked into the wardrobe room and did a double take at my hair and said, 'Oh,' and then looked at my suit and said, 'Oh.'

"But the wardrobe lady jumped in and said, 'It's wonderful; it'll work.' She sold him on it, but Chris said, 'We're going to have to bring your hair down a little,' so it wasn't as bright yellow as I wanted. He also said, 'I don't like the earring.' I said, 'How about a little stud in the ear?' and he said, 'Okay.' I thought it was perfect for this character who was trying to keep up with the times and still living in the past."

When it came time to shoot his first scene, his one-on-one interview revealing Mike LaFontaine's history and background, Willard had no problem coming up with material for the blustery, dynamic fellow.

"I guess a roll of film goes about twenty-two minutes. I went for twenty-two minutes and then heard 'Cut!' Christopher just walked into the room and said, 'That's one-third of the movie right there."

STAGE FRIGHTS

Back when *Waiting for Guffman* was shot, the most challenging aspect of the shoot had been filming the play, *Red, White and Blaine*. Similarly, on *A Mighty Wind*, it looked as though the most difficult days would involve capturing on film the "Ode to Irving" concert. The show involved, among other things, several hundred extras, actors playing instruments, and lots of music recorded live.

There was minimal blocking devised beforehand in order to keep the events real, and camera crews were armed with handheld cameras, communicating with Guest when he wasn't onstage actually performing in character as one of the Folksmen. "If I was not in a scene I'd have a radio, and the director of photography wore an earpiece, and I'd call out the shots I wanted as we were going,"[22] he told the *Star Tribune*.

The first element of getting the concert right had been to create the appropriate mood and atmosphere for the venue, and that was designer Garrity's task. "We knew it shouldn't be too elaborate, but I thought to use the Greenwich Village Arch," Garrity remembers. "There was a city drop behind that and a Washington Square scene."

Also onstage were large, two-dimensional representations of musical instruments. "These instruments were so important," Garrity says. "[These] acoustic instruments leaned kind of casually against this arch. Chris went for it, and then we brought in each of the band logos.

"The Folksmen logo was reminiscent of the sign Eat at Joe's, so we used the same shape with the arrow, as if it were a highway sign on the road. We used the heart as the shape for Mitch and Mickey, and we used the colors of turquoise and yellow in a round shape for the New Main Street Singers."

Harry Shearer remembers the concert as a complex set-up, and one that might have vexed less experienced directors. "When we were shooting the concert sequences, [Guest] had a film crew and a video crew, because he was shooting videotape for the video of the concert.

"He had two crews, two lighting teams, and all these actors," Shearer recalls. "He had to be nervous, because he said we were going to do it live, and we had to be ready and able, yet he was the calmest presence on that day. Whatever tumult he was going through — and I saw some of it — he just never passed it on to anybody else that I saw. He was able to contain it and keep giving the actors what we needed to do these performances. I was really impressed with that. He was the soul of calmness in those situations."

"It was a few-week period, at least a week, for sure, that I was there," Theaker remembers of her participation in the audience. "I couldn't stop laughing because every once in a while, Chris from the stage would say, 'Okay, the guy in the third row — he's got to go,' because he was sleeping through it. A lot of the extras weren't familiar at all with his movies or work and found it so tedious and boring that they would go to sleep. I couldn't believe it.

"There was one point during the playback with the Folksmen — I can't remember the song — where Chris forgot the lyrics," Theaker recalls. "We were all laughing because we were punchy by that point."

IT'S UP TO YOU, NEW YORK

Although *A Mighty Wind*'s events ostensibly occurred in the Big Apple, the production company had gotten by just staying on the West Coast, using California as a double throughout the shoot. The company filmed not just at the Orpheum Theater, but in Pasadena (for the Crabbe's Albany residence), at the Natural History Museum in Los Angeles (as New York City Hall), at Hollywood Park (as the Meshak Notin Casino's Little Big Room in upstate New York), and Mount Saint Mary's College (as Jonathan Steinbloom's ritzy apartment). Still, it was felt that to lend the production verisimilitude, some New York location shooting was required.

So, after the majority of the film was shot in L.A., the cast and crew made a beeline for the East Coast in the summer of 2002 and shot in New York for two incredibly fast-paced days. Waiting there was Rob Covelman, a graduate of the Philadelphia College of Art who had worked on many independent films. Covelman served as property master on such projects as *Living in Oblivion* (1995), *Big Night* (1995), *The Big Kahuna* (1999), and the HBO presentation of *The Vagina Monologues* (2002). He was looking forward to his stint on a Christopher Guest film, even though he understood it would be a rush job.

"Everybody that came out from Los Angeles was really, really nice," Covelman remembers. "I was very happy to be working on the film, because I liked Guest's films, and I thought they were funny, and I liked their sensibility. The designer [Garrity] was great. Eugene Levy, Michael McKean, and Harry Shearer — they couldn't have been nicer."

But time was of the essence on this whirlwind shoot. "The pace of filming was fast, because we were only shooting for two days, and had a lot to cover," Covelman remembers. "They had to get all their locations in." The pace was uncomfortably fast, actually, with the company making two company moves a day, meaning that they were in three locations in a single day of shooting.

Covelman's responsibilities as property master in New York included a week and a half of preparation leading up to the two days of shooting. He had to locate a remote broadcasting truck to place outside Town Hall for the concert, and then get the correct PBN signage on it. All the actors' musical instruments were shipped out to New York from Los Angeles, except that Covelman needed to find a cello case he could tie to the roof of the station wagon that Alan Barrows was seen driving in one scene.

An uncomfortable incident in New York involved a taxi acquired for the film. On the day they were to shoot a scene with Bob Balaban in the cab, the air conditioning didn't work in the vehicle, leaving cast and crew sweltering in a hundred degree heat. Reportedly, Guest was not happy.

Although he saw Guest for only a few days (the film's director arrived a day or two before shooting commenced), Covelman confirms what other talent have also (respectfully) said about Mr. Guest, specifically that he is a man with tremendous *gravitas*, who takes his work very, very seriously.

"His actual personality was a million miles away from what you would think a comedian would be," Covelman describes. "I never saw him smile, never heard him crack a joke."

"We only went to New York for a week and shot some things," Garrity remembers of the stint, "and then proceeded not to use most of it, but we did shoot outside the Town Hall."

After the hectic schedule in New York City, *A Mighty Wind* was officially a wrap.

MIGHTY SCISSORS

Just like *Waiting for Guffman* and *Best in Show*, a tremendous amount of material was trimmed for the final cut of *A Mighty Wind*. The whittling process this time took the film from eighty hours of footage down to less than ninety minutes. Whole performances, whole story arcs, were trimmed from the proceedings.

"There were a lot of characters who did not survive the final edit because they ultimately weren't needed to serve the story," Deb Theaker says. "Chris's character, Alan Barrows, was married to a beautiful Asian woman. Much like Yoko Ono broke up the Beatles, the sense you got was that she broke up the Folksmen."

Another character, the late Irving Steinbloom's trophy wife, was also trimmed from the final cut. "What was missing from the movie is that our father married a bit of a grasping showgirl. He found this happy marriage with this other woman who wasn't our mother. I don't know if we all decided this, or it was something I decided, I can't remember, but there was a sense that he had left the bulk of his fortune to his second wife, so all the kids felt jilted by that," Theaker remembers, "but in the end, it wasn't needed."

Actress Freda Foh Shen played Melinda Barrows, Darlene Karden portrayed Shirley Steinbloom, and their entire presence in the film was excised but for momentary glimpses of them in the audience at the concert.

"Freda was there for all of the shoot, so I was very sad to see her and Darlene not ending up in the final cut," Theaker says. "Ultimately, they didn't need [their roles] and it didn't serve the story, much like my story in *Best in Show*."

Fred Willard remembers one of Mike LaFontaine's scenes that also didn't make the final cut. "There was a wonderful scene where [the New Main Street Singers] was rehearsing, and I just walked through them and I had a cup of coffee in my hand and I would talk to them, and I was completely oblivious to the fact that they were singing a song. In fact, I shook one of the kids' hands and said, 'I'm Mike LaFontaine, welcome to the group.'"

Another deleted scene that didn't make the final cut was a clip of Mitch and Mickey's appearance on a seventies-era detective series like Peter Falk's *Columbo* (1971–77) or *McMillan and Wife*. *Seinfeld*'s (1990–1998) Patrick Warburton played the detective in the scene, and the joke was that past-their-prime musical acts like Sonny and Cher (or in this universe, Mitch and Mickey), often ended up guesting on detective shows as a ratings stunt.

A news conference in which Mitch artfully compares folk and rap music was also left on the cutting room floor, along with some rehearsals by the New Main Street Singers at the Smashbox studios in Culver City, where they tormented Chris Moynihan's "newbie" with demeaning songs like "XYZ."

Of the songs, Mitch and Mickey's "Killington Hill," and the Folksmen's "Children of the Sun" and "Corn Wine," disappeared from the movie, and subsequently, the soundtrack.

A MIGHTY PERFORMANCE

A preview screening of *A Mighty Wind* was held on Wednesday, April 9,

2003, at 7:30 PM at the American Film Institute's Silver Theatre and Cultural Center in Silver Spring, Maryland, with Christopher Guest, Eugene Levy, Harry Shearer, and Michael McKean all scheduled to attend.[23]

The film opened in fourteen major cities on April 16, before going wide in May and taking the country by storm. During its spring run at the box office, *A Mighty Wind* repeated the financial success of *Best in Show*, grossing nearly eighteen million dollars in just a few months.

Fred Willard remembers the premiere that he attended. "I saw Chris afterward, at the party, and Chris always gets mad at me because I don't come to the screenings. He must think I'm above it all, but I just don't want to know what got in. So I went up to him sincerely and said, 'This is a wonderful movie.' Chris said, 'Oh, you didn't walk out?' and I said, 'I'm serious, this is a wonderful movie.'"

By and large, critics agreed. Many were wowed by the efforts of Guest and his talented band of improvisors, and some viewers even noted that "it appears that as each mockumentary gets made, it's turning more into a movie."[24] This expression of praise not was meant to demean *Waiting for Guffman* or *Best in Show* as being somehow less than real movies, only an acknowledgment that *A Mighty Wind* delved so much deeper in expressing resonant and poignant emotion, as well as humor. It had a transcendental quality, and the film's characters were so involving that it didn't matter when — or if — the next joke came. Jokes weren't important; audiences were invested in the story.

Another critic, Mike LaSalle of the *San Francisco Chronicle*, joyously proclaimed "*A Mighty Wind* arrives as a breath of fresh air, with its smart ensemble, subtle wit, and careful observation of humanity."[25]

Matt Zoller Seitz, writing for the *New York Press*, called Guest's latest opus "a great comedy — Guest's most nuanced, controlled, expertly acted so far, and perhaps his deepest."[26]

Other critics also detected that the film was much more than a laugh-a-minute comedy and recommended *A Mighty Wind* almost wholly on the basis of its deeply touching emotional resonances. "*A Mighty Wind* is glutted with inspired details ... but it boils down to Mitch and Mickey, whose culminating performance onstage verges on the transcendent,"[27] wrote Michael Atkinson in the *Village Voice*.

Writing in *USA Today*, Mike Clark declared that "the movie itself displays such twisted affection for its performers that it's unexpectedly moving when the entire cast sings onstage in a preppy grand finale."[28]

Others, including the *Atlanta-Journal Constitution*, praised the film's "tender heart,"[29] and *Christian Century* enthused that it was "the Mitch-and-Mickey kiss that stops the show" and provided the most wonderful ending in movies of the year 2003.[30]

The film's music was singled out, too, with the *Hollywood Reporter* noting that "not since *Nashville* [1975] has a cast done such a good job of providing their own tunes."[31]

Some dissenters included Roger Ebert, who awarded the film just two-and-a-half stars because he felt it crossed the line from being a comedy to being a straight musical performance. In the *New York Observer*, Andrew Sarris also commented that in his opinion the satirists had lost "their bite," and as a result "we are all a little less free."[32]

"You're never going to please everyone," says Michael Hitchcock, who was amused at the double standard applied to these documentary-style comedies. The very same critics who felt *Best in Show* and *Waiting for Guffman* were clever but cruel, now seemed to adopt the opposite stance. "*A Mighty Wind* is absolutely an affectionate film, and what's so funny about that is that I've read critics and some of them were angry that *A Mighty Wind* wasn't as mean as they thought it should be!"

When it came time to hand out awards at year's end, however, the critical majority did not forget *A Mighty Wind*. The Broadcast Film Critics Association selected the anthem "A Mighty Wind" by Levy, Guest, and McKean as best song of the year. The film also won a best music award from the Seattle Film Critics Circle.

Then, in early February 2004 came the best news thus far: the song "A Mighty Wind" picked up a Grammy Award for best song written for a motion picture, television or other visual medium.

But there was more to come. The Boston Society of Film Critics nominated *A Mighty Wind*'s cast as best ensemble. The film was also nominated (along with all its cast members) for a best screenplay award by the Independent Spirit Awards. The Golden Satellites nominated "A Kiss at the End of the Rainbow" as best song for a movie or television program, and made note of Levy and O'Hara as nominees in the categories of best supporting actor and best supporting actress.

Finally, when the Academy Awards were announced, nobody was surprised to hear that "A Kiss at the End of the Rainbow" had been nominated as one of the year's best achievements in music written for a motion picture: original song. Levy and O'Hara memorably performed the song on the Academy Awards show broadcast to a huge worldwide audience.

For those who couldn't get enough of the film's smart, funny folk tunes, the groups reunited in a series of concerts that played across the country, including in Los Angeles and New York. At some shows, Bob Balaban was present to introduce the singers, and Willard, Hitchcock, and Theaker all made appearances. Fans flocked to these events, pleasing all the cast members who had worked so hard to forge something special.

"It was magnificent," Deb Theaker describes one concert. "The audience was rabid and die-hard. Mike Hitchcock and I got mobbed and had to pose for pictures and sign autographs for a good forty-five minutes before the show began. The audience was going bananas. It was like being at a U2 concert.

"Some of the cast of *Will and Grace* (1998–) and John Goodman were there," Theaker recalls. "They were giddy with excitement. By the time Mitch and Mickey closed the show, much like the concert in the film, their harmonies were so beautiful and so lush — they'd gotten so good at it, that it was breathtaking."

Also, it must be noted these concerts attempt to be as accurate to the events of the film as is possible, and that means, among other things, Harry Shearer now appears on stage as Mark Shubb during these concerts wearing a dress and a blond wig. It's almost poetic.

GUEST SHOTS

LOCO MAN: One of the Folksmen tunes is the very funny calypso song, "Loco Man."

"This is about as far from real calypso as you can possibly get," Harry Shearer, the song's composer, explains. "We say in the live show that we were trying to introduce this thing called *folk-lypso*.

"Real calypso music has a totally different tempo and it's sort of the rap music of the islands, because as it's grown up in the last fifty years, it's very topical and always commenting on things, and it's kind of sassy. It has nothing in common with 'Loco Man.' What Americans have heard of calypso and what 'Loco Man' is sort of making fun of is what Harry Belafonte's hits were — 'Mathilda,' 'Day-O.' Trying to put a little island sauce on basically a fairly New York concept."

OUTLAWIN' "G": There is apparently no letter *g* in the folk music alphabet, and Christopher Guest, ever the stickler for accuracy, adheres to that fact with the songs sung by the Folksmen, as Mark Shubb notes in a deleted scene.

For example, the Kingston Trio performed songs with titles such as "Hard Travelin'," "Early Mornin' Train," "I'm Goin' Home," and "Rovin' Gambler, This Train." Arlo Guthrie has sung *g*-deficient tunes like "Stealin'" and "Walkin' Down the Line." Even Peter, Paul, and Mary got in on the fun and sang "Blowin' in the Wind," sans *g*.

Not to be outdone, the Folksmen willfully subtracted the letter *g* from all of their album titles, including *Pickin'*, *Wishin'*, and *Wanderin'*. Their sales went down when they broke this covenant with the audience, releasing an album entitled *Saying Something*. That's a double no-no, as Mark Shubb reports.

REAL PEOPLE — SORT OF: As in the other documentary-style comedies of Christopher Guest, many of the characters were based in part on people that the actors were familiar with.

"Leonard Crabbe is actually based on someone I know," Jim Piddock explains. "Incredibly hail-fellow-well-met. Incredibly boring. Will just talk and talk about anything, a very specific sort of English character."

Jennifer Coolidge's bizarre character, Amber, also had a basis in real life. "Amber's accent was based on a foreign exchange student I met in college," she reported. "Then [the accent] turned into something else; it sounds like a combination of a Scandinavian, Czechoslovakian, and a deaf baby."[33]

Naomi Steinbloom, Deborah Theaker's character, was not based on any one person, but she recalls that Guest had some strict requirements for the role. "When Chris called me, he said, 'She's really emotional.' And I went, 'What do you mean?' And he said, 'I need you to cry.'"

Theaker complied, playing Naomi as not just a weeper, but in her own words, "A big, lumpy malcontent. She probably grew up with the family fortune and didn't really have any skills. Even though she had really expensive clothes and stuff, she was just a lumpy, unhappy person."

Interestingly, in both *Waiting for Guffman* and *A Mighty Wind*, Theaker portrays characters who shed a great many tears, and also end up in the audience watching the third act's big show. This is probably no coincidence.

"I think [Guest] does gravitate in a sense to casting people the way he perceives them," Theaker suggests. "Everybody has a comfort zone, and I think mine runs to vulnerable. I play vulnerable better than I play tough, and maybe that's where that comes from."

Michael Hitchcock's character, Laurence E. Turpin, was not based on any real person, but he had an interesting history. "One of the things that was cut from the film was that Laurence's mother was an opera singer that had Tourette's syndrome. So he came from a musical family, even though his mother had a bit of a flaw."

On the other hand, one of Turpin's most memorable lines came out of the actor's real life experience.

"I remember I said something in the final cut about, 'Maybe I should just get some carnations and put them in a beer stein.' That came from real life because one time, my dad forgot my mom's anniversary, and he brought her carnations in a beer stein, and I've always remembered that. She was not too pleased about having that as her anniversary gift. That's always been the nadir of flower giving, so that's where my mind went."

UNCURIOUS GEORGE: Paul Dooley took the joke about disinterested George Menschell to the *n*th degree, especially in the live concerts performed around the country after *A Mighty Wind* premiered.

"At the end of our set, the string players threw their picks into the audience," he says. "I guess that's something that's done in the music world. You have your name on the pick, and it's a big souvenir for a kid in the front row. So I started throwing my pick to the audience, even though I never even touch my guitar. In one instance in Vancouver, I just broke my guitar over a chair."

SELF LOVE: A running joke in *A Mighty Wind* involves Mitch as he attempts to practice his guitar in a seedy motel. In the next room, passionate lovers expressively moan and gasp, even shaking the wall with their fervent lovemaking. The funny thing about this is that Guest is the one on the soundtrack giving voice to both participants, male *and* female lovers. You can tell, because they both sound like ventriloquists.

BEE FLAT: The same day that *A Mighty Wind*'s crew filmed Crabbeville and its malfunctioning miniature train, there was another problem to contend with. "That was the same day we shot the New Main Street Singers at [Six Flags] Magic Mountain in front of the roller coaster," Garrity explains. "We got a shot of the roller coaster behind them, and it was kind of pathetic seeing this has-been group in the middle of a park where nobody's really paying attention to them, and people are screaming and yelling and they're trying to sing these sweet songs.

"But a whole swarm of bees came around at the base of the ride and they had to clear it, so the roller coaster had to stop," Garrity reveals. "Chris was bummed out about that."

BABA GHANOUJ ANYONE? "There was a scene of the three Folksmen walking in Greenwich Village," Rob Covelman explains, "going to a place where they had performed, but now it was a falafel shop. They pointed to a brick wall and said something like, 'This is where we performed,' and all the customers are eating falafels behind them. It's a very funny scene."

Covelman also remembers a few other scenes set in New York City that didn't make the final cut. "There was a scene of Christopher Guest in Central Park walking around, which didn't get in, and scenes of Michael McKean in the Village, reminiscing."

THE LOLLIPOP GUILD: Fred Willard got a kick out of a one-liner that didn't make it into the final cut. In the Big Apple, Mike LaFontaine spoke at a press conference to publicize the New Main Street Singers, and in it, he demeans and bulldozes a long-suffering deputy mayor.

"That guy who was the deputy mayor, he's kind of a short guy with a moustache," Willard explains, "and in one of the takes I said, 'Well, thank you, Mr. Deputy Mayor, and give my regards to the rest of the Lollipop Guild.' Which I thought was wonderful, and in the movie it got right there, and he cut that line. Maybe the guy felt hurt. He wasn't a midget, he was just a short guy. I have to ask Chris, but he's a tough guy to question."

Another Willard quip that didn't get into the movie involved him suggesting to LaFontaine's off-screen interviewer: "Listen, if you're in town for long, there's a wonderful restaurant. It's so good that they have their own vomitorium."

NOT SUCH A DUMMY: The Guest aficionado will recognize and relish throughout the filmmaker's canon his self-reflexive jokes about previous films and characters. In *Waiting for Guffman*, an alien wore a costume with the number eleven emblazoned on his chest. In *A Mighty Wind*, Alan Barrows briefly adopts a falsetto to sing a portion of "Skeletons of Quinto." After doing so, Alan notes that he sounds like a ventriloquist, a direct reference to Harlan Pepper's chosen hobby in *Best in Show*.

FOLK BOOM: Intentionally or not, the composers of all the songs in *A Mighty Wind* have ignited a mini-folk boom among music fans, as well as their fellow actors, many of whom just can't get enough of *A Mighty Wind*'s soundtrack.

Paul Dooley is particularly fond of "Potato's in the Paddy Wagon." "That's my favorite song. It's so catchy," he says. "When I'm in my car, I play it. I track back, and play it two or three times. It's so authentic sounding. It sounds like it was written a hundred years ago in the Appalachians."

Like many fans, Willard harbors a soft spot for the Oscar-nominated "A Kiss at the End of the Rainbow." "I love that song. Michael McKean invited us [Willard and his wife] to a Christmas party and we went, and there was just so much talent there," Willard recalls. "People would get up and sing songs and I went up like a kid and asked him, 'Michael, will you and Annette do "A Kiss at the End of the Rainbow?"' He said, 'Sure, Fred.' I just love that song. I said, 'Michael, that could be a huge hit!'"

AND THE JOE GARAGIOLA SENSE OF HUMOR AWARD GOES TO: Peter, Paul, and Mary's Paul Stookey, who told reporter Tim Shellberg that he thought *A Mighty Wind* "could've been funnier." Though Stookey acknowledged that the film was believable, he noted there were a whole lot of areas that Guest "missed," and that there "could've been greater animosity between characters."[34]

A TASTE IS IN THE AIR

Bluntly stated, *A Mighty Wind* is Christopher Guest's finest film. *Waiting for Guffman* and *Best in Show* may arguably be judged funnier in the final analysis, but *A Mighty Wind* is surely the best presentation overall, blending laughs, catchy music, and most important, finely crafted characterizations.

Though each of the documentary-style comedies evoke a sense of sympathy for the *dramatis personae*, *A Mighty Wind* goes further and digs deeper, adopting a sensitive approach that makes the audience truly feel the pathos of Mitch and Mickey's story, and their exquisite, timeless kiss. In some fashion, *A Mighty Wind* aims higher than the other observational comedies, and the result is a film that is often downright suspenseful because viewers feel invested in the people, the story, and its ultimate outcome.

Crafting a film like this is like assembling all the right building blocks in the right order, and as has hopefully been demonstrated throughout this book, for Guest that equation is reality plus one step further. So forget about being funny or emotional for a moment, the success of *A Mighty Wind* begins with its solid foundation, a detailed and accurate re-creation of the world of the early 1960s, an epoch right before the British invasion and the ascension of the Beatles, a time when folk music reigned supreme in America. The film employs real archival footage from the era where appropriate and then crafts a world around that footage to resemble the real thing.

"The attention to detail is excellent,"[35] wrote critic Margaret Agnew in New Zealand's *The Press*, and she was referring not just to the carefully created album covers, or the footage meant to represent early TV appearances.

Indeed, the atmosphere of reality enveloping *A Mighty Wind* emanates from the attention paid to making these groups representative of the era. That bailiwick includes song titles and lyrics, group costumes, and much more.

Christopher Guest and his cohorts have gone into considerable detail to disavow any sense that the groups in the film are meant to represent one particular band in the history of folk music, but on a more global scale, he has paid close attention to the genre and its players. For instance, his distinctive neuftet, the New Main Street Singers, boast a special sound, thanks to the harmonies of their nine vocalists. Tellingly, there were also nine Serendipity Singers and nine New Christy Minstrels back in the day. As a group, the former was characterized by their "youth, energy, and feelings."[36] They also wore blue sweaters and ties as a kind of ad hoc uniform (like the sweater vests of the fastidious New Main Street Singers).

Like Terry's group, the Serendipity Singers and the New Christy Minstrels also had a ratio of two women to seven men. And once more like the New Christy Minstrels, the New Main Street Singers very clearly "spread light-heartedness and prompt you to fling your cares to the wind," according to the liner notes on their album *The Wandering Minstrels*.[37]

In fact, those relentlessly upbeat sentiments are transmitted in the New Main Street Singers' staple, "Just That Kinda Day," which admonishes listeners neither to fret, nor frown, lest they bruise their hearts.

A Serendipity Singers tune, "Sailin' Away" could be the antecedent of the New Main Street Singers' sea chanty, "Fare Away," with its peculiar lyrics, "This is where I long to be; sailin' away on the lonely sea."

In general, the vibe is similar, and yet it is also clear that the New Main Street Singers, while not representing either the New Christy Minstrels or the Serendipity Singers in particular, are clearly meant to come from the same school of thought and music. Like *This Is Spinal Tap*, it's a more a genre thing than a particular person or band.

It's very much the same story with the delightful Folksmen. They could very well be the Kingston Trio, the Brothers Four, the Chad Mitchell Trio, the Lettermen, or the Tripjacks. They inherit the qualities of a different style than do the New Main Street Singers, but one altogether common in the ethos of 1960s folk music. They are self-described troubadours — composers and performers who are traveling men and bring culture and music to far-flung towns and cities.

Like the Brothers Four, the trademark of the Folksmen could be "Having fun with a good song."[38] Like the Chad Mitchell Trio, the Folksmen sing with "vigor and enthusiasm."[39] One of the Chad Mitchell Trio even refers to one of his bandmates as a historian before performing the song "Lizzie Borden," a disarming ditty (literally) about the hatchet murderer in Massachusetts, just as Alan Barrows introduces Mark Shubb as the group historian prior to their aborted performance of "Skeletons of Quinto."

Not unlike the Lettermen, the Folksmen can perform a "rare variety of styles, both pop and folk,"[40] their repertory boasting diverse songs including the politically conscious "Children of the Sun" and "Skeletons of Quinto"; the calypso "Loco Man"; their ages-of-man song, "Corn Wine"; their audience participation piece, "Barnyard Symphony"; and their pop hit, "Old Joe's Place."

The great thing about such groups is that they actually did play a variety of musical styles within the rubric of "folk" and thus Guest, McKean, and Shearer are granted opportunities to write and perform variations on many different brands of music under the same catch-all umbrella.

One such style is seen in the song that might colloquially be termed "wanderin'," or the road tune. For the Tripjacks, this style might have been represented in the composition "Lonesome Traveler," which concerned a rambling fellow who traveled in the mountains, down in the valley, here and yonder, and alongside the rich and the poor.

"Every folk singer worth his salt talks about being a hobo on the tracks and wandering, and sings about where he went," explains Paul Dooley. "But [the Folksmen's] 'Never Did No Wanderin'" is all about where they *never* got to go. 'Never did no wandering after all. Never rode the river. Never climbed the mountain, never did no wanderin' high, never did no wanderin' low,'" he recites.

It's a comical variation on a song like "Lonesome Traveler," to be certain, but not a blatantly outrageous one, and that's why the humor is clever rather than stupid. The song is authentic-sounding.

"I love the line [in 'Old Joe's Place'], 'I often stop and think about a place I've never seen,'" Dooley adds. It's not so funny by itself, but within the context of folk music, it is very humorous indeed.

"They're really very good songs," Dooley says. "They're all satiric, but if you take that away, many people would just hear 'Never Did No Wanderin'" and think it's a really catchy song."

Another staple of the folk scene is the railroad disaster song. The Folksmen belt out "Blood on the Coals" on *A Mighty Wind*'s soundtrack, a tune about doomed Irish miners working in Kentucky who are accidentally mowed down by a train. Similarly, the Tripjacks sang "Drill, Ye Tarriers, Drill," a composition originally conceived in the nineteenth century, playing off the old adage that "there's an Irishman buried under every tie"[41] on the railroad.

Mitch and Mickey come from yet another tradition: the romantic couple. As such, they could be Sonny and Cher, Ian and Sylvia, or Richard and Mimi Farina. Like Sonny and Cher, Mitch and Mickey split up not just professionally, but personally. Interestingly, Mitch and Mickey first got together after Mitch had gotten beaten up and spent some time recuperating in a hospital, and Ian Towson initially learned guitar while convalescing in a hospital after a physical injury.

"A Kiss at the End of the Rainbow" isn't precisely the same thing as "I've Got You, Babe," but the song plays on the same principle: the perceived romantic dynamic between the two lead singers. Audiences like to believe that there is such a thing as true love, and that the petty irritations inherent in all relationships somehow don't exist among the rarified strata of performing stars on stage.

A Mighty Wind plays lightly with that notion, as expert witness after expert witness testifies to the cultural significance of the Mitch and Mickey kiss, an event heralded as perhaps penultimate in human experience. Of course, that balloon of pretension is punctured after the touching climax, when both artists back away from the kiss, and deny its importance in their emotional lives.

The climactic song "A Mighty Wind" plays on two interesting notions. First, "mighty" is a popular folk adjective (i.e., "Mighty Day"), and second, "wind" is a popular folk noun, present both in Ian and Sylvia's "Four Strong Winds" and Peter, Paul, and Mary's cover of the immortal Dylan tune, "Blowin' in the Wind." Considering such antecedents, "A Mighty Wind" is a safe and appropriate choice for a song title. It also happens to be very funny, a flatulence reference in the tradition of the *Spinal Tap* number "Break Like the Wind."

"The lyrics are clever, and if you listen to the lyrics, you get the joke," Fred Willard explains. "Like in 'A Mighty Wind,' that final line: 'It's blowing you and me.' If you listen, you go, 'God, do you think he realized what he was saying?'"

As Willard states, the lyrics are funny, but not at the expense of the film's reality, and that's such a hallmark of Chrsitopher Guest's films: the humor emerges from real contexts, not from comic flights of outrageous exaggeration, what Harry Shearer calls "what if" scenarios.

One of *A Mighty Wind*'s greatest strengths is that its songs, its characters, its very world are close enough to the real thing that the audience buys it as such. That aesthetic distance is reduced, and audiences don't twitch about, looking to detect the fakery.

Another clever decision by Guest also makes *A Mighty Wind* feel very realistic: the music is vocalized and performed live by the actual actors involved, not merely lip-synched by somebody else at a later date. This is a critical distinction.

"As actors, it does give us a leg up in portraying these people," Harry Shearer reveals. "As opposed to a performer who doesn't have the talent and the passion, just to sort of mime it, that's a very different relationship to the characters, I guess, than what you have if you can do it.

"It's something we enjoy doing, and if you can do it, why not?" Shearer considers. "There are a lot of different stories to tell, but we're able to tell stories about these people because we can deliver the goods in terms of that aspect of their lives. I think as actors we can connect with these characters because even though they're very different from us, and make wildly different choices than we would make, we do relate to the weirdly twisted passion that they have, because it's one that we share."

With such a carefully erected sense of reality, *A Mighty Wind* achieves something very special and rare: a genuinely autumnal feel. There's a deep melancholy to this film because many characters are past their prime, but still dreaming of a moment when they might again capture the spotlight with their out-of-style music.

"I think people have said there's a slightly elegiac quality to *A Mighty Wind*," Shearer says. "It's about people who have spent a great deal of their adult lives looking backward at that little golden moment that they felt was going to go on much longer. The spark of the movie is the shard, the little thread of hope, that history might repeat itself with a longer moment this time. That's more poignant than what's going on in *Spinal Tap*, for sure."

Indeed, to make a comparison Christopher Guest himself might not appreciate, watching all the acts together onstage at the end of *A Mighty Wind* is a little bit like watching one of the *Star Trek* movies featuring the original cast. Everybody's a little older than the last time we saw them, but the camaraderie among the players is still visceral, and there's a sense of nostalgia — essentially transmitted in "doubly."

First, the music harkens back to a world of forty years ago, one that doesn't really exist anymore. And secondly, who can keep a dry eye watching Catherine O'Hara and Eugene Levy, at the top of their form here, without meditating on the fact that they have been acting together for thirty years? Or that it's been twenty years since *This Is Spinal Tap*, and we first became aware of the Guest, Shearer, and McKean magic? Sure, they're all playing unfamiliar characters within the drama itself, but we still know these guys from their other work, and there is a special alchemy at play on a nearly subatomic level. It feels like a valedictory moment, both for the characters and the actors essaying them.

"You get goose bumps when all the groups are up on stage singing," Willard says. "It almost brought a tear to my eye."

There's a lot of hope, nostalgia, and love playing out on that stage, and that fact may explain the considerable sense of tension evident in the film's final act. Unlike the hapless if enthusiastic cast of *Red, White and Blaine* in *Waiting for Guffman*, these folk groups certainly have the musical chops necessary to stage a comeback, and indeed the New Main Street Singers wheedle their own new TV series out of the concert. Because the audience is invested in these characters, it wants to see if that golden moment will emerge again.

Will Mitch return to Town Hall on time, or end up in a cock-fighting arena, as Mickey fears? What song will the Folksmen finally play, and will they be ready to play it? How will Jonathan's compulsions reveal themselves before a live audience? These are important questions and Guest builds suspense through the film's very structure. He cuts away to the show's director (Scott Williamson), and to the satellite van several times, to impress upon the audience the enterprise's magnitude. He cross-cuts between Olfen, Mickey, and Steinbloom searching the streets for Mitch, and the acts in the ongoing concert. The message is visually quite clear: This is live folks, and time is running out.

"It's like going home to visit your folks on Thanksgiving when you come back to do a concert after many, many years," Dooley considers. "Part of it is you like getting back together, and another part is that all of the old things that were going on between you come back. It could be positive, or it could be ambivalent. If you've been a hit in the sixties, and then you don't work very much, except on a cruise ship occasionally, it's going to change your perspective about coming back."

In *A Mighty Wind*, there is little fraternal battling among or between the groups (though the New Main Street Singers do steal "Never Did No Wanderin'"), and so two elements really float to the forefront. Will this concert be enough to bring these groups back to a more permanent limelight, and on a more personal level, will Mitch and Mickey kiss and thereby re-ignite that age of innocence and love that made them so important, so popular in the first place?

This is not just about nostalgia, this is about true love, and how true love between two people changes substantially from 1963 to 1973, to 2003. Writing for *Knot* magazine, columnist Tim Grierson described the "Ode to Irving" kiss in this way:

> This moment ... is shockingly poignant, natural, and blessedly free of easy laughs. Suddenly the song takes on a sadness that was missing thirty-five years before. Rather than going for a pot shot, Levy and O'Hara ... approach a melancholy and regret that is truly beautiful. His tentative playing and her nervous singing only bring out the heartache in the tune's hope of a happily ever after ... But the genius of this scene is how those cliched words now carry so much meaning.[42]

The kiss is beautiful and a little sad because it is, like folk music itself, about a moment in time that has long since past, an age when the world believed in ideals such as peace, freedom, romance, and true love.

"While the times were a-changing, it blew these singers straight into the strange world of middle age without a life preserver, dog-paddling like mad, staying in the same place but still growing older,"[43] wrote Chuck Graham in the *Tucson Citizen*, and perhaps there has been no better a description of the feelings of nostalgia and poignance this movie generates.

The movie's namesake, the song "A Mighty Wind," offers the "wondrous" tale of a world "where people cared." It concerns "peace and freedom," and a taste that was in the air, spreading from sea to sea. It is a song, then, written and sung by idealistic people who, at least once, believed that a tune like this could actually make a difference. That it was possible for a feeling of peace and freedom to sweep America from coast to coast, and indeed the world. Many critics have complained that *A Mighty Wind* overlooks or ignores the political impact of folk music, but that may not really be the case. Even if by accident.

In March and April 2003, as *A Mighty Wind* premiered in theaters around America, President George W. Bush launched the first pre-emptive war against a sovereign country in U.S. history. As the Folksmen, the New Main Street Singers, and Mitch and Mickey gathered on stage at Town Hall and sung about "peace and freedom," America instead acted as an aggressor and waged war on the international stage.

While these strange folkies vocalized about the 1960s and a wondrous world "where people cared," the President of the United States dismissed war protesters as nothing but a "focus group" and took absolutely no heed of their message or their desire for peace.

This was the context of *A Mighty Wind* when it was released. Was it coincidental? Surely, because the film was shot in the spring and summer of 2002, and conceived even before that. Still, in April 2003, as American war machines rolled into Baghdad to find nonexistent weapons of mass destruction, the climactic song in *A Mighty Wind* petitioned viewers to remember a more innocent time when people believed in a peace movement, and in the principle that people could care about others. It was a stark contrast to real life, and intentional or not, one that added to the film's strong melancholy feel.

All of Christopher Guest's documentary-style comedies are meaningful, true, and funny, but *A Mighty Wind* is the apex of the director's career because it is all those things and more. It evokes nostalgia for a time that many people who saw the film never actually experienced. It pulls at the heartstrings as well as the funny bone, and wraps the package with toe-tapping music and gentle laughs. As much as it looks at the past and evokes a world now extinct, it also calls into question the precepts of the cynical world we inhabit today.

Because don't we all really wish that somehow, some way, a mighty wind of peace and freedom could swell up, and in one great gust, blow each and every one us?

You know what I mean.

SIX MONTHS LATER ...

A CONCLUSION TO THE FILMS OF CHRISTOPHER GUEST AND COMPANY

WITH THE EXPERIENCE HE GLEANED FROM WORKING ON *This Is Spinal Tap* back in 1984, director Christopher Guest went on in the late nineties and early twenty-first century to direct and co-create three of the "mockumentary" genre's most notable *cause célèbre*: *Waiting for Guffman*, *Best in Show*, and *A Mighty Wind*.

These films are successful, and nearly always critically praised, because Guest and his companions have given the material their hearts and minds, and furthermore, vetted all the hard work that the documentary-style entails; making certain that their observations about everything from the Westminster Kennel Club to the tropes of folk music are accurately observed. Then, through a long and arduous editing process, the artist has made certain that the finished products move quickly and tell a fascinating story.

If there's a lesson for filmmakers embedded in the unique cinema of Christopher Guest, it is that research and preparation are necessary steps in the process and must precede the laugh. In fact, research and preparation actually pave the way for the laugh. That's why those exaggerated student films are so funny in *The Big Picture*; that's why *Attack of the 50 Ft. Woman* accurately captures the texture of a 1950s era sci-fi cult film, and so on.

Christopher Guest's characters always feel true, and even universal, because of the talents of those he has gathered together in his informal repertory company, but also because, with the groundwork laid so ably, he can just step back and let the improvisors do their thing. As a result, his characters may stammer or exhibit circular logic, but they also feel more authentic than the programmed stiffs who populate conventional movies. That's why we always root for these dreamers to succeed against all the odds.

"To me, any movie succeeds or fails on whether or not you're involved in the characters," June Chadwick says. "I think everything, whether it's period, a comedy or a musical, if you don't care about who's in it … there's zero attachment, and there's no movie, or I'm bored by it. To me it's such a primary ingredient that seems so obviously missing from certain projects. It's surprising that with the amount of money that sometimes is put into them that somebody hasn't paid more attention."

Indeed, there have been many so-called mockumentary films released in the last decade (*Drop Dead Gorgeous* [1999], among them), and many of those without the name Christopher Guest listed in the credits simply don't cut the mustard.

"I've seen a couple of mockumentaries that people have given to me, and right from the start, they're over the top," says Willard. "They're being funny, they're being zany, they're being nutty. But I don't think any of Chris's characters are trying to be nutty. They just take on characteristics that are a bit eccentric. I completely believe Catherine and me as a couple who are travel agents, and who have never been out of this small town, and it's no big thing, and she drinks too much, and takes acting notes from me, and you just see the friction there."

"If you think what you've observed is amusing, then your job is just to get it down as believably as you can," Harry Shearer says, focusing in on the skills necessary to create a good documentary-style comedy. "Take the dull parts out, and what you're left with is funny. Especially if you've edited well and observed well."

In that regard, hopefully there will be further chances to study in cinemas this format and its methodology from the practitioner that straight-shooter Jim Piddock terms "the master of the genre," Mr. Guest.

But will that next opportunity come?

"I don't know if Chris is going to do another movie," Willard says. "I just hear rumors and then hope that I get a phone call."

"I think he wants to put a little spin on the next one," Garrity hints. "I'm getting wind of something slightly different, but still having improv and maybe more scripted stuff. I'm not sure."

"Chris isn't really repeating himself," Hitchcock considers. "He does something different each time, in different worlds, so it's not a cookie-cutter thing."

Whatever that project is, and whenever it materializes, Fred Willard is certain it will be worth the wait.

"Every young actor I talk to now is planning to, or has done, their own mockumentary, and either wants me to be in it or look at it, and I say to them, 'It better be awfully good — *awfully, awfully* good, because this has been done, and Christopher Guest has put his stamp on it.' So if we do a fourth one, it won't be, 'Oh dear, here we go again,' it'll be, 'Oh, let's see what he's got up his sleeve this time.'"

Audiences can rest assured that whatever quirky notion is nestled up that creative sleeve, it won't result in what Corky St. Clair would call a "stinky" product.

APPENDICES

YOU KNOW YOU'RE IN
A CHRISTOPHER GUEST FILM WHEN ...

THE CHARACTERS SPEAK IN A WORD SALAD.

In the films of Guest and company, many of the *dramatis personae* actually seem to confuse themselves about what they are saying, or attempting to say. In *A Mighty Wind*, the Folksmen debate their dickies, and toss out a word salad of now-and-then adjectives like "retro" and "now," ending up with the new and catchy buzzword, "nowtro."

This gag can also be detected on the DVD commentary from *This Is Spinal Tap*, wherein the British rockers play off each other, discussing one song that is first "anthemic," then "endemic," and finally "pedantic."

This joke style reveals how Guest, McKean, Shearer, Levy, and the others really boast a love of language, and the original ways they can twist it to be funny.

THERE ARE BIZARRE REFERENCES THAT DON'T SEEM QUITE ACCURATE.

In *Waiting for Guffman*, Corky St. Clair references Sherlock Holmes,

D'Artagnan, Zen philosophy, the Lunts, Alfred Hitchcock, and other interesting sources — all incorrectly. Often, the allusions in these Guest films are so clever that just getting the joke at all makes you feel pretty smart.

Give yourself bonus points if, on the *Spinal Tap* commentary, you catch the joke about Jerome Kern (1885 – 1945), the composer of some seven hundred popular songs in the last century. He was famous for cranking 'em out fast, and that's what David St. Hubbin's joke is all about.

These bizarre references have a notable purpose within the Guest documentary-style canon, too. They reveal that these characters, in the incomparable words of David St. Hubbins, probably believe "virtually everything" they read, and secondly, that they have pretensions to be intellectual, to come off as well-read and knowing.

YOU SEE A FAMILIAR FACE DOING A FAMILIAR THING

A true repertory company features familiar players in different roles in different productions, but always ones that play to their individual strengths. This is also true of Guest's company in the doc-style movies.

Deborah Theaker is nearly seen weeping (*Waiting for Guffman*, *A Mighty Wind*), or as the audience's emotional barometer during touching stage performances (*Waiting for Guffman*, *A Mighty Wind*). By contrast, Bob Balaban is often seen as the relatively humorless heir of an important personality (*Best in Show*, *A Mighty Wind*). The hurricane known as Fred Willard is nearly always a dominant, loquacious fellow, and so forth.

YOU SEE MUTT AND JEFF

Much humor is derived in the Guest oeuvre from the chemistry between two complementary personalities. In *Best in Show*, the humor "goes to eleven" when careful, deliberate Jim Piddock teams with brassy Fred Willard. In *A Mighty Wind*, the laughs come hot and heavy when a put-upon Michael Hitchcock is needled by an obsessive-compulsive, dour Bob Balaban. In *Waiting for Guffman*, Corky is a Mutt *playing* a Jeff. He is a mincing effete, but forced by circumstances to appear as a manly stud on stage in *Red, White and Blaine*. "Oh Emma ..."

A PUBLIC PERFORMANCE GONE AWRY (A.K.A. STAGECRAFT 101)

Performances don't always come off without a hitch, a truism proved repetitively by the hapless Spinal Tap. In the documentary-style trilogy, however, public performances and appearances also go off-track sometimes.

In *Waiting for Guffman*, Dr. Pearl appears on stage as pioneer Blaine Fabin, but his eyes are crossed because he can't wear his glasses. He also bumps his head on the alien spaceship in "Nothing Ever Happens on Mars."

In *A Mighty Wind*, the New Main Street Singers steal the Folksmen tune, "Never Did No Wanderin'," causing panic backstage. Likewise, Mitch disappears from Town Hall, necessitating a near-disastrous performance of "Skeletons of Quinto."

Finally, in *Best in Show*, Beatrice breaks stride and attacks a judge on live television, and Buck Laughlin makes numerous gaffes about American history (Christopher Columbus, the Mayflower, etc.) while emceeing.

A CARD FLASHES ON THE SCREEN INDICATING TIME HAS PASSED (USUALLY SIX MONTHS LATER)

This is the standard Guest epilogue, the coda wherein the audience learns that even after some difficulties and disappointments, all the characters who appeared in the film are generally doing well, and perhaps even happy with their new stations in life. This is the most direct evidence that Guest doesn't mock people. Why bother with such narrative closure if the characters are merely props for humiliation-style humor?

SOMEONE'S PUTTING ON A SHOW

All of Guest's documentary-style comedies adhere to the same overarching structure. There's the preparation for the show, the assembly of the show, and the actual show itself. This is a terrific structure because it has a built-in mood of suspense. The first act introduces the weird characters and their quirks. The second act reveals the details and scope of what they will be doing. And the third is the payoff, showing them actually doing it — often with hijinks and mishaps in the mix.

WEIRD HOBBIES GET PROMINENT PLACEMENT

In *A Mighty Wind*, Leonard Crabbe has erected a shrine to miniature trains. In *Best in Show*, Harlan's storage shed is overstocked with beach balls. In *This Is Spinal Tap*, Nigel collects guitars, but he won't let anybody touch them, or even look at them. In *Return of Spinal Tap*, he discusses his love of pets — and his agenda is to provide them passports so they may travel the world more freely.

People who are dog lovers, people who love movie memorabilia, experts who devote their life and profession to a history of folk music singers — they're all here, and all over the place in Christopher Guest's work.

THE CHRISTOPHER GUEST FILMOGRAPHY

AS DIRECTOR: FEATURE LENGTH FILMS

The Big Picture (1989) director Christopher Guest; producers Richard Gilbert Abramson, William E. McEuen, Michael Varhol; writers Michael Varhol, Christopher Guest, Michael McKean.

Attack of the 50 Ft. Woman (1993) director Christopher Guest; producers Chuck Binder, Joseph Dougherty, Daryl Hannah, Debra Hill; writers Mark Hanna, Joseph Dougherty.

Waiting for Guffman (1997) director Christopher Guest; producer Karen Murphy; writers Christopher Guest, Eugene Levy.

Almost Heroes (1998) director Christopher Guest; producers Denise Di Novi, Mary Kane; writers Mark Nutter, Tom Wolfe, Boyd Hale.

Best in Show (2000) director Christopher Guest; producer Karen Murphy; writers Christopher Guest, Eugene Levy.

A Mighty Wind (2003) director Christopher Guest; producer Karen Murphy; writers Christopher Guest, Eugene Levy.

AS DIRECTOR: TV SERIES
Likely Stories (1983)

Morton and Hayes (1991)

D.O.A. (1999)

AS ACTOR: FILM
The Hot Rock (1972) director Peter Yates; producers Hal Lander, Bobby Roberts; writers William Goldman, Don Westlake.

Death Wish (1974) director Michael Winner; producers Dino De Laurentiis, Hal Lander, Michael Winner, Bobby Roberts; writers Brian Garfield, Wendell Mayes.

The Fortune (1975) director Mike Nichols; producers Don Devlin, Hank Moonjean, Mike Nichols; writer Carol Eastman.

Girlfriends (1978) director Claudia Weill; producer Claudia Weill; writer Vicki Polon.

The Last Word (1979) director Ray Boulting; producers Richard Gilbert Abramson, Michael Varhol; writers L.M. Kit Carson, Greg P. Smith, Michael Varhol.

The Long Riders (1980) director Walter Hill; producers James and Stacy Keach, Tim Zinnemann; writers Bill Bryden, Steven Smith, James and Stacy Keach.

Heartbeeps (1981) director Allan Arkush; producers Douglas Green, John Hill, Michael Phillips; writer John Hill.

This Is Spinal Tap (1984) director Rob Reiner; producer Karen Murphy; writers Christopher Guest, Michael McKean, Harry Shearer.

Little Shop of Horrors (1986) director Frank Oz; producer David Geffen; writers Howard Ashman, Charles B Griffith.

Beyond Therapy (1987) director Robert Altman; producers Roger Berlind, Steven Haft; writers Robert Altman, Christopher Durang.

The Princess Bride (1987) director Rob Reiner; producers Norman Lear, Rob Reiner, Andrew Scheinman; writer William Goldman.

Sticky Fingers (1988) director Catlin Adams; producers Catlin Adams, Sam Irving, Melanie Mayron; writers Catlin Adams, Melanie Mayron.

A Few Good Men (1992) director Rob Reiner; producers Dan Brown, William S. Gilmore, Rob Reiner, Andrew Scheinman; writer Aaron Sorkin.

Waiting for Guffman (1997) director Christopher Guest; producer Karen Murphy; writers Christopher Guest, Eugene Levy.

Small Soldiers (1998) director Joe Dante; producers Walter F. Parkes, Colin Wilson; writers Adam Rifkin, Gavin Scott, Ted Ellott, Terry Rossio.

Best in Show (2000) director Christopher Guest; producer Karen Murphy; writers Christopher Guest, Eugene Levy.

A Mighty Wind (2003) director Christopher Guest; producer Karen Murphy, writers Christopher Guest, Eugene Levy.

AS ACTOR: TV MOVIES

It Happened One Christmas (1977) director Donald Wyre; producers Joel Freeman, Carole Hart, Marlo Thomas; writers Jo Swerling, Frank Capra, Lionel Chetwynd, Frances Goodrich, Albert Hackett, Philip Van Doren Stern.

Blind Ambition (1979) director George Schaefer; producer David Susskind; writers Stanley R. Greenberg, John Dean.

The T.V. Show (1979) director Tom Trbovich; producers Phil Mishkin, Rob Reiner, Harry Shearer, Paul Waigner; writers Christopher Guest, Billy Crystal, Tom Leopold, Phil Mishkin, Martin Mull, Rob Reiner, Harry Shearer.

Haywire (1980) director Michael Tuchner; producer William Hayward; writers Ivan and Peter Davis; Frank Pierson.

Million Dollar Infield (1982) director Hal Cooper; producers Peter Katz, Rob Reiner; writer Dick Wimmer.

A Piano for Mrs. Cimino (1982) director George Schaefer; producers Tony Converse, Roger Gimbel, George Schaefer; writers John Gay, Robert Oliphant.

Close Ties (1983) director Arvin Brown; producer Harlan P. Kleiman; writer Elizabeth Diggs.

AS ACTOR: TV SERIES

Laverne and Shirley (1976)

All in the Family (1977)

St. Elsewhere (1982)

Saturday Night Live (1984–85)

Morton and Hayes (1991)

The Simpsons (1992)

Mad TV (2003)

AS WRITER: FILM

This Is Spinal Tap (1984) director Rob Reiner; producer Karen Murphy; writers Christopher Guest, Michael McKean, Harry Shearer.

The Big Picture (1989) director Christopher Guest; producers Richard Gilbert Abramson, William E. McEuen, Michael Varhol; writers Michael Varhol, Christopher Guest, Michael McKean.

Waiting for Guffman (1997) director Christopher Guest; producer Karen Murphy; writers Christopher Guest, Eugene Levy.

Best in Show (2000) director Christopher Guest; producer Karen Murphy; writers Christopher Guest, Eugene Levy.

A Mighty Wind (2003) director Christopher Guest; producer Karen Murphy, writers Christopher Guest, Eugene Levy.

AS WRITER: TV SERIES AND SPECIALS

The Lily Tomlin Special (1975)

The T.V. Show (1979)

Likely Stories (1981 – 1983)

Saturday Night Live (1984 – 85)

Morton and Hayes (1991)

D.O.A. (1999)

FULL MOVIE CREDITS FOR OTHER CHRISTOPHER GUEST FILMS

THIS IS SPINAL TAP (1984)

CHRISTOPHER GUEST: Nigel Tufnel

MICHAEL MCKEAN: David St. Hubbins

HARRY SHEARER: Derek Smalls

ROB REINER: Marty DiBergi

JUNE CHADWICK: Jeanine Pettibone

TONY HENDRA: Ian Faith

FRED ASPARAGUS: Joe "Mama" Besser

ROBERT BAUER: Moke

ED BEGLEY JR.: John "Stumpy" Pepys

PAUL BENEDICT: Hotel Clerk

BILLY CRYSTAL: Marty the Mime

FRAN DRESCHER: Bobbi Flekman

GLORIA GIFFORD: Airport Security Officer

HOWARD HESSEMAN: Terry Lad

Anjelica Huston: Polly Deutsch
Bruno Kirby: Tommy Pischedda
Patrick Macnee: Sir Denis Eton-Hogg
Paul Shaffer: Artie Fufkin
Paul Shortino: Duke Fame
Fred Willard: Lt. Bob Hookstratten

Directed by: Rob Reiner
Written by: Christopher Guest, Michael McKean,
    Rob Reiner and Harry Shearer
Produced by: Karen Murphy
Executive Producer: Lindsay Doran
Director of Photography: Peter Smokler
Music and lyrics by: Christopher Guest, Michael McKean,
    Rob Reiner and Harry Shearer
Casting by: Eve Brandenstein
Film Editors: Kent Beyda and Kim Secrest
Production Design: Bryan Jones

THE BIG PICTURE (1989)

An Aspen Film Society Production

Kevin Bacon: Nick Chapman
J.T. Walsh: Allen Habel
Emily Longstreth: Susan Rawlings
Jennifer Jason Leigh: Lydia Johnson
Michael McKean: Emmet Sumner
Kim Miyori: Jenny Sumner
Teri Hatcher: Gretchen
Dan Schneider: Jonathan
Jason Gould: Carl
Tracy Brooks Swope: Lori
Don Franklin: Todd Marvin
Gary Kroeger: Mark
Fran Drescher: Polo Habel
Eddie Albert: MC
June Lockhart: Janet
Stephen Collins: Attorney
Roddy McDowall: Judge
Elliott Gould: Prosecutor

ROBERT BAUER: Wounded Soldier

JOHN CLEESE: Bartender

SCOTT WILLIAMSON: Restaurant Manager

MARTIN SHORT: Neil Sussman, Talent Agent

DIRECTED BY: Christopher Guest

WRITTEN BY: Michael Varhol, Christopher Guest, Michael McKean

PRODUCED BY: William E. McEuen, Richard Gilbert Abramson,
     Valen Watson, Richard Luke Rothschild.

DIRECTOR OF PHOTOGRAPHY: Jeff Jur

MUSIC: David Nichtern

CASTING: Nina Axelrod

FILM EDITOR: Martin Nicholson

PRODUCTION DESIGN: Joseph T. Garrity

ATTACK OF THE 50 FT. WOMAN (1993)

IN ASSOCIATION WITH WARNER BROTHERS TELEVISION

DARYL HANNAH: Nancy Archer

DANIEL BALDWIN: Harry Archer

WILLIAM WINDOM: Hamilton Cobb

FRANCES FISHER: Dr. Theodora Cushing

CHRISTI CONAWAY: Honey

PAUL BENEDICT: Dr. Loeb

O'NEAL COMPTON: Sheriff Denby

VICTORIA HAAS: Deputy Spooner

LEWIS ARQUETTE: Mr. Ingersoll

KYE BENSON: Alien Woman #2

XANDER BERKELEY: Second Man

HAMILTON CAMP: Prospector Eddie

SCOTT WILLIAMSON: Pilot #2

DIRECTED BY: Christopher Guest

WRITTEN BY: Joseph Dougherty

BASED ON THE MOTION PICTURE WRITTEN BY: Mark Hanna

PRODUCED BY: Debra Hill

EXECUTIVE PRODUCER: Joseph Doughery

CO-PRODUCERS: Daryl Hannah, Chuck Binder

DIRECTOR OF PHOTOGRAPHY: Russell Carpenter

MUSIC BY: Nicholas Pike

CASTING BY: Mary Gail Artz, Barbara Cohen
FILM EDITING BY: Harry Keramidas
PRODUCTION DESIGNER: Joseph T. Garrity
VISUAL EFFECT SUPERVISOR: Gene Warren, Jr.

ALMOST HEROES (1998)

TURNER PICTURES PRESENTS A DI NOVI PICTURES PRODUCTION

CHRIS FARLEY: Bartholomew Hunt
MATTHEW PERRY: Leslie Edward
EUGENE LEVY: Guy Fontenot
KEVIN DUNN: Hidalgo
BOKEEM WOODBINE: Jonah
LISA BARBUSCIA: Shaquinna
DAVID PACKER: Bidwell
STEVEN PORTER: Higgins
HAMILTON CAMP: Pratt
PATRICK CRANSHAW: Jackson
SCOTT WILLIAMSON: William Clark
FRANKLIN COVER: Nicholas Burr
ROBERT TITTOR: Priest
CHRISTIAN CLEMENSON: Father Girard
HARRY SHEARER: Narrator

DIRECTED BY: Christopher Guest
WRITTEN BY: Mark Nutter, Tom Wolfe, Boyd Hale
PRODUCED BY: Denise Di Novi
CO-PRODUCER: Mary Kane
DIRECTORS OF PHOTOGRAPHY: Adam Kimmel, Kenneth McMillan
MUSIC BY: Jeffery C.J. Vanston
CASTING BY: Mary Gail Artz, Barbara Cohen
PRODUCTION DESIGNER: Joseph T. Garrity
COSTUME DESIGNER: Durinda Wood.

NOTES

INTRODUCTION

1. Todd R. Ramlow, "Film: Interview with Christopher Guest, Writer/Director of *Best in Show*," *Pop Matters*, 2000, http://www.popmatters.com/film/interviews/guest-christopher.html

2. Stuart Klawans, "Reel Men," *The Nation*, May 5, 2003, 34.

3. Philip McCarthy, "Seriously Funny," *The Sunday Star-Times*, July 6, 2003, 4.

4. Elvis Mitchell, "Christopher Guest, Plucking Strings for the Camera Again," *The New York Times*, March 19, 2003, E1.

5. Melissa Olson, "U. Southern California: Film Review: *Mighty Wind* will excite mockumentary director's fans," *The America's Intelligence Wire*, April 17, 2003.

6. Roberta Bernstein, "Christopher Guest: former fake rock star explodes on spot scene," *Shoot*, October 16, 1998, 45–46.

7. David Ansen, "Dog Treats. Sit! Stay! Good Comedy!" *Newsweek*, October 2, 2000, 72.

8. Genevieve J. Roth, "Christopher Guest," *Esquire*, May 2003, 68.

9. David Denby, "Private Worlds," *The New Yorker*, May 5, 2003, 106.

10. Bob Strauss, "Extended Play," *The Daily News of Los Angeles*, April 13, 2003, U4.

11. Richard Meran Barsam, *Non-Fiction Film: A Critical History* (Clarke, Irwin and Company, Ltd., 1973), 2.

12. Richard Meran Barsam, *Non-Fiction Film: A Critical History* (Clarke, Irwin and Company, Ltd., 1973), 4.

13. Georgia Brown, *Village Voice*, September 19, 1989, 68.

14. Paula Nechak, "The Laughs Blow in Filmmaker Guest's Love for Passionate People, Hurls him into *A Mighty Wind* of Folk Music," *The Seattle Post-Intelligencer*, April 5, 2003, C1.

15. Louis B. Hobson, "Guest Star," *Calgary Sun*, May 7, 2003.

16. Mikes Standish, "Interview: The Cast of *A Mighty Wind*," *MovieNews*, March 10, 2003. http://movies.go.com/news/2003/3/mightywindinterview031003.html

17. Louis B. Hobson, "Guest Shots," *Edmonston Sun*, October 10, 2000.

18. Thomas Doherty, "The Sincerest Form of Flattery: a brief history of the mockumentary," *Cineaste*, Fall 2003, 22–26.

19. Beth A. Fhaner, ed., *Magill's Cinema Annual 1998*. 17th edition (Gale Group, 1998), 589.

20. Bill Higgins, "*Wind*-Swept Preem (Christopher Guest debuts *A Mighty Wind* at Director's Guild of America)," *Daily Variety*, April 17, 2002, 27.

21. Jess Cagle, "The Lord of Loser: a British noble married into Hollywood royalty, Christopher Guest chronicles ever hopeful wannabes," *Time*, October 9, 2000, 106–107.

22. David Edelstein, *The New York Post*, September 15, 1989, 23.

23. Phillip Lopate, *Totally, Tenderly, Tragically: Essays and criticism from a lifelong love affair with the movies* (Anchor Books/Doubleday, 1998), 263.

24. Kevin Lally, "*A Mighty Wind*," *Film Journal International*, May 2003, 35.

25. Adam Sternbergh, "Too Funny to Be Famous; pay no attention to Christopher Guest. He prefers it that way," *The National Post*, April 19, 2003, SP1.

26. Paul Clinton, "Entertainment: Two Paws Up! *Best in Show* Is Howlingly Funny," *CNN*, September 29, 2000. http://www.cnn.com/2000/SHOWBIZ/Movies/09/29/review.best.in.show/index.html

1. A MAN OF CHARACTERS

1. Philip McCarthy, "Seriously Funny," *The Sunday Star-Times*, July 6, 2003, 4.

2. "Good Lord!" *People Weekly*, April 29, 1996, 56.

3. Elias Savada, "*Best in Show*: Interview with Christopher Guest," *Nitrate Online*, October 13, 2000. http://www.nitrateonline.com/2000/fbestinshow.html

4. Christopher Guest, "Peter Sellers was really one of my idols. (Actors We Love)," *Back Stage West*, June 5, 2003, 10.

5. Gavin Edwards, "The Mighty Grouch. Christopher Guest blows comic wind," *Rolling Stone*, April 16, 2003. http://www.rollingstone.com/features/featuregen.asp?pid=1621

6. Jeff Simon, "Cult of Guest: Christopher Guest explains his brand of comedic movies," *The Buffalo News*, May 9, 2003, G6.

7. *Waiting for Guffman* Online, About the Cast. www.guffman.warnerbros.com/cast.htm

8. Elvis Mitchell, "Christopher Guest, Plucking Strings for the Camera Again," *The New York Times*, March 19, 2003, E4.

9. Andrew Milner, "Folk of Ages," *New City*, September 18, 2003.
   http://citypaper.net/articles/2003-09-18/music2.shtml

10. Michael A. Lipton, "Life as the Unsquiggy: *Laverne & Shirley*'s Michael McKean is ready for a Spinal Tap reunion," *People Weekly*, December 21, 1993, 55–56.

11. Chris Hicks, "McKean shines in folksy spoof *A Mighty Wind*," *Deseret Morning News*, September 19, 2003, W01.

12. Elvis Mitchell, "Christopher Guest, Plucking Strings for the Camera Again," *The New York Times*, March 19, 2003, E4.

13. "Alice Playten Reminisces," *iClassics.com — Classical Music and More*,
   http://www.iclassics.com/iclassics/

14. Bob Woodward, *Wired*, (Pocket Books, 1984), 63.

15. Tony Hendra, "Morning in America: the rise and fall of the *National Lampoon*," *Harper's Magazine*, June, 2002.

16. Christopher Claro and Julie Klam, *Comedy Central: The Essential Guide to Comedy. Because There's a Fine Line Between Clever and Stupid* (Byron Preiss Visual Publications Inc., 1997), 107–108.

17. R.J. Smith, "Harry Shearer's made comedy history, and his radio show is celebrating its 20th birthday. But if you think he's about to mellow, you've got to be joking," *Los Angeles Magazine*, December 2002.

18. Robert Lloyd, "Sketch Artists — The Credibility Gap's one-night stand," *L.A. Weekly*, November 12–18, 1999.

19. Keith Phipps, contributor, *The Onion AV Club: The Tenacity of the Cockroach. Conversations with Entertainment's Most Enduring Outsiders* (Tree Rivers Press, New York, 2002), 380.

20. Will Hodgkinson, "Tapper's Delight," *Guardian Unlimited*, August 17, 2002.
   http://film.guardian.co.uk

21. Andrew Milner, "Folk of Ages," *New City*, September 18–24, 2003.
   http://www.citypaper.net/articles/2003-09-18/music2.shtml

22. Elias Savada, "*Best in Show*, Interview with Christopher Guest," *Nitrate Online*, October 13, 2000.

23. Phil Hall, "King of the Jungle," *Wired*, May 2003.
   http://www.wired.com/wired/archive/5.03/streetcred.html?pg=7

24. Karl French, *This Is Spinal Tap: The Official Companion* (Bloomsbury, 2000), 206.

25. Frank N. Magill, ed., *Magill's Cinema Annual, 1985: A Survey of 1984 Films*, (Salem Press, 1985), 487.

26. Karl French, *This Is Spinal Tap: The Official Companion*, (Bloomsbury, 2000), 258.

27. Keith Phipps, "Interview with Michael McKean," *The Onion AV Club*, Vol. 36, Issue #30, August 30, 2000.

28. Ira Hellman, "This Is Spinal Tap," *People Weekly*, April 16, 1984, 12.

29. John Nange, *Films in Review*, May 1984, 308.

30. David Ansen, "Rocky Road," *Newsweek*, March 5, 1984, 81–82.

31. "Spinal Analysis: Deranged but True (The 100 Greatest Moments in Rock Music — *This Is Spinal Tap* — film versus reality," *Entertainment Weekly*, May 28, 1999, 96.

32. Tasha Robinson, "Interview with Harry Shearer," *The Onion AV Club*, Volume 39, Issue #15, April 23, 2003.

33. Gavin Edwards, David Fricke, Douglas Pratt, Rob Sheffield, Kerry L. Smith, Peter Travers, "Rock! Action! Scares! Plus bonus bling-bling to blow your mind, Rolling Stone inserts the DVDs, hits 'play' and names the golden dozen," *Rolling Stone*, November 27, 2003, 71.

34. Adam Sweeting, "D.A. Pennebaker: No Spinal Tap jokes, please...," *The Independent*, November 9, 2003. http://www.enjoyment.independent.co.uk/low_res/story.jsp?story=462451&host=5&dir=213

35. Michael Cader, ed., *Saturday Night Live: The First Twenty Years* (Houghton Mifflin, 1994), 159.

36. Paul Dudley, "Getting that Synch-ing Feeling," *The Online Daily of the University of Washington*, March 5, 1996.

37. Tom Shales and James Andrew Miller, *Live from New York: An Uncensored History of Saturday Night Live* (Little, Brown and Company, 2002), 265.

38. Tim Appelo, "Interview: Christopher Guest," *Seattle Weekly*, March 16, 2003. http://www.seattleweekly.com/features/0316/film-appelo2.php

39. Ralph Novak, "The Big Picture," *People Weekly*, October 2, 1989, 12.

40. Christopher Claro and Julie Klam, *Comedy Central: The Essential Guide to Comedy. Because There's a Fine Line Between Clever and Stupid* (Byron Preiss Visual Publications, Inc., 1997), 67.

41. Michael Wilmington, *The Los Angeles Times*, September 15, 1989, 8.

42. Stuart Klawans, "*The Big Picture*," *The Nation*, October 9, 1989, 398–399.

43. Ken Tucker and Benjamin Svetkey, "Television: The Week," *Entertainment Weekly*, December 20, 1991, 62.

44. Andrew Milner, "Folk of Ages," *New City*, September 18, 2003. http://citypaper.net/articles/2003-09-18/music2.shtml

45. Ken Tucker, "A Spinal Tap Reunion," *Entertainment Weekly*, December 18, 1992, 50.

46. Michael Quinn, "Gimme a Break," *Time Magazine*, April 6, 1992, 73.

47. "The Funniest Movies on Video — The Mirth of a Nation," *Entertainment Weekly*, October 16, 1992, 16.

48. Pat H. Broeske, "A 'Few' Bucks," *Entertainment Weekly*, November 6, 1992, 9.

49. Kathi Maio, "The Passivity of a Post-Feminist 50 Ft. Woman," *Fantasy and Science Fiction*, July 1994, 98.

50. Ginia Bellafante, "*Attack of the 50 Ft. Woman*," *Time*, December 13, 1993, 85.

51. John Stanley, *Creature Features Strikes Again Movie Guide* (Creatures at Large Press, 1994), 29.

52. Laura Kay Smith, "Always a 'Friend,' Almost a Hero," *People Online*, 1998. http://people.aol.com/people/

53. *Almost Heroes* Online "Production Notes." www.almostheroes.com

54. Gary Eng Walk, "Heroic Encounter — Matthew Perry Remembers Chris Farley," *Entertainment Weekly*, June 1, 1998. http://www.ew.com/ew/

55. "Spring Movie Preview," *Entertainment Weekly Online*, February 27, 1998. http://www.ew.com/ew/

56. Michelle Banks, ed., *Magill's Cinema Annual 1999: A Survey of the Films of 1998.* 18th Edition. (The Gale Group, 1999), 10.

57. Cate McQuaide, *Boston Globe*, May 30, 1998, C7.

58. Owen Gleiberman, *"Almost Heroes," Entertainment Weekly*, June 12, 1998. http://www.ew.com/ew/

59. Enrique Rivero, "Spinal Tap in Video Comeback," *Video Business*, June 5, 2000, 4.

60. Rick Clark, *"This Is Spinal Tap," Video Business*, September 1, 2000. http://mixonline.com/mag/audio_spinal_tap/index.html

61. "LC Adds 25 Films to National Registry," *Library Journal*, January 10, 2003. http://www.libraryjournal.com/article/ca268736

62. Holly Aguirre, *"This Is Spinal Tap* rocks," *Knight Ridder/Tribune News Service*, November 11, 2003, K7992.

63. Jesse Green, "Passing the Bra: The Search for a New Edna," *The New York Times*, February 15, 2004, Section 2, 1 and 10.

64. Ting Yu, "Chatter. To Dye For," *People Weekly*, October 2, 2000, 166.

65. "Mastermind behind *This Is Spinal Tap* shares writing secrets with UK's budding filmmakers," *PR Newswire*, October 29, 2003.

2. THE ARCANE ART OF IMPROVISATION

1. Philip Williams, "Moviemakers Leigh, Jaglom, Duvall and Loach are latest in a long line of 'naturalistic' directors," *Movie Maker Magazine: The Art and Business of Making Movies*, Issue #51, 2003. http://www.moviemaker.com/issues/51/naturalistic.html

2. Luaine Lee, "The Folksmen at home with improv movie," *The Halifax Daily News*, April 16, 2003, 28.

3. Karen Heller, "Eugene Levy hits the big time," *Knight/Ridder/Tribune News Service*, August 8, 2003, K4940.

4. W. Hugh Baddely, *The Technique of Documentary Film Production* (Communications Arts Books, 1976), 14.

5. Devin Faraci, "Interview: Christopher Guest," *CHUD.com*, April 9, 2003. http://www.chud.com/news/

6. Dave Karger, "Off-the-cuff and onto the screen (Comedian, movie director and actor Christopher Guest)," *Entertainment Weekly*, February 14, 1997, 43.

7. Gary Arnold, "The Jokesmen: Comics pick on folks; *Spinal Tap* actors go unplugged," *The Washington Times*, April 19, 2003, D04.

8. Moira McDonald, "Improv actors bond making 'mockumentaries.' *Best in Show* crew reunites in film poking fun at folk singers," *The Seattle Times*, April 13, 2003, L5.

9. Craig Mathieson, "Mighty Serious Comedy," *The Age*, July 25, 2003, 3.

10. Demetrios Matheou, "Festival Diary, Day Eleven," *BFI: The Times 47th London Film Festival*, November 1, 2003.

11. Anthony Breznican, *"Mighty* Mockumentary. No script or rehearsal forms basis of Guest's new comedic film," *The Olympian*, April 17, 2003. http://www.theolympian.com/home/news/20030417/living/44453.shtml

12. Fred Cisterna, "Two Worlds," *Shoot*, October 27, 2000.

13. Gavin Edwards, "The Mighty Grouch. Christopher Guest blows comic wind," *Rolling Stone*, April 16, 2003. http://www.rollingstone.com/features/featuregen.asp?pid=1621

14. Eric Harrison, "Guest at home with offbeat comedy. *Spinal Tap* creator back with new film," *The Houston Chronicle*, May 5, 2003, 10.

15. Greg Adkins, "Ditz Hits: Who's that airhead? Jennifer Coolidge cleans up as Hollywood's go-to-goof," *People Weekly*, August 11, 2003, 63.

16. Sacha Molitorisz, "Strike a Posey," *Sydney Morning Herald*, July 18, 2003, 7.

17. John Griffin, "One Project Down, umpteen to go. Bob Balaban talks about his next film role in Christopher Guest's *A Mighty Wind*; it called for some improvisation," *The Gazette*, May 3, 2003, D2.

18. Andrew L. Urban, "Heaps of Talent: Christopher Guest — *A Mighty Wind*," *Urban Cinefile*, Summer 2003. http://www.urbancinefile.com.au/home/view.asp?a=7678&s=Interviews

19. Elias Savada, "Best in Show: Interview with Christopher Guest," *Nitrate Online*, October 13, 2000. http://www.nitrateonline.com/2000/fbestinshow.html

20. Tim Lammers, "*Best* Puts Christopher Guest Above Rest," *Channel 2000*, October 13, 2000. http://www.channel2000.com/sh/entertainment/atthemovies/stories/atthemovies-20001013-131001.html

21. Chris Hewitt, "Frequent Guest star Catherine O'Hara is full of surprises," *Saint Paul Pioneer Press*, April 18, 2003, K2578.

22. Louis B. Hobson, "Blowing in the Wind, Spinal Tap Reunites for the Folksy Mockumentary *A Mighty Wind*," *The Winnipeg Sun*, May 9, 2003, 21.

23. David Spaner, "Mighty May Be Another Best: *Best in Show* was made without a lot of hype but its success bodes well for *A Mighty Wind*," *The Vancouver Province*, May 4, 2003, D4.

24. Christopher Guest, Eugene Levy, Harry Shearer, Michael McKean, Richard Corliss, Josh Tyrangiel, "Mighty Funny," *Time Magazine*, April 21, 2003, 68+.

25. Jason Middleton, "Documentary Comedy" (Abstract), *Media International Australia, Incorporating Culture and Policy*, August 2002, 55.

26. Louis B. Hobson, "Blowing in the Wind, Spinal Tap Reunites for the Folksy Mockumentary *A Mighty Wind*," *The Winnipeg Sun*, May 9, 2003, 21.

3. WAITING FOR GUFFMAN

1. Jake Tapper, "Interview: Christopher Guest," *The Sundance Channel*, May 2003. http://www.sundancechannel.com/24fn/index.php?ixContent=4882

2. Richard Meran Barsam, *Non-Fiction Film: A Critical History* (Clarke, Irwin and Company, Ltd, 1973), 249.

3. Richard Grant, "Not so Queer as Folk," *The Guardian*, Saturday, January 10, 2004. http://film.guardian.co.uk/

4. J. Simon, "Cult of Guest: Christopher Guest explains his brand of comedic movies," *The Buffalo News*, May 9, 2003, G6.

5. Jamie Painter Young, "Guest Roles: Christopher Guest has carved out a niche that allows him and his actors free to truly play," *Back Stage West*, April 10, 2002.

6. Holly Aguirre, "From *SCTV* to MTV: The Second Coming of Levy," *Zap2It*, July 24, 2003. http://www.zap2it.com/movies/features/scenes/story/0,1259,---17824,00.html

7. Barry Koltnow, "Eugene Levy is busier than ever, with four films this year," *Knight Ridder/Tribune News Service*, June 11, 2003, K2392.

8. Dave Thomas with Robert Crane and Susan Carney, *SCTV: Behind the Scenes* (McClelland and Stewart Inc., 1996), 23.

9. Evan Smith, "Triumph of the Willard," *Texas Monthly*, 1997. http://www.texasmonthly.com

10. Richard Corliss and Jeffrey, "Queen of the Indies," *Time*, February 17, 1997, 82.

11. Rebecca Louie, "Parker Posey is queen of the indies, but studio stardom eludes her," *Knight Ridder/Tribune New Service*, November 18, 2002, K0487.

12. Michael D. Reid, "No Laughing Matter: There's only one actor who can keep a straight face amid such hilarity," *Times Colonist*, May 20, 2003, C4.

13. Mark Remy, "Insider Q & A: Eugene Levy," *TV Guide*, December 27, 2003, 6.

14. Evan Smith, "Triumph of the Willard," *Texas Monthly*, 1997. http://www.texasmonthly.com

15. "The Wait is Over! From the creators of *Best in Show*, *Waiting for Guffman* has arrived ... and takes its DVD bow," *Business Wire*, July 23, 2003.

16. James Cochran, "*Waiting for Guffman*: the director's cut we'd like to see," *Entertainment Weekly*, August 15, 1997, 84.

17. Michael Medved, *The New York Post*, January 31, 1997.

18. David Ansen, *Newsweek*, February 10, 1997, 66.

19. Roger Ebert, *The Chicago Sun-Times*, February 22, 1997. http://www.suntimes.com/ebert/ebert_reviews/1997/02/022105.html

20. Justin Elias, *The Village Voice*, February 11, 1997, 74.

21. Owen Gleiberman, "Guffaw-filled *Guffman* Hears the Greasepaint Roar," *Entertainment Weekly*, February 14, 1997. http://www.ew.com/ew/

22. "Screen Queen," *The Advocate*, March 18, 1997.

23. Gerald Mast, *The Comic Mind: Comedy and the Movies*, Second Edition (University of Chicago Press, 1973), 26.

24. Bob Thompson, "At the Festival — Catherine O'Hara's so bad, she's great," *Jam Canoe*, September 12, 1996. http://jam.canoe.ca/JamMoviesArtistsO/ohara_catherine.html

25. Sarah Vowell, "The mockumentary cometh," *Salon.com*, July 28, 1999. http://www.salon.com/ent/col/vowe/1999/07/28/mock/

26. Tom Gliatto, "Waiting for Guffman," *People Weekly*, March 17, 1997, 21.

4. BEST IN SHOW

1. Rob Thomas, "It's about people, it has nothing to do with dogs — An interview with Christopher Guest," *Varsity Review*, September 25, 2000. http://varsity.utoronto.ca:16080/archives/121/sept25/review/its.html

2. Bert Osborne, "Dog Dish: Christopher Guest targets dog lovers in new mockumentary," *Creative Loafing Atlanta*, October 14, 2000. http://atlanta.creativeloafing.com/2000-10-14/flicks_interview2.html

3. Westminster Kennel Club. www.Westminsterkennelclub.org

4. James Mottram, "BBC-Films-Interview-Christopher Guest," *BBC*1, March 5, 2001. http://www.bbc.co.uk/

5. Kevin Conley, "Dog Star," *The New Yorker*, September 11, 2000, 76.

6. Todd R. Ramlow, "Interview with Christopher Guest Writer/Director of *Best in Show*," *Pop Matters*, 2000. http://www.popmatters.com/film/interviews/guest-christopher.html

7. Millie Takaki, "Dir. Christopher Guest on a Roll in Atlantic City," *Shoot*, August 27, 1999, 15.

8. Harry Haun, "Shearer Madness," *Film Journal International*, April 2002, 24.

9. Nicole LaPorte, "Jennifer Coolidge funny girl: High Laugh quotient puts a determined actress center stage," *American Theatre*, May 2002, 52–53.

10. Karen Lurie, "126th Annual Westminster Kennel Club Dog Show," *Flak Magazine*, February 15, 2002. http://www.flakmag.com/tv/kennelclub.html

11. "About Production," *Best in Show Online* http://bestinshowonline.warnerbros.com/about/production.html

12. "Christopher Guest's 'Untitled Dogumentary' Projects Beings Production in Vancouver," *PR Newswire*, November 12, 1999.

13. "The Buzz: Gay Man's Best Friend," *The Advocate*, October 24, 2000, 22.

14. James Mottram, "Christopher Guest on Going to the Dogs," *Channel4.com*, http://www.channel4.com/film/reviews/

15. Liane Bonin, "Dogged Determination," *Entertainment Weekly*, October 9, 2000. http://www.ew.com/ew/

16. Roger Ebert, *The Chicago Sun Times*, October 13, 2000. http://www.suntimes.com/ebert/ebert_reviews/2000/10/101301.html

17. Susan Stark, *The Detroit News*, October 13, 2000. http://www.detnews.com

18. Lou Lumenick, "Guest's *Best* Is," *The New York Post*, September 27, 2000, 52.

19. David Edelstein, *Slate*, September 29, 2000. http://slate.msn.com/id/90528

20. Eddie Cockrell, "*Best in Show*," *Variety*, September 11, 2000, 24.

21. Rita Kempley, "The Dogs and the Wag," *The Washington Post*, October 13, 2000. http://www.washingtonpost.com/

22. Michael Wilmington, "*Best in Show* Howls at the Dog Show Crowd," *The Chicago Tribune*, October 13, 2000, 1.

23. Carla Meyer, "Tongues, Tails Wag in *Best in Show*," *The San Francisco Chronicle*, September 29, 2000.

24. Liane Bonin, "Dogged Determination," *Entertainment Weekly*, October 9, 2000. http://www.ew.com/ew/

25. Mark Easterbrook, "Entertainment — Movies: *A Mighty Wind* — No 'Mockumentary,'" *Xtra MSN*, July 30, 2003. http://xtramsn.co.nz/entertainment/

26. Rob Neyer, "The Interview: Fred Willard," *ESPN*, July 8 – 9, 2001.
    http://espn.go.com/mlb/columns/neyer_rob/1403750.html

27. "Morning News: Announcer Joe Garagiola Discusses Westminster Kennel Club Dog Show,"
    (Interview with Daryn Kagan)," *CNN.com Transcripts*, February 12, 2001.
    http://www.cnn.com/TRANSCRIPTS/0102/12/mn.11.html

28. "Dog Daze," *Sports Illustrated*, October 16, 2000, 44.

29. Steven Rea, "Christopher Guest: from *Spinal Tap* to *Best in Show*," *Knight Ridder/Tribune News
    Service*, October 6, 2000, K438.

30. Todd R. Ramlow, "Interview with Christopher Guest writer/director of *Best in Show*,"
    Pop Matters, 2000. http://www.popmatters.com/film/interviews/guest-christopher.html

31. *The St. Petersburg Times*, July 19, 2001. http://www.sptimes.com/

32. Steve Dale, "Real Dog Life Funnier Than *Best in Show*," *Pet World*, 2000–2001.
    http://www.goodnewsforpets.com/

33. Ben Walker, "Norfolk Terrier, Newfoundland Lead Westminster," *USA Today*, February 9, 2004.
    http://www.usatoday.com/sports/

34. Carla Meyer, "*Spinal Tap* for the folk crowd — *A Mighty Wind*, Christopher Guest's
    latest 'mockumentary,'" *SF Gate*, April 13, 2003. http://sf.gate.com

35. Richard Linett and Ann Marie Kerwin, *Advertising Age*, September 22, 2003, 39.

5. A MIGHTY WIND

1. Carla Hay, "Christopher Guest (aka Spinal Tap's Nigel Tufnel) is directing an as yet-untitled
   mockumentary film about folk music for Castle Rock Entertainment," *Billboard*, March 2, 2002, 75.

2. Lynn Hirschberg, "Good Humor Man," *The New York Times*, April 20, 2003,
   http://www.nytimes.com/

3. Zorianna Kit, "Folksie Reunion for *Show* men Levy and Guest," *Hollywood Reporter*,
   January 31, 2002, 1.

4. Lynn Hirschberg, "Good Humor Man," *The New York Times*, April 20, 2003.
   http://www.nytimes.com/

5. Shanda Deziel, "Quick wit, slow talker (actress Parker Posey)," *Maclean's*, December 9, 2002, 82.

6. Bonnie Laufer-Krebs, "Interview: *A Mighty Wind* (Interview with Christopher Guest,
   Michael McKean, Harry Shearer)," *The Tribute*, April 2003.
   http://www.tribute.ca/tribute/0403/interview_a_mighty_wind.htm

7. Gary Arnold, "The Jokesmen: Comics Pick on Folk. *Spinal Tap* Actors Go Unplugged,"
   The Washington Times, April 19, 2003, D04.

8. Sean Chavel, "Interview: Michael McKean, Harry Shearer, Christopher Guest of *A Mighty Wind*,"
   Cinema Confidential, April 15, 2003. http://www.cinecon.com/news.php?id=0304151

9. Bob Strauss, "Extended Play," *U-Daily News*, April 12, 2003. http://u.dailynews.com/

10. David Eimer, "Interview, Christopher Guest — actor, director, politician,"
    Times Online — Entertainment, January 1, 2004. http://www.timesonline.co.uk/

11. Patrick Naugle, "DVD Verdict Interviews Michael McKean," *DVD Verdict*, October 6, 2003.
    http://www.dvdverdict.com/specials/michaelmckean.php

12. Rebecca Murray and Fred Topel, "Interview with Harry Shearer and Michael McKean," *Dramatic/Romantic Movies*, 2003–2004. http://www.romanticmovies.about.com

13. Len Righi, "*Mighty Wind* tour whipping up renewed excitement," *The Morning Call*, September 18, 2003. http://www.mcall.com

14. "O'Toole, McKean making beautiful music together," *Gwinnett Daily Post Online Edition*, January 2004. http://www.gwinnettdailyonline.com

15. Jim Bessman, "McKean's Folk Evokes Legendary American Composers," *Billboard*, January 10, 2004.

16. "Top Artist C.J. Vanston Gets Folky with Logic," *Emagic*, 2003. http://www.emagic.de/home/artists/

17. Christopher Walsh, "Spinal Tap Reunites with Vanston for Folk Spoof," *Billboard*, March 22, 2003, 54.

18. Erin Cullin, "Eugene Levy is on top of the world," *Empire Movies*, April 14, 2003. http://www.empiremovies.com/interviews/a_mighty_wind/eugene_levy_01.shtml

19. "*A Mighty Wind*: Interview with Christopher Guest, Eugene Levy, Catherine O'Hara and Harry Shearer," *Film Features on My Movies — For the Full Picture*, 2003. http://www.mymovies.net/

20. Brian D. Johnson, "A one-time folky is now blowing in the wind," *MacLean's*, April 21, 2003, 59.

21. Gred Adkins, "Seriously Funny: With earnestness — and eyebrows — Eugene Levy wins laughs," *People Weekly*, August 11, 2003, 64.

22. Jeff Stickler, *The Star Tribune*, April 18, 2003, 13E.

23. "AFI Silver Theatre and Cultural Center to Host Special Preview Screening of Christopher Guest Film *A Mighty Wind*; (Cast Members Christopher Guest, Eugene Levy and Harry Shearer to Attend Screening)," *PR Newswire*, April 7, 2003, LAM09507042003.

24. Jack Schneider, "*Wind* powers mockumentary advancements," *On-line 49er*, Volume LIII, Number 113, May 5, 2003, http://www.csulb.edu/~d49er/archives/2003/spring/diversions/v10n113-win.shtml

25. Mike LaSalle, "Howling in the Wind," *The San Francisco Chronicle*, April 16, 2003, D1.

26. Matt Zoller Seitz, "Film — Folk Explosion — Loving send-up of aging hippies is a real gas," *The New York Press*, Volume 16, Issue #16, 2003. http://www.nypress.com/16/16/film/film.cfm

27. Michael Atkinson, "Taking Wing," *The Village Voice*, April 16–22, 2003. http://www.villagevoice.com/

28. Mike Clark, "*Wind* spoofs folk music with a lingering twang," *USA Today*, April 16, 2003. http://www.usatoday.com

29. Eleanor Ringle Gillespie, "Lovable pranksters poke gentle fun at folk music," *The Atlanta-Journal Constitution*, April 16, 2003, E1.

30. Steve Vineberg, "Where have all the folkies gone?" *The Christian Century*, May 31, 2003, 51.

31. Michael Rechtshaffer, *The Hollywood Reporter*, April 14, 2003. http://hollywoodreporter.com

32. Andrew Sarris, "I Wasn't Blown Over by Soft, Vague *Mighty Wind*," *The New York Observer*, May 5, 2003, http://observer.com/pages/story.asp?ID=7315

33. David Schmader, "Killing Babies: An Interview with Christopher Guest and Company," *The Stranger*, Volume 12, Number 31, April 17–23, 2003. http://www.thestranger.com/2003-04-17/film.html

34. Tim Shellberg, "Peter, Paul and Mary bringing 40 years of folk to Star Plaza," *The NWI Times*, November 7, 2003. http://www.nwitimes.com/articles/

35. Margaret Agnew, "*A Mighty Wind*," *The Press*, August 23, 2003, 5.

36. Bob Kline, *Serendipity* (Liner Notes), The Serendipity Singers, Philips Records, a Divison of Mercury Record Productions, Produced by Fred Weintraub and Bob Bowers.

37. Mort Goode, *The Wandering Minstrels* (Liner Notes), The New Christy Minstrels, Columbia Records, Produced by Sid Garris.

38. Bob Morgan, *The Brothers Four* (Liner Notes), The Brothers Four, Columbia Records.

39. Bob Bollard, *Mighty Day on Campus* (Liner Notes), The Chad Mitchell Trio, Kapp Records, Produced by Bob Bollard.

40. Nick Venet, *The Letterman in Concert* (Liner Notes), *The Lettermen*, Capitol Records.

41. Tris Campbell and Bob Freedman, *When I Was One and Twenty* (Liner Notes), *The Tripjacks*, Squire Records, Produced by Tris Campbell and Bob Freedman.

42. Tim Grierson, "*A Mighty Wind*: The Ballad of Mitch and Mickey," *Knot Magazine*, April 24, 2003. http://knotmag.com/

43. Chuck Graham, "Spinal Tap unplugged, satirical *A Mighty Wind* hits folk music's false notes," *The Tucson Citizen*, May 9, 2003. http://tucsoncitizen.com

SELECTED BIBLIOGRAPHY

BOOKS

Baddeley, W. Hugh. *The Technique of Documentary Film Production*. A Communication Arts Book, 1976.

Banks, Michelle, ed. *Magill's Cinema Annual 1999. A Survey of the Films of 1998*, 18th ed. The Gale Group, 1999.

Barsam, Richard M. *Non-Fiction Film: A Critical History*. Indiana University Press, 1973.

Brooks, Tim and Earle Marsh. *The Complete Directory to Prime Time Network TV Shows 1946–Present*, 3rd ed. Ballantine Books, 1984.

Cader, Michael, ed. *Saturday Night Live: The First Twenty Years*. Houghton Mifflin, 1994.

Claro, Christopher and Julie Klam. *Comedy Central: The Essential Guide to Comedy. Because There's a Fine Line Between Clever and Stupid*. A Byron Preiss Visual Publications, Inc., 1997.

Fhaner, Beth A., ed. *Magill's Cinema Annual 1998. A Survey of the Films of 1997*, 17th ed. The Gale Group, 1998.

French, Karl. *This Is Spinal Tap: The Official Companion*. Bloomsbury Press, 2000.

Langman, Larry. *The Encyclopedia of American Film Comedy*. Garland Publishing Inc., 1987.

Lopate, Phillip. *Totally, Tenderly, Tragically. Essays and criticism from a lifelong love affair with the movies*. Anchor Books/Doubleday, 1998.

Mast, Gerald. *The Comic Mind: Comedy and the Movies*, 2nd ed. University of Chicago Press, 1973.

SELECTED BIBLIOGRAPHY

Matthews, Nicole. *Comic Politics: Gender in Hollywood comedy after the new right.* Manchester University Press, 2000.

Nicholls, Bill. *Introduction to Documentaries.* The Indiana University Press, 2001.

Phipps, Keith, contrib. *The Onion AV Club: The Tenacity of the Cockroach. Conversations with Entertainment's Most Enduring Outsiders.* Three Rivers Press, 2002.

Shales, Tom and James Andrew Miller. *Live from New York: An Uncensored History of Saturday Night Live.* Little, Brown and Company, 2002.

Stanley, John. *Creature Features Strikes Again Movie Guide.* Creatures at Large Press, 1994.

Thomas, Dave, with Robert Crane and Susan Carney. *SCTV: Behind the Scenes.* McClelland and Stewart, Inc., 1996.

Terrace, Vincent. *Radio Programs, 1924–1984, a Catalog of over 1800 Shows.* McFarland and Company, Inc., 1999.

——. *Television 1970–1980.* A.S. Barnes Company Inc., 1981.

Woodward, Bob. *Wired: The Short Life & Fast Times of John Belushi.* Pocket Books, 1984.

PERIODICALS

Adkins, Greg. "Ditz Hits: Who's that airhead? Jennifer Coolidge cleans up as Hollywood's go-to goof." *People Weekly*, August 11, 2003, 63.

——. "Seriously Funny: With earnestness — and eyebrows — Eugene Levy wins laughs." *People Weekly*, August 11, 2003, 64.

"AFI Silver Theatre and Cultural Center to Host Special Preview Screening of Christophger Guest Film *A Mighty Wind*; Cast Members Christopher Guest, Eugene Levy and Harry Shearer to Attend Screening." *PR Newswire*, April 7, 2003, LAM09507042003.

Agnew, Margaret. "*A Mighty Wind.*" *The Press*, August 23, 2003, 5.

Ansen, David. "Dog Treats. Sit! Stay! Good Comedy!" *Newsweek*, October 2, 2000, 72.

——. "Gotta Sing, Gotta Dance! A small town gets bitten by the Broadway bug." *Newsweek*, February 10, 1997, 66.

——. "Rocky Road." *Newsweek*, March 5, 1984, 81–82.

Arnold, Gary. "The Jokesmen: Comics pick on folk; Spinal Tap actors go unplugged." *The Washington Times*, April 19, 2003, D04.

Atkinson, Michael. "Taking Wing." *The Village Voice*, April 16–22, 2003. http://www.villagevoice.com/

Bellafonte, Ginia. "Fifty-Foot Feminist." *Time*, December 13, 1993, 78.

Bessman, Jim. "McKean's Folk Evokes Legendary American Composers." *Billboard*, January 2004.

Bonin, Liane. "Dogged Determination." *Entertainment Weekly*, October 9, 2000. http://www.ew.com/ew/

Breznican, Anthony. "*Mighty* Mockumentary. No script or rehearsal forms basis of Guest's new comedic film." *The Olympian*, April 17, 2003. http://www.theolympian.com/home/news/20030417/living/44453.shtml

Broeske, Pat H. "A 'Few' Bucks." *Entertainment Weekly*, November 6, 1992, 9.

Butler, Robert W. "Mockumentaries have a long and mostly funny history." *The Kansas City Star*, May 16, 2003, K3063.

"The Buzz: Gay Man's Best Friend." *The Advocate*, October 24, 2000, 22.

"Christopher Guest's 'Untitled Dogumentary' Projects Beings Production in Vancouver." *PR Newswire*, November 12, 1999.

Cisterna, Fred. "Two Worlds." *Shoot*, October 27, 2000.

Clark, Mike. "*Wind* spoofs folk music with a lingering twang." *USA Today*, April 16, 2003. http://www.usatoday.com

Clark, Rick. "*This Is Spinal Tap*." *Mix*, September 1, 2000. http://mixonline.com/mag/audio_spinal_tap/index.html

Cockrell, Eddie. "*Best in Show*." *Variety*, September 11, 2000, 24.

Conley, Kevin. "Dog Star." *The New Yorker*, September 11, 2000, 76.

Corliss, Richard and Jeffrey Ressner. "Queen of the Indies." *Time*, February 17, 1997, 82.

Deziel, Shanda. "Quick wit, slow talker." *Maclean's*, December 9, 2002, 82.

"Dog Daze." *Sports Illustrated*, October 16, 2002, 44–45.

Doherty Thomas. "The Sincerest Form of Flattery: A Brief History of the Mockumentary." *Cineaste*, Fall 2003, 22–26. http://www.cineaste.com/

Dudek, Duane. "A Mighty Performance; Levy's mentally battered singer-songwriter gives folkie 'mockumentary' a three star twang." *The Milwaukee Journal Sentinel*, May 9, 2003, 03E.

Dudley, Paul "Getting that Synch-ing Feeling." *The Online Daily of the University of Washington*, March 5, 1996.

Ebert, Roger. *The Chicago Sun Times*, October 13, 2000. http://www.suntimes.com/ebert/ebert_reviews/2000/10/101301.html

Edwards, Gavin. "The Mighty Grouch. Christopher Guest blows comic wind." *Rolling Stone*, April 16, 2003. http://www.rollingstone.com/

Edwards, Gavin, David Fricke, Douglas Pratt, Rob Sheffield, L. Kerry, Peter Travers. "Rock! Action! Scares! Plus bonus bling-bling to blow your mind. *Rolling Stone* inserts the DVDs, hits 'play' and names the golden dozen." *Rolling Stone*, November 27, 2003, 71–73.

Eimer, David. "Interview, Christopher Guest — actor, director, politician." *Times Online — Entertainment*, January 1, 2004. http://www/timesonline.co.uk/

Feiffer, Jules. "Twenty Questions: Jules Feiffer is a New York-based dramatist and cartoonist whose plays include *Little Murders* and *Knock Knock*. His latest play, *A Bad Friend*, premieres at Lincoln Center Theater in New York on May 15." *American Theatre*, May–June 2003, 88.

"The Funniest Movies on Video — The Mirth of a Nation." *Entertainment Weekly*, October 16, 1992, 16.

Garcia, Chris. "Mighty Friends — McKean, Guest and Shearer — aka The Folksmen, aka Spinal Tap, tell how they turn the satire up to 11." *The Austin-American Statesman*, May 9, 2003, E3.

Gillespie, Eleanor Ringle. "Lovable pranksters poke gentle fun at folk music." *The Atlanta-Journal Constitution*, April 16, 2003, E1.

Gliatto, Tom. "*Waiting for Guffman*." *People Weekly*, March 17, 1997, 21.

Glieberman, Owen. "*Almost Heroes*." *Entertainment Weekly*, June 12, 1998. http://www.ew.com/ew/

Graham, Chuck. "Review: *A Mighty Wind*; Spinal Tap Unplugged." *Tucson Citizen*, May 9, 2003.
http://tucsconcitizen.com/

Grant, Richard. "Not so Queer as Folk." *The Guardian*, Saturday, January 10, 2004.
http://film.guardian.co.uk/

Griffin, John. "One Project Down, Umpteen More to Go. Bob Balaban talks about his next film role in Christopher Guest's *A Mighty Wind*." *The Gazette*, May 3, 2003, D2.

Guest, Christopher, Eugene Levy, Harry Shearer, Michael McKean, Richard Corliss, Josh Tyrangiel. "Mighty Funny." *Time Magazine*, April 21, 2003, 68+.

Harrison, Emily. "Guest at Home with offbeat comedy; *Spinal Tap* creator back with new film." *The Houston Chronicle*, May 4, 2003, 10.

Haun, Harry. "Shearer Madness: *Spinal Tap* co-creator hosts *Teddy Bears' Picnic*." *Film Journal International*, April 2002, 24.

Heller, Karen. "Eugene Levy hits the big time." *Knight Ridder/Tribune News Service*, August 8, 2003, K4940.

Heller, Steven. "Feiffer's Last Dance." *Print*, September 2000, 26.

Hendra, Tony. "Morning in America: the rise and fall of the *National Lampoon*." *Harper's Magazine*, June 2002, 59–56.

Hewitt, Chris. "Frequent Guest Star Catherine O'Hara is full of surprises." *The Saint Paul Pioneer Press*, April 18, 2003, K2578.

Hicks, Chris. "McKean shines in folksy spoof *A Mighty Wind*." *The Deseret Morning News*, September 19, 2003, W01.

Hirschberg, Lynn. "Good Humor Man." *The New York Times*, April 20, 2003. http://www.nytimes.com/

Hitchcock, Michael. "Spencer Tracy is one of the actors I most admire." *Back Stage West*, June 5, 2003, 8.

Hobson, Louis B. "Blowin' in the Wind; Spinal Tap reunites for the folky mockumentary *A Mighty Wind*." *The Winnipeg Sun*, May 9, 2003, 21.

Hodgkinson, Will. "Tapper's Delight." *Guardian Unlimited*, Saturday, August 17, 2002.
http://film.guardian.co.uk/

Johnson, Brian D. "A one-time folky is now blowing in the wind." *Maclean's*, April 21, 2003, 59.

Kelly-Saxenmeyer, Anne. "Little Murders." *Back Stage West*, March 14, 2002, 18.

Kempley, Rita. "The Dogs and the Wags." *The Washington Post*, October 13, 2000.
http://www.washingtonpost.com/

Killorn, Donnie. "Christopher Guest great again; With *A Mighty Wind*, this movie genius shows he can put out one top notch comedy after another." *The Guardian*, June 20, 2003, C4.

Kit, Zorianna. "Folksie reunion for *Show* men Levy and Guest." *Hollywood Reporter*, January 31, 2002, 1.

Klawans, Stuart. "*The Big Picture*." *The Nation*, October 9, 1989.

——. "Reel Men." *The Nation*, May 5, 2003, 34.

Koltnow, Barry. "Eugene Levy is busier than ever, with four films this year." *Knight Ridder/Tribune News Service*, June 11, 2003, K2392.

Kristal, Nicole. "Ever Eccentric." *Back Stage West*, June 28, 2001, 6.

Lacey, Liam. "A folk-mock star: Eugene Levy never blows *A Mighty Wind*." *The Globe & Mail*, Tuesday, April 15, 2003, R3.

LaPorte, Nicole. "Jennifer Coolidge funny girl: High laugh quotient puts a determined actress center stage." *American Theatre*, May 2002, 52–54.

LaSalle, Mike. "Howlin' in the Wind." *The San Francisco Chronicle*, April 16, 2003, D1.

"LC Adds 25 Films to National Registry." *Library Journal*, January 10, 2003. http://www.libraryjournal.com/article/ca268736

Lee, Luaine. "The Folksmen at home with improv movie," *The Halifax Daily News*, April 16, 2003, 28.

Linett, Richard, Ann Marie Kerwin. *Advertising Age*. September 22, 2003, 39.

Lipton, Michael A. "Life as the unsquiggy, *Laverne and Shirley*'s Michael McKean is ready for a Spinal Tap reunion." *People Weekly*, December 21, 1992, 55–56.

Lloyd, Robert. "Sketch Artists — The Credibility Gap's one-night stand." *L.A. Weekly*, November 12–18, 1999. http://www.laweekly.com/

Louie, Rebecca. "Parker Posey is queen of the indies, but studio stardom eludes her." *Knight Ridder/Tribune News Service*, November 18, 2002, K0487.

Lumenick, Lou. "Guest's *Best* Is." *The New York Post*, September 27, 2000, 52.

Maio, Kathi. "The Passivity of a Post-Feminist 50 Ft. Woman." *Fantasy and Science Fiction*, July 1994, 96.

"Mastermind behind *This Is Spinal Tap* shares writing secrets with UK's budding filmmakers." *PR Newswire*, October 29, 2003.

Mathieson, Chris. "Mighty Serious Comedy." *The Age*, July 25, 2003, 3.

McCarthy, Phillip. "Seriously Funny." *The Sunday Star-Times*, July 6, 2003, 4.

McDonald, Moira. "Improv actors bond making 'mockumentaries.' *Best in Show* crew reunites in film poking fun at folk singers." *The Seattle Times*, April 13, 2003, L5.

McQuaide, Cate. "Almost Heroes." *The Boston Globe*, May 30, 1998, C7.

Meyer, Carla. "Tongues, Tails Wag in *Best in Show*." *The San Francisco Chronicle*, September 29, 2000.

Middleton, Jason. "Documentary Comedy." *Media International Australia*, August 2002, 55–67.

Mitchell, Elvis. "Christopher Guest, Plucking Strings for the Camera Again." *The New York Times*, March 19, 2002.

Molitorisz, Sacha. "Strike a Posey." *Sydney Morning Herald*, July 18, 2003, 7.

Nange, John. *Films in Review*, May 1984, 38.

Nechak, Paula. "The Laughs Blow in: Filmmaker Guest's Love for Passionate People Hurls Him into *A Mighty Wind* of Folk Music." *The Seattle Post-Intelligencer*, April 5, 2003, C1.

Olson, Melissa. "*Mighty Wind* will excite mockumentary director's fans." *The America's Intelligence Wire*, April 17, 2003.

Osborne, Bert. "Dog Dish: Christopher Guest targets dog lovers in new mockumentary." *Creative Loafing Atlanta*, October 14, 2000. http://atlanta.creativeloafing.com/2000-10-14/flicks_interview2.html

Quinn, Michael. "Gimme A Break." *Time*, April 6, 1992, 73.

Rea, Steven. "Christopher Guest: from *Spinal Tap* to *Best in Show*." *Knight Ridder/Tribune News Service*, October 6, 2000, K438.

Rechstshaffer, Michael. *The Hollywood Reporter*, April 14, 2003. http://hollywoodreporter.com

Reid, Michael D. "No Laughing Matter. There's only one actor who can keep a straight face amid such hilarity." *The Times-Colonist*, May 20, 2003, C4.

Remy, Mark. "Insider Q & A: Eugene Levy." *TV Guide*, December 27, 2003.

Richards, Rand. "American Voices — *A Mighty Wind* & *Spellbound*." *Commonwealth*, May 23, 2003, 21–22.

Rivero, Enrique. "*Spinal Tap* in video comeback." *Video Business*, June 5, 2002, 4.

Rooney, David. *Variety*, April 14–20, 2003, 19.

Ross, Bob. "Guest's Mighty Career; He rates as a top comedian, actor, songwriter, and satirist." *The Richmond-Times Dispatch*. May 15, 2003, D8.

Roth, Genevieve J. *Esquire*. May 2003, 68.

Russo, Francine. "A Matter of Medium: Writer Jules Feiffer recalls the forces that redirected his career." *Time*, May 21, 2001, G8

The St. Petersburg Times. July 19, 2001. http://www.sptimes.com/

Sarris, Andrew. "I Wasn't Blown Over By Soft, Vague *Mighty Wind*." *The New York Observer*. http://www.newyorkobserver.com

"Screen Queen." *The Advocate*, May 18, 1997, 27.

Shellberg, Tim. "Peter, Paul and Mary bringing 40 years of folk to Star Plaza." *The NWI Times*, November 7, 2003. http://www.nwitimes.com/articles/

Simon, Jeff. "Cult of Guest. Christopher Guest explains his brand of comedic movies." *The Buffalo News*, May 9, 2003, G6.

Smith, Laura Kay. "Always a 'Friend,' Almost a Hero." *People Online*, 1998. http://people.aol.com/people/

Smith, R.J. "Harry Shearer's made comedy history, and his radio show is celebrating its 20th birthday. But if you think he's about to mellow, you've got to be joking." *Los Angeles Magazine*, December 2002.

Soeder, John. "Singin' out about the '60s. Actor-director of folk-music spoof knows which way the wind blew." *Plain Dealer*, May 13, 2003, E1.

Spaner, David. "Mighty may be another Best; *Best in Show* was made without a lot of hype, but its success bodes well for *A Mighty Wind*." *The Vancouver Province*, May 4, 2003, D4.

Spencer, Alan. "Allan Arkush *Heartbeeps* Director with a Heart." *Starlog #52*, November 1981, 26–29;64.

"Spinal Analysis: Deranged But True. (The 100 Greatest Moments in Rock Music — *This Is Spinal Tap* — film vs. reality.)" *Entertainment Weekly*, May 28, 1999, 96.

Stark, Susan. *The Detroit News*. October 13, 2000. http://www.detnews.com

Steelman, Ben. "Ben on Film: Guest ranks as our nation's top mockumentarian." *The Star-News* (Wilmington, NC), May 2003, 33.

Sternbergh, Adam. "Too Funny to be Famous: Pay No Attention to Christopher Guest. He prefers it that way." *The National Post*, April 19, 2003, SP1.

Stickler, Jeff. "Folk-music parody strikes a chord with creator Guest." *The Star Tribune*, April 18, 2003, 13E.

Strauss, Bob. "Extended Play." *The Daily News of Los Angeles*, April 13, 2003, U4.

Sweeting, Adam. "DA Pennebaker: No Spinal Tap jokes, please..." *The Independent*, November 9, 2003. http://www.enjoyment.independent.co.uk/low_res/story.jsp?story=462451&host=5&dir=213

Szalay, Jeff. "The Special Effects of *Heartbeeps*." *Starlog* #53, December 1981, 16–21

Takaki, Millie. "Dir. Christopher Guest on a Roll in Atlantic City." *Shoot*, August 27, 1999, 15.

Talley, Lori. "Jennifer Coolidge: Best in comedy." *Back Stage West*, June 6, 2002, 11.

Thomas, Rob. "Wacky Ensemble Again Delights in *Mighty Wind*." *Wisconsin State Journal*, May 8, 2003, 4.

Thompson, Ian. "Mastermind behind *This Is Spinal Tap* shares writing scerets with UK's budding filmmakers." *PR Newswire*, October 29, 2003.

Tucker, Ken and Benjamin Svetkey. "Television: The Week." *Entertainment Weekly*, December 20, 1991, 62.

"The Wait Is Over! From the creators of *Best in Show*, *Waiting for Guffman* has arrived ... and takes its DVD bow, August 21." *Business Wire*, July 23, 2003.

Walker, Ben. "Norfolk Terrier, Newfoundland Lead Westminster." *USA Today*, February 9, 2004. http://www.usatoday.com/sports/

Walsh, Christopher. "Spinal Tap Reunites with Vanston for Folk Spoof." *Billboard*, March 22, 2003, 54.

Wilmington, Michael. "*Best in Show* Howls at the Dog Show Crowd." *The Chicago Tribune*, October 13, 2000, 1.

——. *The Los Angeles Times*, September 15, 1989, 8.

Wloszcyna, Susan. "Parody Team Stirs up *A Mighty Wind*." *USA Today*, April 13, 2003, 6D.

Yu, Ting. "Chatter. To Dye For." *People Weekly*, October 2, 2000, 166.

INTERNET

"About Production." *Best in Show Online*, http://bestinshowonline.warnerbros.com/about/production.html.

Aguirre, Holly. "From *SCTV* to MTV: The Second Coming of Levy." *Zap2It*, http://www.zap2it.com/movies/features/scenes/story/0,1259,—-17824,00.html

"Alice Playten Reminisces." *Iclassics.com — Classical Music and More*, http://www.iclassics.com/iclassics.

Amen, Jessica. "Library of Congress selects *This Is Spinal Tap* and Others for Preservation." *Audio Revolution*, December 30, 2002, http://www.audiorevolution.com/news/1202/30.spinaltap.shtml.

Applebaum, Stephen. "Christopher Guest on *A Mighty Wind*." *Channel4.com*, http://www.channel4.com/film/.

SELECTED BIBLIOGRAPHY

Chavel, Sean. "Interview: Michael McKean, Harry Shearer, Christopher Guest of *A Mighty Wind*." *Cinema Confidential*, April 15, 2003, http://www.cinecon.com/news.php?id=0304151.

Clinton, Paul. "Entertainment: Two Paws Up! *Best in Show* is Howlingly Funny." *CNN*, September 29, 2000, http://www.cnn.com/2000/SHOWBIZ/Movies/09/29/review.best.in.show/index.html.

Cullin, Erin. "Eugene Levy is on Top of the world." *Empire Movies*, April 14, 2003, http://www.empiremovies.com/interviews/a_mighty_wind/eugene_levy_01.shtml.

Dale, Steve. "Real Dog Life Funnier Than *Best in Show*." *Pet World*, 2000–2001, http://www.goodnewsforpets.com/petworld.archive.

Edelstein, David. *Slate*. September 29, 2000, http://slate.msn.com/1d90528.

Easterbrook, Mark. "Entertainment: Movies: *A Mighty Wind* — No 'Mockumentary.'" *Xtra MSN*, July 30, 2003, http://xtramsn.co.nz/entertainment/.

Grierson, Tim. "*A Mighty Wind:* The Ballad of Mitch & Mickey." *Knot Magazine*, April 24, 2003, http://www.knotmag.com.

Hall, Phil. "King of the Jungle." *Wired*, May 2003 http://www.wired.com/wired/archive/5.03/streetcred.html?pg=7.

Harry Shearer, www.harryshearer.com.

Lurie, Karen. "126th Annual Westminster Kennel Club Dog Show." *Flak Magazine*, February 15, 2002, http://www.flakmag.com/tv/kennelclub.html.

Matheou, Demetrios. "Festival Diary, Day Eleven." *BFI: The 47th London Film Festival*, November 1, 2003, http://www.lff.org.uk/films_editorials.php?EditorialID=44.

Meyer, Carla. "*Spinal Tap* for the folk crowd — *A Mighty Wind*, Christopher Guest's latest 'mockumentary.'" *SF Gate*, April 13, 2003, http://sf.gate.com.

"Morning News: Announcer Joe Garagiola Discusses Westminster Kennel Club Dog Show." (Interview with Daryn Kagan). *CNN.com Transcripts*, February 12, 2001, http://www.cnn.com/TRANSCRIPTS/0102/12/mn.11.html.

Mottram, James. "Christopher Guest on Going to the Dogs." *Channel4.com*, http://www.channel4.com/films/.

Murray, Rebecca and Fred Topel. "Interview with Harry Shearer and Michael McKean, Two of *A Mighty Wind*'s Folksmen." *RomanticMovies.about.com*, http://romanticmovies.about.com/.

Naugle, Judge Patrick. "DVD Verdict Interviews Michael McKean." *DVD Verdict*, October 6, 2003, http://www.dvdverdict.com/specials/michaelmckean.php.

"O'Toole, McKean making beautiful music together." *Gwinnett Daily Post Online Edition*, http://www.gwinnettdailyonline.com.

Phipps, Keith. "Interview with Michael McKean." *The Onion AV Club*, Volume 36, Issue #30, August 30, 2000. http://www.theonionavclub.com/.

"Production Notes." *Almost Heroes* Online, www.almostheroes.com.

Righi, Len. "*Mighty Wind*" tour whipping up renewed excitement." *The Morning Call*, September 18, 2003. http://www.mcall.com

Robinson, Tasha. "Interview with Harry Shearer." *The Onion AV Club*, Volume 39, Issue #15, April 23, 2003. http://www.theonionavclub.com.

Savada, Elias. "*Best in Show*: Interview with Christopher Guest." *Nitrate Online*, October 13, 2000. http://www.nitrateonline.com/2000/fbestinshow.html.

Schneider, Jack. "*Wind* powers mockumentary advancements." *Online 49er*, Volume LIII, Number 113, May 5, 2003. http://www.csulb.edu/~d49er/archives/2003/spring/diversions/v10n113-win.shtml.

Seitz, Matt Zoller. "Folk Explosion; Loving send-up of aging hippies is a real gas." *New York Press*, Volume 16, Issue 16, 2003, http://www.nypress.com/16/16/film/film.cfm.

Smith, Evan. "Triumph of the Willard." *TexasMonthly.com*, March 1997. http://texasmonthly.com.

Standish, Mike. "Interview: The Cast of *A Mighty Wind*." *Movies.com*, March 10, 2003, http://movies.go.com/news/2003/3/mightywindinterview031003.html.

Strauss, Bob. "Extended Play." *U-Daily News*, April 12, 2003, http://u.dailynews.com/

Streett, Bill. "Christopher Guest, Saturn and the Art of the Mockumentary." *Astrology for the Soul*, 2003, http://www.astrologyforthesoul.com/billstreett/christopherguest.html.

Tapper, Jake. "Interview: Christopher Guest." *The Sundance Channel*, 2003, http://www.sundancechannel.com/24fn/index.php?ixContent=4882.

Thompson, Bob. "At the Festival — Catherine O'Hara's so bad she's great." *Jam Canoe*. September 12, 1996. http://jam.canoe.ca/JamMoviesArtistsO/ohara_catherine.html.

Urban Andrew L. "Heaps of Talent: Christopher Guest—*A Mighty Wind*." *Urban Cinefile*, Summer 2003, http://www.urbancinefile.com.au/home/view.asp?a=7678&s=Interviews.

Vowell, Sarah. "The mockumentary cometh. Documentaries are huge. Their perverse cousins are nipping at their heels." *Salon.com*, July 28, 1999, http://www.salon.com/ent/col/vowe/199/07/28/mock.

Waiting for Guffman Online, www.guffman.warnerbros.com/cast.htm.

Westminster Kennel Club, www.Westminsterkennelclub.org.

Williams, Phillip. "Improvising the Perfect Script; Moviemakers Leigh, Jaglom, Duvall and Locah are latest in a long line of 'naturalistic' directors." *MovieMaker — The Art and Business of Making Movies*, Issue #51, http://www.moviemaker.com/issues/51/naturalistic.html

INDEX